D0097884

WE ARE LIKE THAT ONLY

praise for the book

'One of the most insightful books on how a multinational company can win in India by managing the diversity, complexity and affordability of Indian consumers. My congratulations to Rama Bijapurkar for writing a reader-friendly book with captivating case studies based on her highly successful consulting experiences.'

—Jagdish N. Sheth, Charles H. Kellstadt Professor of Marketing, Goizueta Business School, Emory University

'Rama Bijapurkar is one of the very few global minds who doesn't paint emerging markets with a developed country brush. In this book, she uses her deep understanding of India to deliver a highly informative piece of work. Anyone looking to profit from the boom in developing countries such as India would be well advised to first read this very thoughtful exposition.'

—Ruchir Sharma, Head of Global Emerging Markets, Morgan Stanley Investment Management

'India is a "chaos" market with many layers of opportunity beyond the obvious. This book has the rare insight and courage to describe the Indian market as it truly is and will be in the future. It is essential reading for anyone who is serious about doing business in India.'

—Kishore Biyani, Founder and Group CEO, Future Group

we are like that only
understanding the logic of
Consumer India

Rama Bijapurkar

**PENGUIN
PORTFOLIO**

PORTFOLIO

Published by the Penguin Group

Penguin Books India Pvt Ltd, 11 Community Centre, Panchsheel Park, New Delhi 110 017, India

Penguin Group (USA) Inc., 375 Hudson Street, New York, NY 10014, USA

Penguin Group (Canada), 90 Eglinton Avenue East, Suite 700, Toronto, Ontario, M4P 2Y3, Canada (a division of Pearson Penguin Canada Inc.)

Penguin Books Ltd, 80 Strand, London WC2R 0RL, England

Penguin Ireland, 25 St Stephen's Green, Dublin 2, Ireland (a division of Penguin Books Ltd)

Penguin Group (Australia), 250 Camberwell Road, Camberwell, Victoria 3124, Australia (a division of Pearson Australia Group Pty Ltd)

Penguin Group (NZ), 67 Apollo Drive, Rosedale, North Shore 0632, New Zealand (a division of Pearson New Zealand Ltd)

Penguin Group (South Africa) (Pty) Ltd, 24 Sturdee Avenue, Rosebank, Johannesburg 2196, South Africa

Penguin Books Ltd, Registered Offices: 80 Strand, London WC2R 0RL, England

First published in Portfolio by Penguin Books India 2007

Copyright © Rama Bijapurkar 2007

ISBN 10: 0-67099-944-X   ISBN 13: 978-0-67099-944-6

For sale in India only

Typeset in Bembo by InoSoft Systems, Noida

Printed at Gopsons Papers Ltd, Noida

For my parents, especially my father, who would have marvelled that my 'marketing blah blah' has resulted in a book

contents

foreword

C.K. Prahalad

Few topics elicit as much unwarranted optimism or scepticism as the Indian consumer. Yes, the optimists say that India represents a huge untapped middle class market; a market critical for a global firm. Yes, the sceptics say that India is still too poor by global standards—most getting by on less than $3 per day per person. So this market is not critical for us and won't be for a long time. At a high level of aggregation both are right. However, as Rama Bijapurkar so ably illustrates in this book, any broad generalization about the consumer market in India is bound to be wrong. The market is complex. It is evolving rapidly in ways that few could have predicted, even five years ago.

First, from a consumer market perspective, *there is no single India.* There are the very rich. There are the IT/pharma employees who aspire to global standards and have high expectations. Then there is the aspiring middle class. The self-employed India. The agriculture-dependent subsistent farmers. The urban poor. The rural poor. They all have different approaches to consumption. They construct their consumption basket in distinctly different ways. So firms are better off in creating their 'own India' that they want to serve.

Secondly, GDP *per capita is not a good measure of the capacity to consume; much worse it can be misleading.* Rama articulates an in-depth methodology on how to understand the propensity and the capacity of Indian consumers to consume using primary income survey data. This approach provides a new and broad understanding of the size of the market, once we know *which*

India to go after. She also includes in her analysis an understanding of the demographic (a young India), psychographic and social determinants of the market in India. I believe that the psychographic and social determinants may have as much relevance as expenditure data in segmenting and sizing the Indian market. Such an analysis, therefore may give clues to *which India* a company should target. The interesting aspect of the methodology that Rama provides here is that it is helpful in identifying and sizing the market.

Thirdly, rural India *is not poor; nor is it totally agriculture-dependent.* This is an important insight. Rural India represents 50 per cent of India's GDP (but 70 per cent of its people) and 50 per cent of rural GDP is non-agricultural: it comes from the self-employed in all kinds of services. Although they are rural, they are not very different in their aspirations from the urban consumers. They like two-wheelers, FMCG products, jeans and cell phones. They have their own logic for consumption.

Rama's analysis provides a focus on new questions not just for multinationals entering India but for established Indian firms as well. India is like a kaleidoscope. Every time you turn it, you get a different perspective—enticing, different, and 'real'. The basic requirement for understanding Consumer India is to recognize that there are no simple algorithms to segment it. It is the methodological nuances that allow one to get at the heart of this opportunity. Rama has done a great service by capturing in this book her vast experience for all: from CEOs to market and business development professionals.

While India is undoubtedly complex, there still are some simple truths that managers have to accept. Indian consumers *are very value-conscious. They may be poor, but they are not backward.* Even in media-dark India, consumers are well informed. They are not overwhelmed by western brands. *And they can make a difference to the global positions of individual firms.* Consider cell phones. The Indian market is growing at the rate of 6 million new subscribers per month. The market cap of the top five carriers in India is more than $75 billion. There is a message for multinationals here. If you can understand the Indian consumer right and create appropriate business models (including products), the Indian market will surprise you. You cannot expect to flog old and tried products in India and expect to create a mass base. Rama's prescription is clear. India is not an easy market to understand and operate in. But for anyone who does understand it, the prize can be very substantial. India is an investment opportunity. Therefore, think like a venture capitalist. Invest in innovation.

Rama has developed a very strong case for learning about India on its own terms before investing. This book is a critical read for anyone considering building a large franchise for themselves in India.

C.K. Prahalad
The Paul and Ruth McCracken
Distinguished University Professor of
Corporate Strategy
Ross School of Business
The University of Michigan

preface

A book is both the end of a journey and the beginning of another. This particular book is the culmination of innumerable panel discussions, Power Point presentations, and speeches that I have made around the world on the possibilities, perils and paradoxes of the Indian market and the Indian consumer. The audiences, diverse but always engaged, included groups such as the YPO, the British Business Group, the Alfred Herhausen Society for International Dialogue, the Fortune 500 power women's forum, the advertising agencies association in France, students from leading American and European business schools, corporate business leaders and emerging market strategy teams from large global companies and, of course, lots and lots of fund managers, private equity investors and investment bankers from Bombay to the Bahamas. Some totally agreed with what I had to say, others violently disagreed, some were blown away and quite a few were unimpressed. Whatever be their reaction, they always listened with a deep interest and engagement. Their participation and responses made me realize that what I was saying was new and different because it gave a 360 degree view of the Indian market through the lens of consumers and people, and that it made them think differently about India, in the context of their own work. To them, I owe my greatest debt. With such encouragement, I felt that a book on Consumer India could be of interest to a wider audience, especially at a time when India, despite being the focus of much attention, is confusing more and more people with its oddities and contradictions.

My own consulting experience of the past decade has been very rich and rewarding in terms of lessons that it has taught me about Consumer India and what it takes to develop winning strategies for it. Through examining strategic choices confronting a wide range of business contexts, sectors, company types and nationalities, it has enabled me to distil universal issues related to developing customer-centric business strategy for the new world. It has also come with its share of struggle—persuading Indian companies to get more customer centric in their battle for dreams and markets, and persuading reluctant MNCs to be more open to adopting a 'made for India' business approach.

I also confess that what goaded me to write this book was my complete disagreement with popular methods used by consulting firms and business analysts to evaluate the Indian market opportunity. Done almost entirely using supply-side data, they rely heavily on analogies of how other markets have evolved in the past and assume unquestioningly that there is only one model of evolution for the entire world, and that a uniform looking world is inevitable. I, on the other hand, believe that the top line of a profit and loss (P&L) statement is about consumer choices, not supply-side economics, and that analogies of the kind being used actually do not make much sense. I also believe that emerging markets are not like developed markets the way they were in their infancy. They will eventually walk down a different path of their own, as they get more prosperous. I also disagree with theories about the magic number of per capita income above which consumption in a country is supposed to 'take off'. These, I believe, are theories for the faint hearted. With low-priced innovations, consumption had already taken off in India at far lower income levels. I was puzzled by their analysis of how if the per capita consumption of a widget in America or Brazil was 100, and in India it was 10, then the gap of 90 represented a huge opportunity waiting to happen. I considered the possibility that maybe Indian consumers have use for only 10 units per capita, either because of environmental or cultural factors, or because they have leap-frogged to a new kind of more modern widget and have skipped this stage altogether.

The data and insights for this book have been drawn from a variety of sources—from highly formal survey research to anecdotal and experiential consumer stories from the field to the work of social scientists. The last was particularly difficult, because in India, the world of the social sciences and the world of business are very distant from each other and there are very few people and institutions that bridge the two. Further, during the first fifteen years of my working life, I never had any real need to understand macroeconomics in order to understand consumer markets, since we all lived in a closed and insulated economy. In a tranquil pond there are no unpredictable storms caused by global trade or economic policy. This, however, has changed drastically in the last decade. I have often, this past decade, wished that there was a formal and well-established discipline called *macro-consumer* that I could have drawn ideas and inspiration from. Ubiquitous and akin in scale and scope to macroeconomics, it would focus on the combined effects of macroeconomics, social development, politics, policy, cultural changes, etc., on shaping consumer markets at a national or regional level.

It is from this perspective that this book has been written—to provide a macro-consumer view of the changing Consumer India, for use as an input into developing a winning 'made for India' business strategy. I believe that India and Indians aren't going to become like someplace else or someone else, but will continue to march down their own road to their own future destination. Hence, the title of this book is the phrase that we in India are all familiar with: *We Are Like That Only*.

acknowledgements

My thinking on Consumer India has evolved over the past decade, contributed in no small measure by a whole host of people who have been fellow travellers on this road to discovery and clarity and who have very generously shared their work and their thoughts. That makes it a huge number of people that I need to acknowledge, too numerous to individually name here. There are some, however, who I must specifically mention.

The biggest influence on my thinking has come from Professor C.K. Prahalad, my professor at IIM Ahmedabad who has remained my teacher ever since, through his inspirational work and the intellectual energy that he radiates.

S.L. Rao, former director general of the National Council of Applied Economic Research (NCAER), was the first person to do serious macro-consumer research on Consumer India and put it in the public domain. He showed me what the territory of this could be, and has always been a thoughtful and constructive critic. Dr Rakesh Mohan (presently deputy governor of the Reserve Bank of India, and earlier, director general of NCAER) wrote to me when I published, with trepidation, my first big article on Consumer India based on NCAER data and his 'cold call' with warm praise gave me the confidence I needed to take larger steps on this journey. Since then, he has been a very helpful thought and discussion partner, patiently explaining the nuances of income distribution through squiggly graphs drawn on available scraps of paper, and answering endless Economics 101 questions with simplicity and clarity.

While on the subject of economists, my first big 'aha' about the changing composition of rural India's GDP came from work that Subir Gokarn (chief economist, CRISIL) and I did for Mahindra & Mahindra. Subsequently, I worked further on this with Omkar Goswami and his team at CERG, and I learnt a lot even as we gamely traded economist and consultant jokes. Laveesh Bhandari (founder, Indicus Analytics) helped me achieve a long-standing desire of linking survey income data to GDP by coming up with a conceptually elegant and wonderful piece of analysis that we wrote up in a joint article titled 'Solving the Income Data Puzzle'.

Ashok Das (managing director, Hansa Research Group), in addition to being a special long-time buddy, has been a very important research partner. He has always provided just the right kind of data to explore any hypothesis I might have, and he has also come up with several novel constructs and analyses to push my thinking further. Dr Rajesh Shukla of NCAER has also been most generous with his time, valuable research and insights. Both their footprints are all over the chapter on purchasing power. Santosh Desai (now managing director of Future Brands, formerly president of McCann Erickson) has added a significant dimension to my understanding of changing consumer values and attitudes and has been quoted quite a bit in this book. And a special thank you to Arun Adhikari (presently chairman, Nippon Lever, formerly director, Hindustan Lever) for his thoughtful and deep insights, over ten years, into whatever issue I was grappling with and needed help to think through.

I really owe Mythili Bhusnurmath, a long-time editor of my *Economic Times* edit page column, for making sure that I wrote my column regulary and captured my thoughts over the years. Also a big thank you to Tony Joseph and Indrajit Gupta (formerly with *Businessworld*), for allowing me to write cover stories on Consumer India, and helping me deliver work that got noticed and acclaimed.

Getting this book out has been quite a tortuous process for me; but I suspect that it might have been more tortuous for my many editors who worked hard to beat my manuscript into something fit to be published as a book. Thank you, Sharad Panse, for going well beyond the call of duty and working so closely with me to produce something that was all mine in tone, yet so much better in the way it read. Chapal Mehra has been just fantastic—his insight into what in my writing was not working and why, was so bang on target that correcting it in the next draft was astonishingly easy. He has been an absolute island of calm, yet uncompromising in his demand for excellence; he has been willing to take risks; and I couldn't have asked for better support.

And last but not least, I want to acknowledge those near and dear who have been there with me through the travails of writing this book. Lucy Sutari at my office kept track of every little detail of every part of the book, and never let me know just how disorganized I was. Aparna, my daughter, gave me the best advice I got in the context of this book: 'Mom, please stop trying to write the mother of all books. Just get on with it and write a book please.' Ashoke, my husband, has lived through the house being invaded by untidy stacks of paper, and never once said anything rude when I ceaselessly moaned and groaned about 'the damned book', as if it were his fault that I had to do it! My mother has been terrific—she sympathized when I needed sympathy, goaded me when I needed goading, kicked butt when I was drowning in self-pity as I faced yet another stack of editorial queries. The book started getting written at her dining table in Hyderabad, and finally got finished at my dining table in Mumbai a year later. But she was there throughout it all for me.

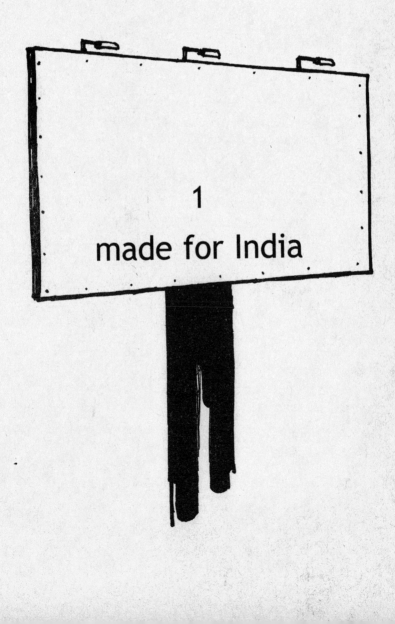

India is undeniably an important future growth market of the world. It is large (it has the fourth largest gross domestic product or GDP in the world in Purchasing Power Parity or PPP terms), it is young (it has 450 million people below the age of 21) and it is just beginning its consumption journey.

In 1991, India made a 180-degree turn in its economic ideology and started the process of economic liberalization. Until then, its consumer markets were governed by the socialistic ideology of Jawaharlal Nehru, its first prime minister. There was a very strong focus on self-reliance and local production and a high degree of protection for small-scale producers. These ideas were partly the legacy of Mahatma Gandhi. During India's freedom movement, Gandhi had positioned British mill-made cloth as a symbol of colonial oppression, and called upon all self-respecting Indians to boycott it and wear Indian-made homespun or *khadi* fabric instead.

Nehru's socialistic model continued even after his death in 1964. Indeed, it reached its zenith in the days of his daughter Indira Gandhi, who was India's prime minister for sixteen years in two spells, from 1966 to 1977 and then again from early 1980 to late 1984. She went to war against the rich with her slogan 'garibi hatao'. She spread the tentacles of state ownership deep and wide through the economy with disastrous moves like nationalization of banks.

Thus, until 1991, when India began its journey towards market capitalism, it was the government that was in charge of business. It was the government that largely determined who produced how much of what, quite unmindful of either the logic of business economics or the sensibilities of consumers. The prices of most items were unreasonably high and few could afford to buy them. Taxes, the largest component of prices, were particularly high, especially on whatever the government decided were luxury items, be it shoes, shampoos, light bulbs, lipsticks, air conditioners or branded apparel.

Television had arrived in India—in Delhi—as early as 1959. Its expansion, however, began only in 1972; but even in 1991, there were only two state-run channels. Extremely stringent currency regulations inhibited most people from travelling abroad. There were severe restrictions on the operations of multinational companies (MNCs) in the country and most of them decided not to set up operations. So global brands were few and far between in India. To top it all, while agricultural income was tax free in the rural hinterland, where people did not have much to buy, the urban Indian paid taxes upwards of 75 per cent. There was an enormous and flourishing black economy, but this wealth could not be spent freely on anything conspicuous for fear of attracting the attention of the taxman.

HIGH HOPES AND BELIED EXPECTATIONS

The socialistic model failed miserably. GDP growth crawled for the first thirty-five years after Independence and per capita income was very low. The latter began to inch up a bit in the mid-1980s when Rajiv Gandhi succeeded Indira Gandhi as prime minister and took a few faltering steps towards economic liberalization. However, it was only in 1991 that an unprecedented financial and balance-of-payments crisis forced the Indian government to open up the Indian economy and initiate the process of liberalization and economic reforms.

Since then, there has been a jump in the GDP growth rate and a spurt in national income. This, however, has not been the only area of growth and change. In place of just two government-owned channels, there are now over 100 television channels, offered at throwaway prices by private cable operators through a ubiquitous, low-cost distribution network throughout the country. Consumer confidence and aspirations have also been upbeat ever since 1991, as consumers have been seeing visible and tangible improvements in their lives each passing year.

That is the scenario on the consumer side. On the supply side, first and foremost, there have been drastic cuts in taxes and import duties. Delicensing has led to competition and a supply-side renaissance has occurred in category after category, at amazing speed. There is now a lot more to buy, it is cheaper, and what's more, it is better than ever before!

The potential of a market of over a billion people, residing in the world's fourth largest economy (in PPP terms) and consistently growing, should be the end of this story. 'Consumer India integrates with the global consumer market scene and is enthusiastically welcomed as a new source of growth by global corporations, smoothly rolling out their global strategies, duly adjusted for cultural sensitivity' is how the story ought to conclude.

Unfortunately, it doesn't. The conclusion actually reads something like this: 'Consumer India has been the source of belied expectations and frustrating resistance to conventional global offerings. Never before has any market been so rebellious about what it will embrace and what it will not. Nokia wins. Coke and Pepsi struggle. Honda wins. Mercedes struggles. LG and Samsung walk away with the market. GE Appliances doesn't. Levis lags behind expectations. Nike limps along. Diageo did not make a big splash, Star TV has had many rethinks, MTV localizes, Kellogg's still struggles. Heinz ketchup doesn't catch on. Beware! Consumer India offers as much pain as gain and there will be no walkover for global big brands that don't think through their India strategy from ground upwards.' Over the past decade and a half, we have learnt many valuable lessons from watching new multinational entrants negotiating the slippery turf of Consumer India. Anyone aspiring to embark on this journey would be well advised not to lose sight of them.

First of all, *the nature of emerging market economies is fundamentally different*. Emerging market economies are large in their total size but small in terms of per capita income, India being a prime example. And *that* is what makes all the 'doesn't everybody know' sort of global ideas, on price–performance points and margin–volume equations, ineffective in such markets. As far as India is concerned, a fundamental rethink around appropriate 'made for India' propositions is needed, which must replace the conventional wisdom of 'global standard' benefits at 'global equivalent' prices.

In fact, the two interesting questions to think about, given the demographic and economic growth characteristics of India and China, are, 'what exactly do we mean when we say *global standards?*' and 'where is the centre of gravity of *global* going to be?'

Second, *emerging markets need not be virgin markets*.

Range of offerings available: Even in an emerging market like India, there can already exist an array of home-grown options in many categories, which can offer incredibly tough competition to new entrants. Such options can be several and diverse, ranging from traditional solutions to hybrid blends of the traditional and the modern, as also to Indianized versions of international options—all available at several price-performance points.

One good example of this is the retailing environment in India. Street markets of every level of sophistication coexist. There are the organized Mumbai pavement shops that locals refer to as 'Fashion Street'. They sell the 'export surplus' stocks of the very latest fashions of big international brands which, thanks to outsourcing, are now manufactured in India. They also sell jeans that are manufactured in India, but which are the exact replicas of the latest styles from Bangkok. Then, there are the mom-and-pop shops or stores ranging from the high end, high service shops to the 'holes in the wall' existing alongside various shades and grades of local supermarkets and hypermarkets.

This range of competition proves to be a very challenging environment for global retailers who always end up with a value disadvantage over one or the other existing option. And since most Indians shop at all options, the question 'why buy me' becomes even more challenging to answer for a global retailer.

Sophisticated distribution and brands: Until 1991, India was certainly not a market that had an ethos of modern consumerism as we know it the world over. Nevertheless, within the framework of the numerous constraints, business practices were quite modern and Indian consumers were exposed to a wide, deep and efficient distribution system comprising a network of over five million (and still growing) small retailers that dotted the country (and still do). Robust and sophisticated Indian brands were built, which, of course, had to compensate for the primitive products they represented. Advertising was, therefore, often the hero of the brand building process and was very creative. The Indian market research and advertising industry was extremely well developed even by acknowledged international benchmarks. All this actually raised the bar for the new entrants into India.

The picture at the time of liberalization, thus, was of a deeply inhibitive regulatory framework that repressed and suppressed all forms of consumption and product innovation, but within which, paradoxically, a sophisticated sales and marketing system existed and operated, doing its best to innovate, develop and tease out whatever consumption it could from the market. A market that was—still is and will always be—mind-boggling in terms of its linguistic, cultural and income diversity.

To best understand these phenomena, consider this analogy: Consumer India is like an experienced hire in an organization, while Consumer China is like a fresh hire. An experienced hire is more difficult to manage and mould, because he already has a set way of doing things that works pretty well and therefore he needs a lot of convincing (by persuasion or clout) to adopt your way of thinking or doing things. A fresh hire, on the other hand, has a clean slate as far as past experiences are concerned. At any rate, his past experiences are fairly primitive and hence, persuading him to adopt your ways is comparatively easy.

Not only China, but also Russia or, for that matter, even most countries of Southeast Asia—when they were emerging—have been like new hires.

Third, *emerging markets today*—such as India—*are not what the developed markets were in their infancy*. Hence, the assumption that Indian consumers today are like what American consumers were twenty years ago, is deeply flawed. Consumers exist in real time and are confronted by all the forces of today, not yesterday. Moreover, they are products of their own unique consumer history and culture.

Let me illustrate this with an example. Indian consumers have not embraced the culture of cola drinking as many other emerging markets have. To begin with, water holds a pre-eminent place in Indian food and drink. Water is loaded with cultural meanings and is seen to be the elixir of life. Offering water to a stranger in the middle of summer is the epitome of hospitality and kindness. Further, there is already a very well developed 'in-home' beverage market of tea and coffee that coexists with a network of out-of-home bottled water distribution as well as tea and coffee bars. Added to this is the fact that American popular culture, of which cola is a prominent symbol, has not had the same influence in this region, as it has, say, in the Philippines. At the same time, all the discourse around the world on health concerns with colas is being transmitted in real time to consumers in India, as much as to consumers anywhere else. So the Indian consumer also knows that there is a move to ban colas in American schools.

If we take all this into account, it becomes rather obvious that Coke's current global strategy or its age-old market penetration strategy cannot win in India. The strategy necessarily has to be different, as cola companies are now discovering.

So would it be with Walt Disney, who must understand that the child of today's India has no parallel elsewhere. This child represents a poor country's Internet generation, its aspirations running riot in a milieu of very scarce opportunities: a situation that has not existed anywhere else, ever before.

To take another example, Intel will have to stop worrying about when PC penetration in India will hit the same levels as it did in developed markets earlier—it will need to fight in an India revolutionized by feature-rich cell phones, which are getting far more deeply entrenched than PCs in a much shorter span of time.

Finally, countries change around their DNA. And the Indian DNA is about continuity with change; it is about 'THIS *as well as* THAT'; about cobbling together clever and low-cost solutions that are ingenious combinations and adaptations of products available in the market. As I often say, for instance, our faith in astrology does not decrease as a result of the rising levels of our scientific education; rather, as a consequence, we effortlessly move to computerized horoscope casting!

Products and services that understand all this, win. Those that don't are bewildered about why consumers process value the way they do and give a 'thumbs down' signal to a product that has been successful elsewhere in the world.

MADE FOR INDIA

It is now clear to all Consumer India watchers that what we have here is a tricky and complex market. It demands strategy complexity and strategy customization way beyond its current worth. The right question to ask here is not 'what is the size of market that India offers for my global strategy', but, rather, 'what should be my local, customized strategy for the Indian market'.

As C.K. Prahalad says in a brilliant article in *Harvard Business Review*,[1]

> While it is true that MNCs will change emerging markets forever, the reverse is also true. Many corporations are beginning to see that the opportunity that big emerging markets represent, will demand a new way of thinking . . . requiring more than developing cultural sensitivity.

He goes on to urge MNCs to 'rethink price–performance equations, rethink the cost of market building'. I would add, rethink business definition and business models.

The Indian experience so far makes it pretty obvious that only those companies that leverage their competencies for creating businesses tailor-made for India are likely to win in India and benefit from its inevitable growth, rather than those that mechanically transplant their best practice strategies from other markets. As Prahalad says, it is not about 'best practice'. It's about 'next practice'.

In order to create this 'made for India' 'next practice' strategy which carefully balances the compulsions of global economics and the comfort of the tried and tested best practices with what is needed to unlock the potential of this distinctive market, a deep understanding of the market is absolutely essential. And the imperative is to gain or obtain this deep understanding from the viewpoint of *shaping* business strategy, not merely of *adapting* existing marketing policies and programmes that may be functioning, and functioning well, elsewhere.

That's what this book attempts to do, by presenting an insightful and in-depth analysis of what Consumer India is all about, and the implications and complications for business-market strategy.

Most investors and new entrants into India have a list of FAQs. Such as, why bother with India when I have China? Is there

---

[1] C. K. Prahalad and Kenneth Liberthal, 'The End of Corporate Imperialism', *Harvard Business Review* (R03086), 1998, 2003.

enough evidence that India can be a consumption powerhouse? Tell us about the Indian middle class. What is the exact purchasing power of the market? Is there really a fortune at the bottom of the pyramid? Why are demand patterns so capricious? Is rural India a sophisticated or a primitive market? This book addresses all these and more.

It looks at Consumer India through multiple lenses, and presents a zero-base, consumer-centric view of India's demand structure and its drivers. It critically examines the demographic, cultural and social trends and identifies the strategic themes and approaches that corporations must think about when addressing Consumer India, so that they may develop their own mental models of it.

2

the mixed messages
from Consumer India

Global businesses have not quite been able to make up their minds about the opportunity offered by the Indian market or what their strategy for it should be. That is understandable given the many mixed messages that Consumer India has been sending out.

Ever since India opened up its markets in 1991, Consumer India has been the source of a fair amount of heartache and headache even for the most seasoned global businesses, including MNCs. Almost all early entrants into the market, ranging from Coke, Kellogg's and Seagram to Reebok and Sony to Mercedes Benz and Booze Allen Hamilton, soon found their business expectations totally belied. So did a host of companies in the specialty chemicals, computers, confectionery and cosmetics businesses, to name just a few. The conclusion was the same in each case, even if the specifics of the story were slightly different—namely that the much-touted, supposedly vibrant, hungry and desperate-to-consume Indian market, the sleeping beauty waiting to be awakened by the kiss of the multinational prince, was more myth than reality.

Yet now, fifteen years later, slow and steady economic growth has created the world's fourth largest economy having just under 6 per cent of the world GDP (on a PPP basis). If you are a PPP non-believer, then, in US dollar terms, India is today the eighth largest economy with a population of over a billion people, 40 per cent of them below the age of 21, a heartening statistic in an otherwise ageing world, and one that would warm the cockles of all marketers' hearts. However, the fact remains that in terms of per capita income, the Indian market ranks a dismal 145 in the world.

The fact also remains that Consumer India coexists in many centuries and at many levels of affluence.

This paradox comes into sharp focus in the media coverage that India gets. For instance, take the period between March and July 2006 and look at the montage of mixed messages put out by foreign as well as Indian media on India's future. *The Economist* did a cover story with a provocative editorial titled 'Can India Fly?' and concluded, '. . . it has taken off at last. Only with further reform can it spread its wings and soar'. It went on to state that it did not look like further reforms were going to happen in a hurry. It elaborated, 'India has been in fashion before, only to disappoint foreign and local companies alike. Despite its huge potential market . . . despite its wealth of English speakers . . . despite its vaunted 15 year old reforms . . .'

Newsweek had a cover story called 'The New India' where it examined the question: 'Is Asia's other powerhouse ready for its moment under the sun?' The article was brutally candid when it said that most people would find it hard to take India seriously despite all the threats to American jobs from outsourcing to Indian information technology (IT) companies. It went on to say, 'anyone who has actually been to India will probably be puzzled . . . India, he or she will say, with its dilapidated airports, crumbling roads, vast slums and impoverished villages? We are talking about that India?'

The article further stated, 'The country might have several Silicon Valleys, but it also has three Nigerias within it, more than 300 million people living on less than a dollar a day . . .' but concluded with a hugely positive pat on the back to the enterprising, energized Indian spirit because of which 'there is change that can be felt even in the slums'.

During the same period, two consecutive cover stories in *Businessworld* made one wonder whether it was the same country that was being talked about. The first story was about the race that Indian pharmaceutical companies were running with their counterparts in the developed world to discover a new molecule, but at a fraction of the costs that the latter were incurring. The second story asked the spine-chilling question: Will the Indian economy crash?

It is little wonder, then, that even as interest in India grows, scepticism about whether or not India will deliver the promised future remains. This never fails to escape anyone who has been on a roadshow overseas to market India as an investment destination. An Indian diplomat posted in London summed up this 'guilty until proven innocent' attitude towards India succinctly. He and I were on a panel at an India conference organized by the London Business School. The conference hall was in the building of the Royal College of Obstetricians and Gynaecologists. The diplomat, tongue firmly in cheek, informed his audience that the venue of the India conference was ironic, as India had been shouting from the rooftops for the past few years that she was pregnant (with economic possibility) and about to deliver a new, attractive and long-term growth market. But the world has mostly looked on impassively and said, 'Please bring us more evidence that this is not a false pregnancy and that you are capable of delivering a fully formed baby that will grow to be a healthy adult.'

It is against this backdrop of mixed messages that businesses need to answer two critical questions: Just how much of business interest does this market hold? And what kind of strategy does it really deserve?

STRATEGIC PERSPECTIVES ON INDIA ARE CHANGING, BUT ARE STILL CONFUSED

The cautious companies (or are they the laggards?), which aren't here yet, are reluctantly beginning to think that since India appears to be here to stay and set to grow on the world's economic and political stage, the Indian market merits a deeper investigation. Over and above the usual questions discussed earlier, they also grapple with some more fundamental questions: Is India a 'nice to have in the portfolio' market, or a 'must have' market without which the future competitiveness of my businesses will be compromised? Is the Indian market really ready for me, or should I wait till it gets more sophisticated and rich and ready to respond to my global strategy?

Several global businesses are already here with varying degrees of strategic and resource commitment. They are beginning to realize that in order to fully exploit the demographics and the GDP of the Indian market, they need to do much more. Many of them have been cautious about investing in their businesses, which they operate with a global or a pan-regional strategy. In fact, they have been waiting for the turning point—when the market evolves into something more recognizable and similar to the developed markets that they are familiar with. However, many of them now feel that the future is taking unexpected twists and turns and seems unpredictable. The turning point may therefore have to come for their strategy and not for the market!

This rather rare flash of realization has been further driven home by the transformational ideas emerging in business thinking during the past five years: the notion of the BRIC (Brazil, Russia, India, China) markets, the concept of the 'fortune at the bottom of the pyramid', the whole discourse around 'disruptive innovation' and offshoring and so on. All this has helped deepen the thought that maybe the question to ask of the Indian market is not 'when will the Indian market be ready for my global "best practice" strategy', but rather, 'when will I be ready to create the next practice strategy for the Indian market?'

It is therefore not surprising that we now see a flurry of emerging market strategy teams in Fortune 500 boardrooms, and more and more board and leadership group meetings are being held in India. Added to this is the return of many highly qualified and high profile non-resident Indians (NRIs) to work or do business in India. Yet, on the other hand, it is also not surprising that the state of India's airports, the invariable stray buffalo in the middle of a main street in Delhi or Mumbai (Bombay), the profusion of mom-and-pop shops cheek by jowl with glass-encased malls, the world class Power Point presentations from Indians and the other-worldly power cuts, make everyone wonder whether this market would ever merit more than a token presence!

THE CONSUMER DEMAND JOURNEY: 1991 TO DATE

So has India been crying wolf? Is there really a market waiting to happen? In all fairness, some of the world's scepticism is with good reason. The roller coaster nature of Consumer India's progress is best described by S.L. Rao, an economist and former director general of the National Council for Applied Economic Research (NCAER). He uses a delightfully accurate analogy and says that it is 'like the walk of a drunken man. You know he will get home eventually, but it will be two steps forward, two steps sideways, one step backwards.'

Since India liberalized, there have been several wrong judgements and major disappointments as well as some pleasant surprises. However, what is still lacking is sufficient understanding of the pattern of this apparently random progress of the Indian economy. It is, therefore, useful, with the benefit of hindsight, to review Consumer India's demand story since 1991. It may, perhaps, help in putting some past bogeys to rest, as well as in having a realistic understanding of the future.

The first few years of hyped expectation: India first started marketing itself as an investment destination in the early 1990s, soon after it began the liberalization of its economy. It had the unenviable task of combating the dominant image the world had of it—a country of snake charmers, temple elephants, the Taj Mahal and millions living in object poverty. Needless to say, India's chief competitor in attracting foreign direct investment

(FDI) was China, with its image of a communist superpower now determinedly and efficiently turning capitalist. China's image only served to exaggerate India's backwardness. Although the size of its economy was a mediocre US$100 billion and its per capita income was abysmal at less than US$10 per month, India portrayed itself as an emerging consumer market powerhouse, an enormous juggernaut marching towards consumerism, but did not bother to put a time-frame on when this would really happen.

The early demand boom: The market growth in the first five years after liberalization was phenomenal and, in retrospect, a red herring. The growth rates for practically every product on offer, from cars to shampoos, were explosive: 20 to 30 per cent volume growth and 15 to 20 per cent value growth were seen as the new 'Hindu rate of growth' (the Indian equivalent of the golfing term, 'par for the course') for consumer markets, in an unshackled economy that had, at last, unconstrained supply.

Market analysts and business strategists extrapolated these early growth rates into the future and the myth of the Great Indian Middle Class was born. Supposedly numbering 250–300 million consumers, it was assumed to be a homogeneous consumer juggernaut rolling on towards mega consumerism, delivering double-digit growth in all categories for many years to come.

The subsequent demand stagnation: Based on this view of the market, the mid-1990s saw large capacity investments and grand business plans. The only trouble was that this large consumption machine failed to materialize. The late 1990s saw disappointment and frustration made worse by a below-average monsoon and retarded rural demand. The market did not yield the expected or predicted results. Not surprisingly, the first among the new entrants who had set up shop in India went through a lot of turmoil. Over the first decade, Coca-Cola ran up losses far exceeding its equity investment of US$268 million, presumably incurred in its effort to get to an equivalent top line. Procter and Gamble reduced the number of stock keeping units it offered, cut its distribution width and depth, and shrank in order to be beautiful and profitable. Even the consulting firms had their share of trouble. Booze Allen closed shop, though McKinsey hung in there and waited for the market to mature—and maybe is still waiting! Despite many of the new MNC entrants declaring that they were in the Indian market for the long haul and would do whatever it took for long-term market development, CEOs' heads rolled, business cases were furiously reviewed, and the Indian market got a bad reputation for being fickle and for being more hype than reality.

Ironically, even in China the expected volumes and profits were not achieved. But given its higher income levels and higher GDP growth rate vis-à-vis India and the visible signs of westernized development, the future seemed more concrete and more comprehensible there.

THE LESSONS LEARNT

The dangerous delusion of pent-up demand: The boom–extrapolation–stagnation cycle has since been repeated many times. It is now clear that there is always an initial starburst of demand as a result of a confluence of one-time events or phenomena. Past examples of this are: Just after liberalization, the release of pent-up demand of the rich who always had the money and the desire but had nothing much to buy; a television ownership boom, when, for the first time, the category was strongly promoted; a distribution boom that causes a spurt when the sought products and services are suddenly available within easy reach; a lowering of a price point with the launch of the miniature pack (the sachet) strategy or instalment schemes that decrease the unit price and make a range of products suddenly affordable to a whole group of consumers.

The rock table: After growth that comes easily from mopping up pockets of pent-up demand or just-below-the-surface demand, the market always hits a rock table and growth grinds to a halt. To continue the growth trajectory, what is needed is not a mop but actually a powerful drill fashioned from a good market strategy, and over time the next layer will appear. At this stage, what makes more sense is to strategically search for weak areas of weathered away rock in the rock table, rather than flogging the sales team with targets based on historical growth as companies usually tend to do.

Zigzag economic growth gives zigzag consumer market growth: Given the large number of variables, from politics and geopolitics to meteorology, each of which has a different impact on the many sub-economies that make up India's economy, India's exact economic growth cannot be taken for granted. Between 1994–5 and 1996–7, the real GDP growth ranged from 7.3 to 7.8 per cent, breaking the 'under 6 per cent' jinx of many preceding years. However, the folly was to assume that it would continue that way. In 1997–8, GDP grew at just 4.8 per cent in real terms, while in the next two years it was at 6.5 per cent and 6.1 per cent respectively. It plummeted again to 4.4 per cent in 2000–1, went up to 5.8 per cent the next year and crashed to 4 per cent in 2002–3. In 2003–4 it was 8.2 per cent, but 2004–5 saw it decline to 6 per cent, and the following year on, it has been at 8 per cent and beyond.

Income growth does not always keep pace with supply-side renaissance: Despite several years of good economic growth, there was a very important trouble-making factor that most market watchers had somehow overlooked. With many new product categories entering the market for the first time, there was an explosion on the supply side. Added to this were the many supply-side revolutions in quality, price and distribution, as well as the sudden easy availability of consumer finance. Therefore the number of things that consumers could buy increased exponentially, while the income of consumers did not. As a result, 'category-collide' or inter-category competition became very strong. The choice now was between paying for a cell phone for yourself and paying for high quality shampoo and ketchup for the family. Unbelievable but true, this choice was a real one.

The fast moving consumer goods (FMCG) business, for example, got hit hard by this phenomenon. As one small town consumer explained, since a refrigerator in one's home or a second-hand car for one's family were such visible signs of status and indulgence, why would one want to use an expensive brand of shampoo that promised the same? Further, with the rise in consumer credit, many households had committed the bulk of their future income to pay for homes and consumer durables that they had acquired. The residual money available had to be stretched to run the home and handle the 'revenue' expenditure. So began the paradox of increasing consumer income and sophistication, but, at the same time, consumers adopting the practice of 'down trading' (i.e. shifting to a lower price-performance point brand) in several categories.

Late 1990s and early 2000s: In the midst of all this churning, the ambitious theory of a huge and homogeneous mass market, made up of the Great Indian Middle Class, which should have been a tireless engine of growth, was officially buried. Companies resigned themselves to very slow top line growth and focused on the middle line of their P&L—operational performance improvement and financial restructuring—in order to shore up their bottom line.

But Consumer India has always been pretty tricky to second guess. Not only has the real GDP grown at a spanking pace since 2003–4 to date (8.5 per cent, 6.9 per cent and 7.5 per cent respectively), with it the national income has also grown substantially. Also, by 2005, a lot of small consumption-friendly changes were taking place in Consumer India. When viewed in isolation, each change, could easily be rejected as not being particularly significant. However, when taken together, they have provided a critical mass of overall change and created a deep and distinctive consumer market. A market that now has more cell phones than bank accounts, more colour TV sets than toilets. And this is a market whose potential and desire to consume have perhaps moved way ahead of marketers' and investors' mental models of it. The number of cars has exploded faster than the roads to drive them on and airports cannot cope with the sharp increase in the number of flights and passengers. Restaurants and movie theatres are full, and recovering from bypass surgery is now a fairly common middle-class pastime.

GOOD NEWS, BAD NEWS

Good News: Consumer India is a market that has evolved in an economy where average per capita incomes have increased more than five times since 1991 and more than doubled in the eight years from 1997, when the market was written off as a mirage of hype and hope, to 2005. It, therefore, is a market that is very high on consumer aspiration and consumer confidence, which is about believing that it's all right to spend and make merry today because tomorrow will definitely be even better. So, are happy times here again, once marketers scramble and catch up with the consumers who have moved way ahead of them? Almost, but not quite!

Bad News: **DANGER! DIVERSION! ROAD UNDER REPAIR!** It is often said of the Indian cricket team that they are experts at snatching defeat from the jaws of victory. They squander away a winning position and paint themselves into a corner and end up struggling with a 'win-some, lose-some' nail-biting finish. So is the case, it would seem, with the Indian market.

Trouble seems to be looming ahead and a supply and infrastructure breakdown may dampen consumption. If the demand slowdown of the 1990s was about too much supply and not enough demand, the slowdown that may happen now is about too much demand, with the groaning infrastructure causing poor quality supply. Calls are dropped as cell phones outstrip network capacity and flying is a nightmare because of air traffic delays and small airports. So why bother to pay more for business class and arrive in terrible shape anyway? Outside every mall a long, long line of cars snakes along at snail's pace into the parking lots, resulting in irritated shoppers in terrible moods—which, as any retailer will tell you, is bad for business.

Even at the top end of pricing, there are not enough hangars for private planes, few as they may be given the size of the population, no jetties for the private yachts that lie anchored outside the Gateway of India and no five-star hotel rooms to be had for love or money in the big cities. Real estate prices are climbing dangerously as there is not enough supply of high quality housing in the market. The stock market is forever yo-yoing and investor confidence is getting adversely affected by left-leaning, anti-free market coalition politics.

Add to this list of woes rising petrol prices and rising interest rates affecting consumer credit and you can see a slowing down, temporarily at least, of demand growth.

Yet, when supply constraints will ease and politics settles down, there will be a return to high consumption growth rates again. It seems quite clear that, once again, Consumer India will outsmart its analysts!

It is a bit like those 'good news–bad news' game shows on television that go somewhat like this: 'Contestant Bernice, we are happy to inform you that you are the winner of the grand prize in this spelling bee contest. The good news, Bernice, is that you get two first class tickets to Amsterdam—Amsterdam, in New York State that is. However, the tickets come to you in the pocket of a beautiful mink coat, here it is—the coat, by the way, is 100 per cent fake mink . . .' Unable to take the pressure of this roller coaster ride, contestant Bernice faints, only to be revived and then told that 'the prize also comprises a million dollar check placed in the other pocket of the coat. However the rules of the contest say that in order to get all this, you have to remain conscious throughout the contest'!

As a Fortune 500 CEO once said to me after a particularly stressful session on the future of Consumer India, 'I have no doubt at all that in the long run I will be fine. But unfortunately I have to first survive in the short run!'

This is the exact opposite of China, where the long-term stability and continuity of policies of a non-democratic regime are in doubt, but in the short run, economic growth is steady and encouraging.

DEVELOPING A PERSPECTIVE ON CONSUMER INDIA

A Mosaic of Tradition and Modernity

- India is a confusing market because it harbours far too many contradictions. We call it the 'bullock cart to business class' economy—except that in India, consumers are forcing business class to get cheaper and demanding bullock carts that are more technologically sophisticated! Modern influences affect different parts of India in different ways and produce a mosaic of modernity that is sometimes quite unexpected and startling.

- Over the last decade, there has been, so to speak, an economic and sociological food processor on full churn in India, with some pretty powerful forces operating the controls and some pretty stubborn contents inside. The resulting compound is yet to be identified—all we can bet on is that it will scarcely be like anything we have seen before in the more developed markets.

- India is a land where contradictions will continue to abound, because there are many Indias that are being transformed, with different levels of intensity, by different forces of globalization. Each of these Indias is responding to them in different ways. Consider these coexisting examples of progress and *status quo*: India is a nuclear-capable state that still cannot build roads that will survive their first monsoon. It has eradicated smallpox through the length and breadth of the country, but cannot stop female foeticide and infanticide. It is a country that managed to bring about what it called the 'green revolution', which heralded food grain self-sufficiency for a nation that relied on external food aid and yet, it easily has the most archaic land and agricultural laws in the world, with no sign of anyone wanting to reform them any time soon. It has hundreds of millions of people who subsist on less that a dollar a day, but who vote astutely and punish political parties ruthlessly. It has an independent judiciary that once set aside even Indira Gandhi's election to parliament and yet, many members of parliament have criminal records and still contest and win elections from prison. India is a significant exporter of intellectual capital to the rest of the world—that capital being spawned in a handful of world class institutions of engineering, science and management. Yet it is a country with primary schools of pathetic quality and where retaining children in school is a challenge. India truly is an equal opportunity employer of women leaders in politics, but it took over fifty years to recognize that domestic violence is a crime and almost as long to get tough with bride burning. It is the IT powerhouse of the world, the harbinger of the offshore services revolution that is changing the business paradigms of the developed world. But regrettably, it is also the place where there is a yawning digital divide.

- As a consumer market too, India is no less a land of conflicting truths. India's domestic demand for everything from motorcycles to colour televisions to mobile phones has surprised a lot of people who think of the Indian market in terms of its abysmal per capita income of US$538. Equally, there are enough people buying American upper end labels and imported Mercedes cars and drinking the finest Scotch to justify the successes that upper end product companies are experiencing despite having modest expectations. The other aspect of consumer complexity is the way Indians belong culturally to many centuries at the same time! A farmer who understands ecological balance and the power of the Internet coexists with a nuclear scientist who insists that he needs a son to light his funeral pyre, so that he is not trapped in yet another cycle of birth and death!

A Strange Amalgam of Old and New

India's small scale marketers and service providers excel at designing their offers for this strange amalgam. My favourite example of this is a story narrated to me by a young lady who worked in a beauty parlour. The institution of arranged marriages is still fairly prevalent in India. Typically, there is a 'girl viewing' ceremony where the boy's family and friends come to the home of the girl and have to be treated to high tea. The girl, formally dressed and coiffured, is made to serve the guests, so that her gait, posture and physical appearance can all be critically examined. Then she is asked a few questions about herself and her abilities. She may be asked to sing if she is musically inclined or questioned about her 'adjustability' if she is a 'working girl' and the 'viewing' comes to a close.

Someone decided that the cost and embarrassment of doing all this was too much—especially for a middle class family, particularly if there is a fussy girl who would need to see several candidates! So there was a business created by a marriage broker who would videotape a mock 'viewing ceremony', with just the girl and her family (and himself, for his own brand awareness to increase), and would show it to prospective candidates. On the basis of this tape they could decide whether or not to move to the next step. It was a huge success because this solution recognized the acceptability of technology, gender-driven decision making (let the boy decide first, then the girl will), and the need to reform the process but not reengineer it!

And here's another sobering, though controversial, thought on this subject: Multinational marketers and big consulting firms favour predicting market evolution by studying more developed markets that they believe are analogous. But that has not been nor will be very helpful in understanding the future of Consumer India. The notion that as GDP per capita increases, all countries will demonstrate a predictable pattern of market structure and consumer behaviour has been disproved already. The fact is that never before in the history of humanity have so many poor and illiterate people been subjected to so much real time exposure to the developed world, via television and the Internet, and never ever before have so many Indians, rich and poor, seen their incomes grow so fast.

And never before have they had so many things to buy and so friendly a consumption discourse. And unlike China, Indian consumers have a halfway-house experience of modern consumerism and are constantly benchmarking what they see new with what they have always been used to—and the new option is not always the obviously better choice For example, a mom-and-pop shop in India provides such sophisticated customer relationship management and free services like home delivery and replenishment on telephonic orders, as would be hard for a Tesco or a Sainsbury to match. And the many housewives in large cities supplying home-cooked, ready-to-eat lunches and dinners at low overheads, high hygiene and low cost, with home delivery, are already inhibiting the growth of the packaged processed food industry.

DEFINE YOUR OWN INDIA

How, then, should businesses be making sense of all this? Shashi Tharoor gives us the first clue in his book *India: From Midnight to the Millennium*, when he writes of how Winston Churchill once barked: 'India is merely a geographic expression. It is no more a single country than the equator.' That is what I tell my clients—that the onus is on them to define what their India is, and translate the geographic idea into a well-defined construct of a consumer market.

Tharoor goes on to say, 'any truism about India can be immediately contradicted by another truism about India. The country's national motto emblazoned on its governmental crest, is *Satyameva Jayate*: "Truth Alone Triumphs". The question remains, however: whose truth?' Again, the message from this is that rather than worrying about finding the absolute, incontrovertible truth about India, marketers should learn to accept that this is a market of contradictions and focus on designing innovative businesses which would or might work in such a market.

The most important thing about dealing with the Indian market, therefore, is to figure out how to think about it in the context of your business strategy, and develop a mental model of what 'my target India' is and then proceed further.

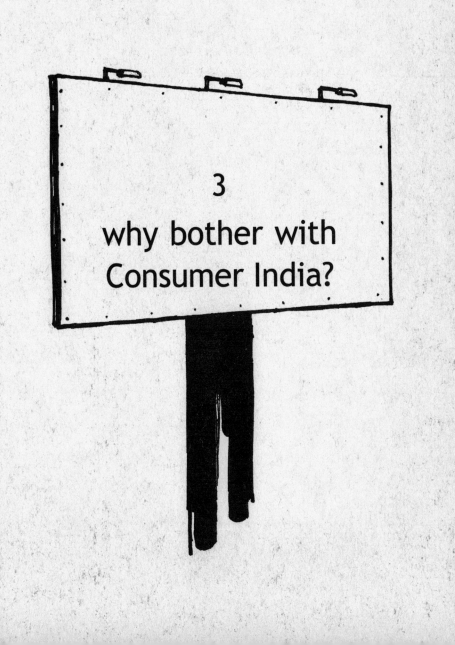

3

why bother with
Consumer India?

Most market analysts and business strategists bark up the wrong tree when they set out to evaluate the India opportunity by asking the question, 'When will India have the per capita income and infrastructure of China, the westernization and per capita consumption of Brazil, the education levels of Russia, the institutional framework and maturity of the US'? What they are actually asking is, 'When will India become like someplace else?'

The correct answer to this incorrect question is 'probably never'; certainly not in the lifespan of most people reading this book! That is the most important truth about India. To use a popular Indian phrase and the title of this book, 'We are like that only! Mind it' (loosely translated, it means 'deal with it'!). Evaluating India through a comparative lens will lead to the inevitable conclusion that 'now' will never ever be a good time to enter a market of a billion consumers, US$700 billion GDP and growing at 8 to 9 per cent, because it will probably never catch up with the benchmark 'someplace else'.

However, when evaluated through a standalone lens there are no surprises here and it is clearly a mixed verdict. The glass of market attractiveness is half full and half empty. However, there are several signs that would lead one to believe that the glass is filling—maybe not as fast as we would like it to, but the water level is definitely rising with each passing year.

THE DARK CLOUD AND THE SILVER LINING

There are a few indisputable truths about Consumer India that will endure for a long time to come and which must form the backdrop against which all mental models about 'my target India' must be built: Consumer India is large, it is mostly poor, it is getting richer and less poor, and it is totally schizophrenic. Not surprisingly, it calls for unusual strategy complexity. Here's a list that I call Consumer India 101.

- **Consumer India is large.** Over one billion people and still growing at about 1.6 per cent annually. India adds to itself a population equivalent to that of Australia each year! It will comprise 18 per cent of the world's population by the year 2030. A fact that global marketers cannot ignore, because in terms of sheer numbers, the centre of gravity of 'global' has to shift towards where the consumers are.
- **It is mostly poor, but is getting less poor.** Unfortunately, these billion people are mostly poor. The good news, however, is that they are getting less poor by the year, as economic growth fuels income growth. This can be seen from the increase in the per capita income from a US$120 in 1991 to US$700 today. Despite the fact that the fruits of the new, improved economy—the fruits of liberalization—have gone far more to the rich and the educated than to the mostly illiterate poor, the bottom of the well of poverty is rising. Between 1993–4 and 2004–5, according to the National Sample Survey, an official government survey, the percentage of people below the poverty line has dropped from 36 per cent to 22 per cent, a significant reduction by any standard, even if the measure of poverty is a very cynical one based on the number of calories consumed, i.e. whether the person has had enough to eat to stay healthy. But the growing population has neutralized the percentage reduction and the number of

the poor has remained roughly the same, at about 230 million.

- **It has some rich people, increasing in number, getting richer.** As we said earlier, the early fruits of liberalization have gone more to those who were already in a position to take advantage of it. Since 2001 to date, the average annual growth rate of high income households has been double that of any other income group. The top 10 per cent of India's population has per capita income levels that are the same as 60 per cent of those in Malaysia and 80 per cent of those in Brazil. This is where the great Indian number trick comes into play where even a small percentage of a large population is a large number of people! And these 100 million people are, by themselves, equivalent to three times the total population of Canada, five times that of Australia, a little less than double that of France, and about 60 per cent of the population of Brazil.

- **Consumer India is totally schizophrenic.** Words like heterogeneous and plural do not even begin to convey the extent of India's diversity and the varied dimensions or aspects of that diversity. And it's not just the twenty-three languages, the geographic and climatic diversity, the different religions living together and the many shades of rich and poor people that exist, or coexist, in this vast, continental country. India has twenty-eight states, and there are wide income and social development disparities among them. Jean Drèze and Amartya Sen, in their book *India: Economic Development and Social Opportunity*, say that some Indian states are worse off than sub-Saharan Africa, while others are better than China. Rural and urban India are at different stages of evolution; even within rural India, often within the same state, there are oases of development poised to leap-frog and become more developed than even urban India.

- Broadly speaking, India has two totally distinct age groups that coexist in sizeable numbers, but whose consumption ideologies are totally different. One is the isolated, post-Independence generation brought up in and conditioned by the Nehruvian socialistic milieu. The other is the free-market, globally integrated, post-liberalization generation. These represent two edges of the spectrum and we discuss this in greater detail later.

- Finally, as many as four separate economies with startlingly different characteristics can be said to coexist in India, ranging from the globally competitive infotech economy, which earns in dollars from overseas markets, to the totally uncompetitive (even in India) agricultural economy that is heavily dependent on the monsoon.

Multiply all these different variables and you have a bewildering patchwork quilt with no apparent grand design or explainable pattern. And to go back to what Shashi Tharoor says, every truism about India and its opposite are both true! As different parts of India get exposed to different economic, social, political and global forces to different degrees, the level of schizophrenia is getting worse, not better.

One of the most common complaints about India from global companies then is that doing business in India demands far greater strategy complexity than any other market of equivalent size.

A 'Guaranteed to Happen' Snowball/IPO Type of Opportunity

As we said earlier, India is hardly likely to become like someplace else in a hurry. But on its own terms, it still offers a fertile ground for long-term, sustainable growth, which is now guaranteed to happen, even if it takes the meandering path of the 'walk of a drunken man'. In short, India offers a large and 'must exploit' opportunity to global businesses for long-term value creation. So let us get back to the question we began with: Why should global businesses bother with Consumer India, an ugly duckling that may never become a beautiful swan? Here's a set of reasons to consider:

- *A 'guaranteed to happen' growth story.* It is a large economy and has a large consumer base growing steadily at a modest and sustainable pace. It has the proven environment for 'guaranteed to happen' growth. Between 1992–3, when the economic reform process had just begun, and 2005–6, India's worst real annual GDP growth rate was between 4 per cent and 4.4 per cent in 1997–8, 2000–1 and 2002–3; and the best was close to 8 per cent (between 7.8 per cent and 8.5 per cent), in 1996–7, 2003–4 and 2005–6. On an average, the 1990s achieved a real GDP growth rate of 6.3 per cent per annum and since the new millennium began, it has been 6.2 per cent. This rate of growth has survived three governments at the centre, countless changes in state governments, the communist parties as central government coalition partners, six years of negative growth in agriculture (a sector that accounts for one-fifth of the economy) and an Asian meltdown. So it seems to be pretty much sustainable, no matter what. With apologies to Shakespeare, 'politics cannot wither her nor change in custom stale her infinite variety'!

- *Young people, virgin market.* For those operating in developed markets that are ageing and saturating, Consumer India offers a guaranteed growth source of 400 million people below the age of 21, and over 20 million new babies each year. Moreover, since incomes are increasing steadily, each year there are more and more new consumers just entering consumption, resulting in significant market expansion.

- *Low country risk.* In addition to interesting demographics, India is a story of inclusive growth that is stable both politically and socially. This is the result of being a democracy. While there may be several arguments about the merits and demerits of the Indian democracy the inevitable answer that emerges is that democracy may be slow but it clearly is the most suitable system for India. The wages of democracy are sometimes hard to deal with but if and when the party does happen, *everyone* will be invited to it and have a stake in it. Consequently, abrupt and unreasonable about-turns in economic or social policy are not a real threat.

- *Strong institutions.* Another key aspect that makes a country attractive for investment is that there are well-developed institutions, with a clear separation between the legislature and the judiciary. Further, there is a continuous modernizing of these institutions as they are being tested constantly and are strengthened in the process. India's courts that have become more activist, its tough Election Commission and the glare of an independent free press enable a variety of voices and viewpoints to be widely heard. This ensures deeper discussion and strengthens the institutional framework of democracy. Voters are becoming more punishing, even if they are not becoming more discerning.

- *Change confluence.* There is a 'change confluence' that is happening, which is creating the tipping point for a vibrant consumer market. We will soon see exponential changes in market growth and sophistication. The average Indian's income is growing, India's economic fundamentals are growing stronger and are unlikely to flounder due to the several areas of weakness. Rural India is decreasing its dependence on agriculture, the self-employed population dominates the process of making India a vibrant nation of strivers, not *status quoist* people in sleepy large companies or government jobs; and consumption is now a huge engine of growth. While private consumption accounts for less than half of China's GDP, it accounts for over 60 per cent in the case of India.

- *China 2005 = India 2015*. In about eight years' time, India will have the same per capita income that China had in 2005 and if China is being considered a 'hot' and attractive consumer market, then India will be just as 'hot' in another eight years.

Taking all of these factors together, there can be no doubt that for growth-hungry corporations, presence in the Indian market is a matter of compulsion, not choice. India is the second biggest game in the world (after China)—the game has just begun and entry tickets are still soing cheap. However, the question is just how much should companies invest in such a market. The best way is to think about it being like an IPO, in that you invest in it early and get in on the ground floor of a 'guaranteed to happen', long-term growth opportunity that is built on solid foundations. Or picture a snowball: it starts off modest in size, but grows at an ever-increasing pace over time. In short, India is likely to offer similar long-term benefits or returns to those who are willing to come in now and be there for the long haul.

It makes sense to pause and examine the journey so far and ask whether there is sufficient evidence to justify the confidence that the promised future will happen, even the way we have just visualized it. How have fifteen years of a liberalized economy and 6 per cent plus growth rate changed Consumer India? What is the change confluence that is now happening, which leads us to believe that Consumer India's tipping point is here, and that the change from now on will be both dramatic and irreversible?

CHANGE CONFLUENCE CAUSING THE TIPPING POINT IN CONSUMPTION

C.K. Prahalad, management guru and author of the book *Competing for the Future*, once remarked that in order to see the

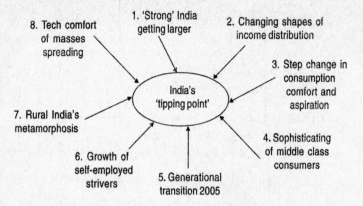

Figure 3.1: Consumer India's Confluence of Change

future and not miss fundamental changes that are about to happen, one needs to look at all the weak signals of change collectively—signals which, when viewed individually, can easily be dismissed as inconsequential but when viewed collectively give a clear message of imminent change. Applying this to Consumer India, it is obvious that it is now fortuitously at the confluence of several changes (Figure 3.1). The coming together of a diverse set of economic, demographic and social change waves, all point towards the fact that a brave new market is here—a market of a billion consumers, a highly fertile ground to sow the seeds of future business creation.

The pace of change is slow, and it is a long-haul market, but the fact that the future will happen and Consumer India will keep its promise is now a concrete reality, not an illusion a created by more optimism.

Let us now turn our attention to the individual change waves that are causing the change confluence, which has resulted in the tipping point for Consumer India.

Strong India is Getting Larger

In January 2000, P. Chidambaram, the present finance minister of India, gave a talk at the University of Michigan. It was titled

'Of Elephants and Tigers: India's Place in an Asian Century'. In that, he said,

> Reforms as implemented thus far have brought to the fore two faces of India. One that is vibrant, full of entrepreneurial and managerial energy, and eager to generate wealth through the use of technology, trade, finance and markets. This India is eager to compete, win and join hands with the best and the brightest in the global marketplace. It is keen on both learning and teaching, and dealing with the world on its own terms. But there is another India that is lonesome, sad and sunk so deep in deprivation and misery that its quest for mere survival has doused any flicker of aspiration that it may have nurtured by mistake. Unfortunately, the second India is many times bigger than the first. Even more worrisome is that these two Indias seem to be moving on parallel tracks. Or to put it in current jargon, there is a strong 'disconnect' between the two. I have no doubt that the first India will participate in and gain from the forthcoming Asian century. But what about the second India? Will it or will it not? Our reforms have still not provided a clear answer to this question. However, one thing is clear: that unless the 'disconnect' is eliminated the second India will limit the promise the first India sees for itself in the Asian century.

The worry which Chidambaram expressed in 2000, that the weak India will swallow the fledgling strong India, has now been proved to have been unwarranted. True, weak India will slow down strong India, but the evidence shows that strong India has now grown large enough and is here to stay. It continues to grow steadily, as it did between 2000 and 2005. This strong India, of Indians with economic opportunity who have experienced visible improvement in the quality of their life in terms of education, healthcare and housing, by my reckoning, now comprises about 60 per cent of urban India and 12–15 per cent of rural India, numbering almost 285 million people. This rural India number varies significantly by state, with strong India being much larger in states like Himachal Pradesh, Gujarat, Maharashtra and Tamil Nadu, but being comparatively smaller in states such as Bihar and Uttar Pradesh. In fact strong

India has realized that it is in its own interest to help weak India rather than ignore it. Therefore, we are seeing a greater push in corporate social responsibility, in public–private partnerships, in innovations in education, healthcare and financial service solutions for the bottom of the pyramid via self-help groups as well as organized charity. Again a set of weak signals, but taken together, giving an unequivocally clear message.

Changing Shapes of Income Distribution

Figure 3.2 is a graphical representation of a very interesting metric, the shape of income distribution, i.e. what percentages of the population are at each of five levels of income, ranging from low to high, and how this has changed over time. This is a valuable indicator because changes in the shape herald changes in consumption patterns: an idea not intuitively difficult to understand, because as these shapes change, the centre of gravity or the reference point of the 'average' consumer behaviour also changes, as also do the reference points and role models where poor consumers peg their aspirations. The figure plots the changes in the shape of income distribution, based on data from the Market Information Survey of Households (MISH) of the NCAER. Since the data was obtained from the same survey and is inflation adjusted, it is comparable over time.

Between 1995–6 and 2005–6 the shape of income distribution in urban India changed from the traditional poor country shape of a triangle or pyramid (indicating far more people at the bottom than at the middle and even fewer at the top) to a diamond, with less people at the bottom and the top but a lot more in the middle.

In 2001–2, the shape of urban income distribution was a diamond but with the middle being low slung, that is, more in the lower middle income level than the middle or upper middle level. However, by 2005–6, this changed to a proper diamond shape, with the middle income level having the highest number

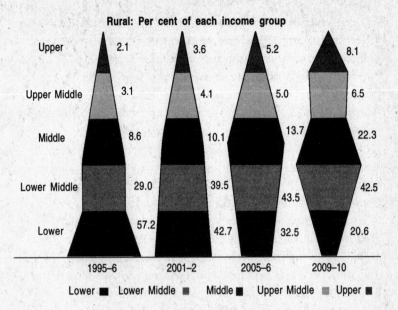

Rural: Per cent of each income group

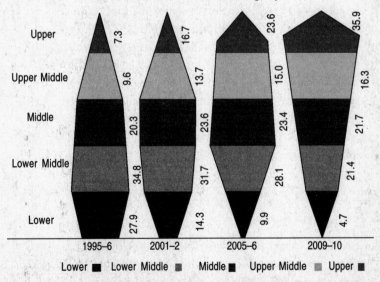

Urban: Per cent of each income group

Figure 3.2: Changing Shapes of Income Distribution

of people. At a 6.5 per cent rate of economic growth, NCAER projects that the shape will become a cylinder standing on a narrow base, with equal numbers in the top four income groups and very few at the lowest income group. This means a sharp increase in demand for the higher performance offerings, even at higher prices. Never before in the history of India has this shape of income distribution been achieved.

The shape of income distribution in rural India has also changed for the better over the years. From a very bottom-heavy triangle in 1995–6, it changed to a better proportioned triangle by 2002–3. By 2005–6, it began to acquire the dimensions of a diamond—with more people at one income rung above the bottom than at the absolute bottom. It is expected that by 2009–10, we will see a distinctly more diamond-shaped income distribution, with a further narrowing of the bottom. The point that ought not to be forgotten is that even a 1 per cent improvement on any count in rural India accounts for close to 6 million people. So the 8 per cent increase in the proportion of rural population in the middle income group, on the increased population base of 2009–10 of rural India, would be an addition of 14.5 million households, which is almost 90 million people. A state by state look at rural income distribution shows that in many states, the shape of income distribution has already changed to that of a diamond and, in some states, even to that of an inverted triangle, suggesting that parts of rural India are poised for a quality consumption boom, if only quality supply could be made available.

Step Change in Consumption Comfort and Aspiration Levels

Actual visible consumption increase: Between 1995–6 and 2003–4, car and two-wheeler sales more than doubled. Those of cell phones increased more than fivefold. These categories are the best combination of functionality and status enhancement and have continuously been making efforts to drop price thresholds—indeed, they are great examples of how responsive the Indian consumer market can be to real value propositions. And also of the fact that it is Nokia's and Honda's experience that defines this market, rather than that of Kellogg's or Coke!

Business Today and *Business Standard*, two of India's leading business publications, also reported that there was a purchasing boom in the smaller towns, outside the large metros. For example, towns that were number 60 and below in terms of population rank, accounted for 20 per cent of the sales of Maruti, from India's largest car maker, and registered a growth of 33 per cent in 2003–4.

If we consider the 250 million-plus population or the 50 million-plus households of urban India, the increase in penetration is across the board for all sorts of products. Between the years 1990 and 1999, television penetration in the country increased by 20 per cent and in the lowest income groups of urban India, it increased by 24 per cent. In the highest income group, washing machine penetration increased by 20 per cent and most of urban India, rich and poor, acquired mixer grinders. Overall, its penetration increased by 16 per cent, uniformly across all but the lowest income group. The same was the story for LPG cylinders. Like television, pressure cooker penetration in the lowest income groups increased by 17 to 20 per cent. In rural India, two-wheeler penetration is quite stunning.

Visible consumption breeds more consumption: Nothing breeds the desire to consume more than consumption itself. For someone who has not taken the consumption road yet, there is less desire and aspiration to consume. But for someone who has begun that journey, there will only be more consumption. Urban India has increased its ownership of durables quite significantly, in all socio-economic classes. It now has a sufficiently large consumption base and enough comfort with it. This will act as a springboard for it to jump to the next stage of its consumption life cycle.

A large enough consumption base now exists to create a springboard for more consumption: The current level of product penetration in any market influences the pace of future penetration. Market penetration is not linear. It accelerates as base penetration increases, up to a point when saturation sets in. If only one out of twenty households in a given socio-economic class has a washing machine or a two-wheeler, adoption will be slow. But when one out of every ten households have them, it becomes something significant on the aspiration radar of the rest. And when it gets to one in every five, it actually serves to rapidly penetrate into the balance households. While this may appear to be a mere 20 per cent penetration, it becomes a 'must have' now for the others. Given the current levels of penetration in the upper income group (enough as a springboard, but far from saturated), increase in penetration will be more in the high income group than in the middle.

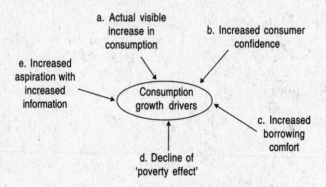

Figure 3.3: Drivers of Consumption Comfort and Consumer Confidence

Step Change in Consumer Confidence

Consumer confidence is all about the belief a person has that tomorrow's income will be greater than today's. This has been the visible pattern for most Indians over the past fifteen years. The biggest social implication of income growth has been the rapid change in the standard of living in just under one generation. In just nine years between 1990 and 1999, an average household saw its nominal income increase by a factor of 2.4. With this change came the climb on to the next rung of the economic and, consequently, social ladder, and to a new self-image and aspiration. Typically, as people will tell you, 'in the old days, I could only hope to start my life at half the lifestyle that my father enjoyed when he retired. Now I start my life at a point above where he ended'. And when people see this steady progress over the last decade in their own homes and the homes of those around them, it unleashes a huge amount of consumer and consumption confidence. Imagine this happening in a country of over a billion people who have seen steady income growth for a decade and a step change in their spending power.

Affordability growth greater than income growth: This consumer confidence has been further fuelled because affordability growth has been greater than income growth for this past decade, due to a sharp drop in prices with an increase in performance, thanks to the pressures of competition, falling interest rates and easier consumer credit.

In real terms the prices of everything from cars to shampoos to air conditioners to telephones to refrigerators have actually come down. As competition intensifies, fresh capacities increase and the 'low cost business' learning improves amongst suppliers, this trend will continue. The prices of many consumer goods have fallen, both in real terms and in nominal terms, and the average price-performance points are unlikely to rise disproportionately beyond the income growth.

Increased comfort with borrowing: At last, consumer comfort with borrowing to fund future consumption is on the rise. Being in debt has always been an area of high discomfort for everybody in India other than the very poor who have no choice but to borrow for survival. In the early years we wondered if this would ever change. However, three things have helped change this—one is the sheer confidence, based on past experience, that tomorrow will be better than today. Therefore being a borrower is now a sign that you are confident about your income rather than that you are living beyond your means (and that's a 'no no' in this country). The second is the low interest rate regime. For example, consumers feel that it makes far more economic sense to buy a home at these rates of interest, rather than rent one. The third is the concept of EMI, equated monthly instalments, which is the most popular form of repayment. EMI acts like magic at legitimizing borrowing, especially for funding future consumption—it creates a sensible and disciplined borrowing method, with predictable and planned outflows. Small wonder, then, that the average age of the home loan taker has come down by ten years in a period of just five years.

Of course, all this would not have happened had it not been for increased lending comfort from the banks. They survived the early phase of taking a leveraged bet on the Indian economy, betting that the potential risks of write-offs from liberal loan policies will be more than offset by the increase in the number of higher quality borrowers—not unreasonable, given the higher-than-average growth predicted of households in the high income group.

This comfort with lending and borrowing is now well internalized socially, and can only increase, on a trend basis, as data on white goods purchases and consumer credit offtake has been showing.

Decline of the poverty effect: Economists talk about the concept of the 'wealth effect', according to which it takes some time before consumption decreases in response to decreasing income. Equally, it takes a while for comfort with consumption to happen, and consumption increase lags behind income increase, especially in a country that has been poor and celebrating abstemiousness for so long. It also takes a supply explosion to spark the desire to consume and to translate it into actual action. Both events have happened.

Rampant Rise in Aspiration

The connectivity, communication and literacy leap that India
has gone through during this last decade has been a major driver
of aspiration. Much has been said about these, as also about how
they drive aspiration. The most lucid explanation for this comes
from the well-known anthropologist Arjun Appadurai, presently
with the New School: 'Imagination is not about individual
escape. It is a collective social activity. Informational resources
are needed for people to even imagine a possible life, weave
a story and a script around themselves and place products in
emerging sequences. Imagination may not always lead to action,
but it is a prelude to action.'

Consumer India now has enough access and exposure to
informal resources and media to concretely imagine or visualize
a better life, inspired both by the real and the make-believe
world around it.

Sophisticating of the Middle Class

In the past five years the performance of the mid-price or
'popular' segment products has improved dramatically, almost
beyond recognition. This has been a long-delayed epiphany for
both multinational and Indian businesses, underscoring the fact
that volumes lie in middle income urban and rural India. Unless
prices drop to a level this India can afford, volumes will not pick
up and markets will not be created. There is also the discovery
across sectors that the arithmetic of lower margins being more
than compensated by increased volumes actually does work.
And finally, the supplier mindset of 'rubbish at low prices' has
changed, especially after a few resounding failures due to
middle income consumer rejection of what manufacturers
thought would be adequate quality for the price. The moped
category died, the chunky cell phone did not move off the shelf
and motorcycles with premium styles and popular price points
were winners. Budget hotels of high quality, budget airlines,

budget apparel brands, prepaid cards for budget cell phone users, low-price basic handsets, budget retail formats that are hybrid superstore-hypermarkets and high-end banking facilities for mid-level customers have appeared on the scene. As this formula gets widely understood and accepted, as more success stories emerge, we will see a whole slew of such new entrants. The result? A middle majority of sophisticated and discerning customers who are joining the consumerism game.

Generational Transition: Liberalization Children Come of Age

Liberalization marked the ushering in of a non-socialist, consumption friendly ideology. The post-liberalization generation is coming of age—the first non-socialist generation of India. Children born around 1990 will be entering the workforce shortly. There are 100 million seventeen- to twenty-one-year-olds[1]—indeed, six out of ten households have a liberalization child. All these youngsters have grown up with no guilt about consumption, even as they have never seen anything like the bad times that the generation before them has seen. Most importantly, these youngsters are now reasonably confident about their future.

Striving, not Resigned: A Nation of the Self-employed

One of the frequently heard comments in the India vs China debate is that change in India is bottom-up, while change in China is top-down. Part of this bottom-up change is the extent of the entrepreneurial energy that exists at the grassroots. India's organized sector accounts for less than 10 per cent of the jobs in the country while the informal sector actually drives

[1] Indian Readership Survey, 2003.

employment. Since most of Consumer India wants to get ahead in a hurry, being self-employed is the means by which they can earn and construct a better life for themselves and their families. The epitome of the 'resigned to life', low energy, *status quoist* mindset is a government job, which used to be the coveted mainstay of employment in the pre-liberalization era.

The self-employed person, in contrast, is a striver and struggles. Entrepreneurial by nature, he does not accept conventional boundaries set by the circumstances of his birth. The rise of the self-employed and the service economy, requiring less capital and more sweat has changed the mindset from one of demanding social justice to one of grabbing economic opportunity—it is an attitude of 'I can and I will', especially visible in urban India. Today, 90 per cent of rural households and 60 per cent of urban households are headed by a self-employed person. In the highest income group of urban India, the proportion of the self-employed is the lowest, at about 45 per cent, while in the lowest income group, it rises to almost 80 per cent.[2]

The employed salary earner has now been replaced by the self-employed as the new 'mainstream market', especially in urban India. Progressive and image-conscious, they use products much more to signal success and quickly adopt any tools that can help increase productivity or profit whether it be cell phones or two-wheelers.

The Morphing of Rural India Beyond Agriculture

One of the problems with rural India till recently has been its dependence on agriculture, and in turn, the dependence of agricultural performance on the monsoons. This led to regular boom and bust cycles and fragile sentiments. Further, in economic terms, agriculture has not been a great proposition for a variety of reasons, and has grown at just 1.9 per cent over the last decade.

[2] MISH Survey, NCAER.

However, rural India has now gone beyond its dependence on agriculture in order to augment incomes from non-agricultural activities. Today, non-agricultural activity in the rural areas is almost equal to the agricultural activity and accounts for a little less than half of the rural GDP. It is growing fast and creating a different kind of rural market where non-agricultural households have higher incomes and spend power. NCAER occupation data shows a decline in cultivators, and there is enough evidence of dual sector households. Add to this the exposure of the top end of rural India through television and other media. In the matter of mindsets, which dictate consumption, the rural market will soon be closer to the urban market. This is already happening in the more developed states with higher incomes.

Comfort with Technology

Awareness of the power and utility of IT, whether in solving problems/improving lives or in creating employment opportunities, has sunk in and trickled down to the lowest socio-economic classes and to much of the rural population. This may be through the demonstration effect of model projects of the NGO kind, the thirty Internet kiosks set up at the Kumbh Mela, or by watching the rich use it and prosper. It has been further enhanced by the mushrooming of call centres and other computer-related services offering employment. Whatever may be the reasons, Indians whether rich or poor, urban or rural are finding some use for IT. Cyber grandmas in the upper middle and upper class, who have become e-mail literate in order to communicate with their scattered flock at no recurring cost, are not uncommon. As the nascent projects of distance healthcare as well as village kiosks offering varied services gather scale, this phenomenon of IT awareness will accelerate even further.

There are two key reasons why the vast but scattered rural consuming base has not been tapped by most companies and businesses. The first is that in rural India the number of people who have a large enough income to be counted as high potential consumers are a small proportion of the total rural population. They are scattered over a vast geographic area making them hard to locate and expensive to target. The second reason is the enormous cost of creating a business that can serve such a large geography given such poor infrastructure.

New technologies like the Internet and wireless broadband can solve both these problems, making it economically viable to offer a whole host of services to rural India, from banking to distance education to distance healthcare to remotely supported other services with 'thin' front ends on the ground. This will certainly transform the expectations, aspirations as well as the economy of the rural consumer in India.

BEYOND MARKET POTENTIAL: THE TRIPLE WHAMMY BENEFIT

Long-term sustainable market potential is just one part of the business case for India. There actually is a triple whammy benefit on offer for businesses: (1) interesting and huge demographic-economic opportunity, (2) global cost-cutting opportunities by offshoring business processes and R&D to India, as demonstrated by the IT, BPO and other outsourced businesses and (3) the 'disruptive' innovation capability of a bunch of highly talented scientists and managers, who have cut their teeth in a low-resource environment and prove the point that necessity is the mother of innovation! Leading-edge companies that have set up R&D and innovation centres in India say that they hope to learn a whole new set of 'disruptive' innovation skills that a low-resource, high talent environment like India spawns—the fruits of which can create significant competitive advantage, if deployed, in developed markets.

WHY CHINA AND INDIA?

A decade ago, *McKinsey Quarterly* described China and India as Asia's non-identical twins. As the years roll by, it is very clear that they are indeed so. They offer different capabilities and different sources of risk, have different performance profiles in various sectors and both have 'disruptive' capabilities, but of different kinds. They offer different types of strategic benefit in the portfolio. They have different sources of country risk, as described very eloquently by Arun Maira, Chairman of the Boston Consulting Group India, in his book *Remaking India*. He says that both India and China are trying to cross a river, with each having slippery stones underfoot and a rope overhead for support. In the case of China, the slippery stones are its polity and its institutions and the rope overhead, its economy. In India's case, the situation is the exact opposite.

Most global businesses have stopped asking the question 'Should we be in China OR India'. They now think in terms of Chindia (a phrase coined by Credit Lyonnaise South Asia) to describe the two markets, which complement each other and which are both 'must haves' in the portfolio of any business that considers itself global.

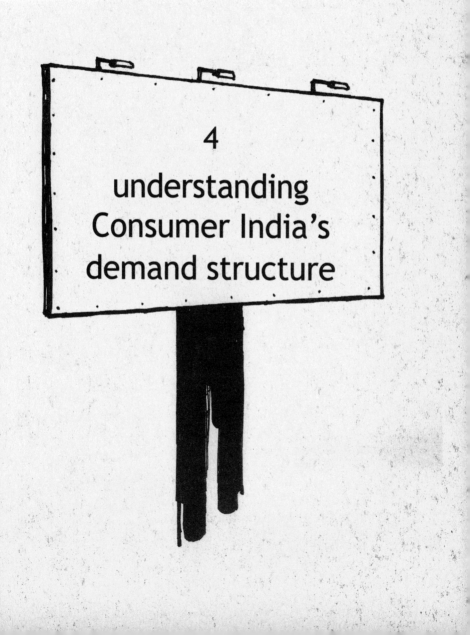

4

understanding
Consumer India's
demand structure

The most startling revelations emerge from the simplest data. Table 4.1 shows the population rank, the GDP rank and the GDP per capita rank of the BRIC economies, in PPP terms, and compares them with the data for the US. On all counts, the US ranks very high. It is the world's largest economy and, using the indicators of per capita GDP, is the tenth richest country in the world after some small countries like Bermuda, Guernsey and Luxembourg. It also has the fourth largest population in the world. China, on the other hand, ranks third in terms of its GDP and first in terms of its population size. However, it ranks 108th in terms of per capita GDP. The pattern for India is the most extreme of all BRIC economies. It is the world's fifth largest economy in terms of its sheer size but ranks a lowly 153rd in terms of its per capita GDP! And even if it clocks a spanking 8 per cent rate of GDP growth over the next ten years, this scenario is unlikely to change.

As *Dreaming with the BRICs: The Path to 2050*, the BRIC Report of Goldman Sachs points out, in the future, the world's

Table 4.1: Population and GDP Ranking of BRIC and the USA

| Country | Population rank | PPP | |
		GDP rank	GDP per capita rank
China	1	5	108
India	2	5	153
Brazil	7	11	97
Russia	10	10	81
USA	4	1	10

Source: *The World Factbook 2007* (2006 data estimates).

largest economies may not be the world's richest economies. It is this characteristic of being individually poor but collectively rich that fundamentally differentiates emerging market economies from developed economies, which are both individually and collectively rich.

The implication of this rather innocuous statistic is that the structure of consumer demand in emerging markets, specifically India, is totally different from that in the developed markets. Consumer demand in the emerging economies is made up of lots and lots of people consuming a little bit each, adding up to a lot. Marketers in developed economies, however, are used to working with an exactly opposite demand structure—a few people consuming a lot each, adding up to a lot. Therefore, neither the pricing paradigms nor the cost structures of their usual, tried and tested global business models are appropriate for India's demand structure.

The organized retailing business is a prime example of this. In developed markets, the store design, store economics and, indeed, the entire science of retailing, is built around the assumption that a geographically focused catchment area or a single high street will have only a few people who will consume a lot each. Their other assumption is that if there are not that many people in a given area to generate the required sales per square foot for economic viability, then a shop far away from the city can be made to generate it, by persuading consumers from a wider catchment area to drive out that far, lured by an attractive discount. Part of that discount can be recovered from the lower costs of the real estate at a non-prime location and part from the increase in the number of people served.

Using this paradigm, the first organized retail forays into the Indian market made by local retailers in collaboration with their global counterparts were a spectacular failure. The high overhead costs of designing and managing a modern store required large outlets in order to generate the sales per square foot required for profitability. However, even highly populated catchment areas did not have enough per capita consumption to generate the required sales per square foot. Low car ownership and a profusion of nearby shops with reasonable goods and services also made the factory outlet or the faraway mega-supermarket model unviable.

A workable solution for food and grocery finally emerged in the form of Subhiksha, a chain of small (mostly around 750 to 1000 square feet) hypermarkets in all the residential areas of a city. Serving the same catchment area as the mom-and-pop store and generally having the same size too, Subhiksha's value advantage was its aggregated backend. As a result, it was able to generate economies of scale in purchases and customer service, which the standalone mom-and-pop store could not. It questioned these 'taken for granted' rules of modern retailing and not just in terms of the prescribed 'ideal' size of a store. Because the stores were so small, they had no labelled aisles for customers to walk through and select what they wanted. Customer interface was provided by way of a computer screen at the counter, and after customers ticked off their choices, the goods (significantly cheaper than at the local store) were home-delivered at no extra cost. Subhiksha thus succeeded in creating a successful retail model that mimicked the structure of the customer demand—a lot of little shops, selling a little bit each, collectively adding up to a lot.

THE GREAT INDIAN ROPE TRICK OF NUMBERS

India's demand structure manifests itself in counter-intuitive ways. I call it the great Indian rope trick of numbers. One of India's leading scientists once said that the advantage of having such a large population is that even if an infinitesimally small percentage of Indians are good scientists, it is still a larger number of scientists than most smaller countries with better education systems can boast of. In the same vein, people are often surprised to hear that the poor Indian consumers, for some categories, consume, in value terms, far more than the rich consumers. The unwritten, unexamined assumption many of us make is that rich consumers offer higher market potential than the poor. That is not quite true.

An example of this was forcefully brought home to me when I was consulting for a two-wheeler (motorcycles, scooters, mopeds) company. Figure 4.1 shows the structure of the demand for two-wheelers in rural India. It also provides the relationship between penetration or ownership of two-wheelers by income group, the number of households in each income group, and hence, the number of two-wheelers bought by each income group.

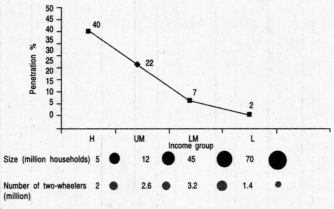

Source: Indian Readership Survey, 2002.

Figure 4.1: Rural India: Two-Wheeler Market

The lower-middle (LM) income group has less than one-fifth of the household penetration of two-wheelers compared to the high income group. But at the same time, it has nine times the number of households in the high-income group. So it actually accounts for 1.6 times the sales of two-wheelers in the high income group. However, marketers are more comfortable focusing on the target market of high income consumers, because the business model that can profitably sell to and service a 7 per cent penetration market needs innovation.

NCAER runs a periodic large-sample survey on household consumption called Market Information Survey of Households (MISH). The results are again counter-intuitive but plausible, if you think about them in terms of the Indian rope trick of numbers. Calculated on a basket of twenty-eight commonly used FMCGs, these findings show that the lowest income group has three times the *value* of consumption as compared to the highest income group. An even more telling statistic is that the value of FMCGs consumed by the lowest rural income group is double the value of the consumption of the highest income group.

Marketing to Such a Demand Structure

So to all those who propagate the theory that there is a magic per capita income number at which consumption in a market 'takes off', it needs to be pointed out that consumption has already 'taken off' in India at far lower income levels. What hasn't taken off is the average marketer's ability to innovate and profitably serve demand structures that are characterized by large populations with low incomes, low to moderate penetration levels, and low per capita consumption levels.

The oft-narrated story of shampoo sachets shows one way of cleverly managing a market that has a demand structure of a lot of people consuming a little bit each, adding up to a lot—and how such a strategy can, in fact, expand the market. The traditional bottled shampoo market had higher unit prices than most people in a poor country could afford, and hence had low penetration and slow growth. Shampoo sachets of 30 ml brought down the unit price dramatically, enabling a large number of users to use the product every once in a while. It also created an expanded user base and additional volume and a value market as big as the bottled shampoo market. Today, there are two shampoo sub-markets in India—the regular use, bottled shampoo market and the special occasion, infrequent use, sachet shampoo market. The latter comprises a large number of women who regularly use shampoo—not at a fixed periodicity but once in a while—for special occasions when they want their hair to look good. The rest of the time they use cheaper traditional products or toilet soap. I call this the 'party pack' market. It would be a mistake to think of this market merely as a small size, trial pack market and focus all effort on trying to 'upgrade' sachet users to become regular users of bottled shampoo. As a matter of fact, the former is the mainstream market for India.

The same demand structure as shampoo also operates for the baby diapers market. Babies are made to wear diapers for special occasions, when they are taken out to a formal function, or for long distance travel, when changing them is a problem. What is inhibiting the growth of this market is the lack of a 'sachet' strategy to enable a large number of parents to use them on occasion, but regularly.

The cost side of the equation for such strategies requires relentless innovation as well as cost reduction. In the case of sachets, the continuous effort is to bring down the cost of packaging while improving its efficacy. An interesting story is how Hindustan Lever (now Hindustan Unilever) had to ensure shampoo sachet margin stability by filling exactly the right amount of shampoo into each sachet—since their conventional filling machines were not precise enough for such small quantities. They had to create attachments for them, learning from fuel injection pumps that were used by the automobile sector to inject exactly the right amount of fuel each time.

THE PREMIUM-POPULAR-DISCOUNT CONSTRUCT OF MARKET STRUCTURE

An age-old construct of market structure that is almost the holy grail of Indian marketers is that there are three broad segments in the Indian market, called premium, popular and discount. These are defined by price-performance ranges and are bought by rich, middle and low income consumers respectively. Every category hitherto, be it FMCGs or durables or even industrial products, has had its rules and conventions about the boundaries of price and performance in each segment. The consumers have also 'obeyed' the rules of not buying into segments above or below their station in life.

While there has been no formal definition of who a premium, popular or discount customer is, the rule of thumb in consumer markets, based on historical data, has been that the top 10 per cent by income of any population constitutes the premium market. Similarly, the next 30 per cent constitute the popular segment and the last 60 per cent is the discount or mass market.

An analysis of the expenditure and income for these three bands at the national level (see Table 4.2) shows that in 2006, the top 10 per cent of consumers in terms of income accounted for 34 per cent of India's income and 30 per cent of India's consumption expenditure. The next 30 per cent accounted for another 36 per cent despite being one-third as rich. The implication of this statistic cannot be overstated. By the rope trick of numbers, three times as many people with one-third of the income create a second tier market of roughly the same size as that of the top tier. Similarly, the bottom 60 per cent of consumers, despite being one-seventh as rich as the top 10 per cent, have a greater share of the total consumption expenditure— because there are so many of them. Translated back into the premium–popular–discount market structure construct that we have been discussing, this means that the premium, popular and discount markets in India are roughly equal in terms of total value. Though they differ vastly in terms of the number of consumers in each and their respective income levels. Welcome to another version of the great Indian number trick!

In industrial or B2B products, the structure of the buyer market is determined by a whole host of supply side issues,

Table 4.2: Consumer Stratification by Income and Expenditure

% of population by income percentile	National income share of each %	Consumption expenditure share %	GDP per capita indexed
Top 10%	34.1	30.0	100
Next 30%	36.1	36.6	35
Lowest 60%	29.7	33.4	14

Source: Bijapurkar and Bhandari, 'Solving the Income Data Puzzle', *Businessworld Marketing White Book 2006.*

specific to an industry, not the least of which is historical regulation. In markets that have historically favoured small producers, the 'unorganized' small-scale buyers are far greater in number than the large-scale, organized sector buyers. Here again, by the magic of the great Indian number trick, a lot of small buyers buying low-priced equipment or services can and do create a market as large in value as that created by large buyers. The former, often catered to by small suppliers, is known as the 'unorganized' segment, while the latter, catered to usually by large companies, is the 'organized' sector. It is not unusual to see many large companies define their target market and report their market share in terms of the organized sector alone and totally miss the point that there is a market, perhaps several times more valuable, at a lower price-performance point. The relative sizes of these markets (organized-unorganized) can range from 10–90 (to as much as 50–50). It must be pointed out, however, that not all these market structures are truly reflective of the customer demand. The history of disproportionate tax subsidies and other cost advantages for certain kinds of products and manufacturing operations has created distortions in the supply segments not matching the demand segments. While this situation has changed to a large extent over the past fifteen years, it has caused enough confusion in the minds of marketers, especially those from overseas. This group does not always remember to make the distinction between free-market product market structures that are indicative of the consumer demand structures and regulated-market product market structures that are quite disconnected from the consumer market structures.

What happens to this market structure, especially in B2B markets, when economies liberalize and the differential duty and tax structures on different kinds of products and producers are rationalized, making it no more extra attractive, beyond market considerations, to operate in the popular segment as compared to the premium segment?

THE BREAKDOWN OF THE PREMIUM-POPULAR-DISCOUNT CONSTRUCT OF MARKET STRUCTURE

The initial assumption, in the early days of liberalization, was that a large part of the popular market would migrate to the premium end and the popular segment manufacturers would die a slow and natural death. However, the reality was different, as is always the case with India. In categories like FMCGs, the reverse happened and the popular segment grew, with richer consumers also opting for it. In personal computers the grey market of system assemblers also grew. Similarly, in industrial water treatment plants, the standard systems market grew faster than the more expensive and more customized products.

The reason for this is that unequal incentives were withdrawn and small marketers were forced to come into open competition with the large premium segment ones. This saw the emergence of 'rogue' marketers especially from within the smaller manufacturers, who refused to respect the unwritten price-performance rules of the category. Hence, consumers now had an explosion of price-performance combinations to choose from. Till recently, it was in everyone's interest to respect the rules of the game and (see Figure 4.2) restrict their innovation to 'fill in the blank' new price-points like mild premium and high end popular, but respecting the 'rules' of how much performance one could provide at how much price.

However, now the rules on what is the 'right' level of performance for a certain price segment are breaking down. This is being especially driven by the popular and discount segment manufacturers who have significantly upgraded their quality, now have access to cheaper imported raw material and better equipment, and are exploiting their low-cost base. In the automotive sector, a 125cc motorcycle is being offered at a 100cc 'popular' price (Victor from TVS). Superior styling that usually comes with a high end popular price tag, is now available at discount segment prices (Boxer from Bajaj). Similarly, a small car that usually belongs in the 'B' or popular product category by historical Indian market rules, is now available with all the features of the premium category (Swift from Maruti). And now

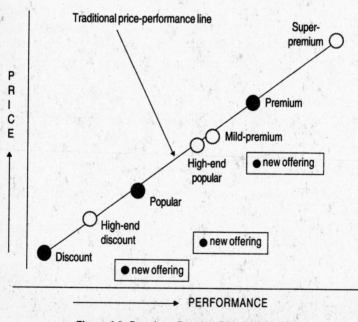

Figure 4.2: Premium–Popular–Discount Market
Structure Construct

there's talk of a car going to be available for Rs 100,000, further lowering the price threshold for the lowest performance segment of cars. This is happening not just in one sector, but across all sectors. With the rigid codes of the market breaking down, consumers too are now liberated in their choices, and are beginning to choose freely, oblivious of the category their station in life merits, as marketers see it in their heads!

In the FMCG sector, this has resulted in rich consumers opting to buy popular and not premium category products. Marketers have christened this as 'down-trading' by consumers, that is buying at price points below where they should. Many have suggested that this is the nature of the Indian consumer —mean and stingy. In fact, it is not the consumer who has 'down-traded' but the supplier who has 'up-traded' his offer and the popular and discount segments, in many cases, now offer a real value advantage in terms of equivalent if not better benefits at a lower price. There are also the shifts in consumer choices affected by changes in related categories, which marketers choose not to notice. For example, rich consumers who are now able to buy, at marginally higher prices, super premium skin creams far superior in performance to what they used to buy. Simultaneously they are happy to settle for basic toilet soaps, now that the quality of these soaps on lather, perfume and fat content has been raised to an acceptable level. Equally, lower middle class consumers are buying high end popular priced anti-ageing and other specific property soaps, which are now available at a price they can somehow afford. And this story repeats across many categories.

It seems the paradigm of premium–popular–discount = rich–middle income–poor is now quite irrelevant. Most old India marketers and marketing service providers including retail audit companies are resisting recognizing this, because the new paradigm that replaces this needs to be found. What's more, all thought and action frameworks in this context have changed as well.

THE NEW MARKET STRUCTURE CONSTRUCT: BY VALUE ORIENTATION

In an effort to find a more realistic way of constructing the structure of the market, NCAER has clustered Consumer India into five types of consumer groups based on what they consume and created a framework called the Consumer Classes Framework.[1] Figure 4.3 shows that there exists five consumer classes based on their consumption patterns.

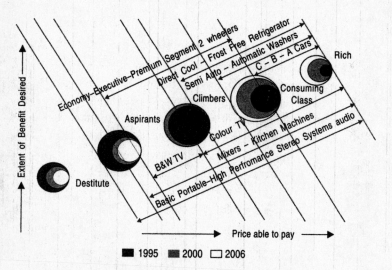

Figure 4.3: Consumer Classes: What are They Buying?

The rich who have most of the luxury goods like cars and PCs and air conditioners and are generally the consumers of premium products.

The consuming class which has about 70 per cent of the 'utility' durables like two-wheelers, refrigerators and washing machines and the bulk of regular FMCGs.

---

[1] S.L. Rao and I. Natarajan, *Indian Market Demographics: The Consumer Classes*, Global Business Press, 1994.

The climbers who have at least one major durable in their homes—either a mixer or a sewing machine or perhaps a television set. They are the main consumers of popular segment consumer goods.

The aspirants who are just entering consumption and have the very basic goods, like a watch, a bicycle, a radio or a table fan.

Finally, there are the **destitute** who own and consume practically nothing, living as they do from hand to mouth.

It is interesting to see that while the same durable is being consumed across the consumption classes, the performance-price points within them are many. For example, the cheaper direct cool refrigerator and the more expensive and more modern frost-free; the 100cc basic economy bike, the 110–125cc performance feature rich bike labelled 'executive' and the premium 150cc bike which is perceived as being more of a 'racing bike'. The semi-automatic and the automatic washing machines are another example.

VALUE ORIENTATION-BASED CONSUMER MARKET STRUCTURE

These consumption-based clusters also harbour a very interesting construct–that of consumer value orientation. The different consumer classes have distinct cost–benefit orientations, that is, distinct orientations about how they think about benefit and cost, when they consume (Figure 4.4).

- The rich consumer class is the benefit maximizer class, oriented towards 'money for value'—willing to pay more for better services and more benefits. One could term this group 'anywhere-in-the-world consumers' who just happen to be in India. Ironically, due to a misreading of their value orientation, in the early days of liberalization

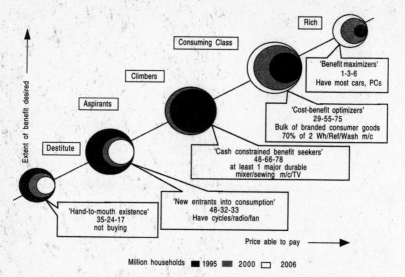

The numbers in the figure refer to the numbers of householders for each class in 1995, 2000 and 2006.
Source: NCAER.

Figure 4.4: Value Orientation-based Market Structure Model

this consumer class was targeted with older (not the latest) models of Mercedes cars and mid-market brands of Scotch, which it rejected. These are people who had come out of a time warp, but rapidly caught up with the world in real time consumption. 'As good as what you can get anywhere in the world' is what loosens their purse strings. Today, they are the target for the latest offerings from all luxury brands, whether in apparel, watches or crystal ware.

- The consuming class is oriented towards 'value for money', in contrast to the rich who are oriented towards 'money for value'. They judiciously balance benefit and price all the time, in order to make 'value optimizing' decisions. This class comprises the cost–benefit optimizers. This segment is not in the market for premium products, but for what we call high end popular products. However, product categories as diverse as skincare, automobiles and footwear have seen that where there is a breakthrough in functional performance available at a much higher price, this consumer class does opt for it. They, however, are very hard to seduce with imagery-oriented brand benefits as the major 'reason why' to buy.

- The climbers are cash-constrained benefit maximizers, who within a confined budget look for the best the market offers. This is the target group that old India hands refer to as 'price-point' buyers, and who form the core and the backbone of the popular segment. Karsanbhai Patel, the legendary Indian marketer who launched Nirma, was the first to target this consumer class. Nirma was a brand of detergent launched in the mid-1980s at one-third the price of the popular Surf from Hindustan Unilever. Nirma gave Unilever a run for its money in India by outselling it ten to one in tonnage terms. Patel offered 'adequate quality at affordable prices' to customers who did not want to pay for a detergent more than what they paid for a laundry soap. A detergent powder at that same price-point was benefit maximization—even if the detergent with 65 per cent soda ash was harsh on the hands and may have ruined clothes in the longer term. The consumers' answer was that they used a stick to stir the bucket of detergent so that their hands were protected. Also, they could not say whether ten years later their bed sheets would disintegrate or not. Moreover, they appreciated the whitening power of detergent over the grey white of laundry soap. Eventually, Unilever also launched a popular brand called Wheel to target this customer. As the market has got more sophisticated, the benchmarks of 'affordable price' and 'adequate quality' may have increased significantly, but the consumer class of this value orientation still exists.

- The aspirants are the new entrants into the consumption arena, and in the mid-1990s fuelled the growth of the FMCGs and durables. The 'paisa' pack of tea and detergent, low-price shampoo sachets, loose glucose biscuits, are some of the offerings aimed at this segment—by virtue of being new consumers, they are occasional consumers. They shampoo hair on special occasions but use bathing soap otherwise. Or use sanitary napkins when going out. Or watch television at their neighbour's house. Or use a payphone only when needed.

- The destitute are not yet into consumption of anything, living as they do from hand to mouth. This category is the wellspring that will fuel growth of the other consumer classes, as incomes increase.

THE GENERIC MODEL OF THE INDIAN MARKET

This value orientation-based consumer class model is a generic Indian model that works for all businesses. In office automation, there are those who are 'anywhere in the world buyers' who will buy the same world standard configuration and brands that their counterparts in other parts of the world will. Then there are the progressive Indian companies that are cost–benefit optimizers. I used to work for a market research company that was just that. We had state-of-the-art computers and software for our data analysis, grey (assembled) but with a high speed Intel chip for the PCs of researchers, and cheap local computers for the office assistants. The many annoyances encountered as a result of this were not considered major, given the overall outcome. Then there are those organizations and shops that have a fixed automation budget and shop for the best deal from the small, one-stop shops in the grey market providing hardware and software. And the 'just entering consumption' aspirants are those who have one computer that is shared by everyone in the office, usually assembled. This segmentation works for hospital service consumers, cell phone subscribers, education, chemicals, and every other category you can think of. Typically, cost–benefit optimizers (the consuming class) have multiple usage between premium–popular–discount products in the same household. For example, there is a very high degree of ownership and usage of both two-wheelers and cars in a household, the idea being to optimize status signalling, comfort as well as running costs.

Farmers in India can also be segmented by this construct, based on their farming 'business model'—the 'return on investment'-oriented farmer who is ready to spend more money to earn more money and does not hesitate to buy an international brand tractor with all the implement attachments. Then there is the 'productivity optimizer' who will settle for the best local brand with the latest technology and mix and match implements and manual operations. The 'cash flow minimizer' is the small farmer whose farm barely supports him and he will buy an assembled tractor—the cheapest one available that does the job adequately. And there is the 'just entering farm mechanization' farmer who custom hires a tractor but does not buy one. Finally, there are all those one and two acre farmers who cannot use anything but bullocks to plough their fields.

Based on this basic generic model, a multi-pronged strategy can be devised for the Indian market for practically any category.

Sizes of Consuming Classes

The NCAER track of consumer classes (Figure 4.4) shows that the two largest consumer classes are the climbers and the consuming class, with about 75 million households each. While one is looking for benefit maximization at a set price point, the other is willing to optimize both benefit and cost until the outcome is satisfactory. It is interesting to see the change in the market structure by this construct, over the past ten years. In 1995, the two major chunks of the market were the aspirants and the climbers. Ten years later, it is the climbers and the consuming class that form the bulk of the market—a very distinct evolution of the market towards greater benefit sensitivity and less price sensitivity.

The rich benefit maximizer has grown at a fast pace, but is still a minor 6 million households as against 75 million each of the other two. These 6 million, by virtue of being geographically concentrated and easy to access with minimal distribution, may be a very good target for luxury product and service brands. However, they represent the sideshow of the mainstay of Consumer India, namely, the climbers and the aspirants. In terms of urban–rural differences, the same pattern as with income classes is applicable.

Structurally, the rural market is eight to ten years behind the urban market in terms of the relative sizes of these different consumption segments. This absolutely does not mean that eight–ten year old urban strategies will work for rural India. The rural consumer's expectations are totally different, since they are exposed to the rest of the world in real time. The urban rich will form a larger part of the urban market than the rural rich will of the rural market. The aspirants (new entrants into consumption) will be a critically significant number in rural Consumer India than in urban Consumer India, where climbers (cash-constrained benefit maximizers) and the consuming class (cost–benefit optimizers) will be the most important groups. This means that we can see far greater volume-driven market growth in rural India and value and upgradation-driven growth in urban India.

DYNAMICS OF FUTURE GROWTH: THE VIRTUOUS SPIRAL OF DEMAND

Different consuming classes drive market growth in different ways (see Figure 4.5), and an appropriate mix of strategies is essential to capture the different sources of market growth.

- *Volume growth due to the destitute transforming into aspirants*: As economic growth occurs, the destitute will

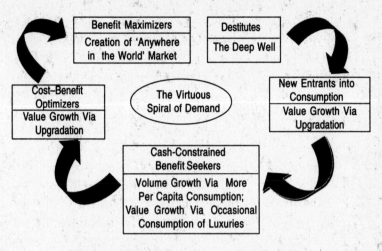

Figure 4.5: Different Growth Levers from Each Class

transform into aspirants and enter the consumption arena, creating an automatic volume growth for several categories. This is the 'do nothing, just wait for the incomes to rise' growth. Categories like toilet soap and detergent and other basic personal care items gained a great deal in the mid-1990s from this source of growth. Now, however, they have almost fully penetrated the market and have to look at other sources of growth.

- *Volume growth due to the climbers increasing their per capita consumption*: As the aspirants become climbers, they fuel volume growth by consuming greater quantities of products than they did earlier. This is true for any category, from textiles (expanding wardrobes) to poultry (chicken twice a week and one piece for everybody in the house, not once a week and only for the men!). There are more occasions for consumption and more quantity is consumed per occasion, of all categories.
- *Value growth due to the climbers occasionally using superior products instead of what they usually use*: Climbers also contribute to volume and value growth through occasional

use of luxury or indulgence items. These are best defined as superior performing substitutes for what they are currently using. Two good examples of this are the usage patterns for disposable diapers and sanitary napkins. Bottled soft drinks that are served to important guests instead of the low-priced squashes and syrups, where the dosage and the quantity of sugar can be controlled depending on how much the drinker is worth! Retailing is another such example, where this category of consumer makes occasional visits to the supermarkets to buy their 'family treat' food products like dry fruits and special spices.

- *Value growth due to the consuming class upgrading to better quality products/brands*: In mature categories like toilet soaps, home care products, refrigerators and two-wheelers, both the growth of the consuming class and their quest for better value drive value growth. They move from scooters to motorcycles, from direct cool to frost-free refrigerators, from popular toilet soaps to premium ones and so on. Most categories of this kind will see growth in the premium segment, functionally superior products and brands. The Indian experience has been that this growth is hard to come by unless marketers make the effort to continue to deliver 'value right' products at the premium end, where the basis of value is superior functionality and user experience. In fact, when this does not happen, we see the reverse phenomenon of down-trading, where the value optimizers decide that they are getting optimal value from a cheaper toothpaste, soap or basic model of television than they are currently using.

It is also here that the biggest category battle is being fought—with some categories being elbowed out of the ranking that cost–benefit optimizers have. The sudden and inexplicable stalling of revenue growth of the FMCG business in 2000–4 was due to down-trading by this consumption group of cost–benefit optmizers who were spending their money upgrading their homes, cars and cell phones. There was not much penetration-driven volume growth since this is now a mature, well-penetrated category.

- *Value growth through creation of a super premium market for the rich benefit maximizer.* This has occured where appropriate 'money for value' offers have been made in segments like cars, apparel, home fittings and accessories, jewellery, watches, etc. The sixfold increase in this consuming class makes it a good market niche for international brands offering 'world class quality at world class prices', and many of them are already here and exploiting it in a focused way.

Implications for Strategy

Consumer India is a multi-tiered consumer base requiring a multi-pronged strategy. One size cannot fit all of it, and any talk of the 'average' of this market is at one's own business peril.

A portfolio of offerings is essential in order to fully capture the multi-faceted market opportunity that India has to offer in the foreseeable future. The premium–popular–discount price performance paradigm that Indian marketers have worked with all these years is here to stay for a while longer, given the income–population structure of Consumer India. However, the behaviour of consumers with respect to this three-tier market paradigm is becoming increasingly complex.

These offerings should ideally span a wide bandwidth of price-performance points, ranging from 'exactly the same thing that you will find in London' to 'paisa packs'. Obviously, each of these will need to be delivered by different business as well as distribution systems. While the consumer-interfacing retail outlets serving the consuming class and the climbers may be the same, the distribution system will need to be different. In the case of the one serving the consuming class, who are value optimizers, the distribution system may need to be a relatively higher margin, higher service, demanding one. In the case of the system serving the climbers or aspirants, it should be a high reach, lower margin and less demanding one.

Consumer India's demand structure is fundamentally different from that of developed markets. It has lots of people consuming a little each, which adds up to a lot of consumption. In fact, an analysis of where the volume estimates in the business plans of most multinationals in the early days went awry showed that it was not so much in the 'penetration' or adoption numbers predicted, but in the assumption that the per capita consumption numbers would be the same as in other countries.

We are, as I once said in an interview to the *Asian Wall Street Journal,* a nation of 'under-dosers'. If the instruction on the pack of any product from detergent powders to baby food says two heaped tablespoons, Indian consumers will use just one. They do this partly because Consumer India cannot afford to consume more, but yet wants to participate in consumption, and partly because there is so much scarcity and deprivation all around that careful consumption is ingrained in everyone's DNA, even in that of the better-off consumers.

The Indian marketer has learnt from watching the behaviour of his consumers that when there are a lot of people consuming a little bit regularly or occasionally, a 'community consumption' strategy is needed to tap them. The success of community use models like cyber cafés and STD/ISD telephone booths is that they amortize the investment across many people and thus effectively create a 'pay as you use' model. A few telephone owners consuming a little are not as attractive as many call booths catering to a lot of people consuming a little each.

The Indian market has always embraced this model—before television sets became affordable, the community television set was its first introduction to media consumption without ownership. The high readership-to-circulation ratio reported for most magazines often makes one wonder if there are any pages left in readable condition! And the latest NASSCOM study shows that access to the Internet is four times the number of connections, a multiplier that can only increase given the success that we are seeing of cyber cafés (and the product for the lower tier consumer—the cyber dhaba).

Cable operators, each of whom has a dish antenna and provides cable connections at a fee of Rs 200–400 a month to a small catchment area of a few thousand homes will together have a larger market than large-scale direct-to-home (DTH) operators. Just like the STD/ISD booths, job shops providing photocopying services also thrive. New tractors are bought by farmers at prices that usually are not justified by the economics of their farm, but there is enough opportunity for custom-hiring or community use, which enables regular payback.

Another model to tap the large potential of occasional consumers is the small pack with low unit price, characterized by the success of the sachet and also cough drops. Thus we have large numbers of people who are 'occasional but regular' consumers of things.

Finally, the consumption logic that drives the lower one-third or half of Consumer India is different from the consumption logic that drives the rest of Consumer India—even for the same product. When gel toothpastes first came into the market, while the marketer intended it to be a statement of modernity and new generation toothpastes, the lower income end of the toothpaste consumers adopted it quickly because in the gel form, a little toothpaste went a long way and that satisfied the child's desire to have the toothbrush full of toothpaste and the mother's need for economy. We squeeze the very last drop out of everything. Housewives will tell you how they control the consumption of expensive food items like ketchup and cheese that are or have been 'finished too fast' by delaying their replacement purchase. And to many a Western mind this may make no sense but we have a culture of thrift and it runs across all kinds of consumers. To an outsider we may seem inscrutable, perhaps even strange, but 'we are' as the title suggests 'like that only'.

5

just how much
purchasing power
does Consumer India
actually have?

How Not to Think About Purchasing Power

Perhaps the most difficult question to answer is the simplest one: 'How much purchasing power does Consumer India actually have?' The answers are always varied and contradictory and the real story is pretty hard to piece together. The obvious answer in terms of a GDP per capita number would lead to the conclusion that there isn't very much purchasing power here to interest marketers of mainstream consumer goods. However, as always, averages about India are misleading and the reality is quite different and far more complex.

A *New York Times* report of 10 December 2005 pointed out that based on the trends of car sales of the last five years, India is 'one of the world's fastest growing car markets'. It went on to say,

Fifteen years after India began its transition from a state-run to a free market economy, a new culture of money—making it and even more, spending it—is afoot. So intense is the advertising onslaught, so giddy the media coverage of the new affluence, that it is almost easy to forget that India is home to the world's largest number of poor, according to the World Bank. Still, India's middle class has grown to an estimated 250 million in the past decade, and the number of super rich has grown sharply as well.

The resurgence of the much-touted Indian middle class always makes me a bit nervous. The myth of the Indian middle class has caused more heartache than happiness to business. It has no clear definition, its size has been hotly contested and it needs

to be understood carefully before it is blindly used as a basis
for investing in the Indian market.

THE MYTH OF INDIA'S MIDDLE CLASS

The popular misconception about the Indian middle class is
that there is a large, homogeneous chunk of people at the heart
of Consumer India (numbering between 200 million and 500
million, depending on whose estimate you choose to believe)
who have the bulk of India's purchasing power and a great
enthusiasm to consume. It is on the back of this juggernaut that
many businesses planned to ride their way to mega profits in
the 1990s—and had their hopes belied, their business plans torn
asunder, and their large new capacities left unutilized.

The truth is that the Great Indian Middle Class was a
seductive idea that was conceived, packaged and sold to the
world by India as part of its sales pitch for foreign direct
investment (FDI) in the early to mid-1990s when all it had to
offer was a GDP per capita of less than US$20 per month, and
a lot of optimistic conjecture about the future. The story put
out was that there was a sleeping beauty called Middle Class
India, comprising 250–300 million people, who had money and
a burning desire to consume, but nothing decent to buy. And
with just one kiss from Prince Charming, that is to say, with
the mere availability of 'previously unseen goods and services,
there would be a huge release of demand pent up for decades'.

Of course, this did not happen, and by early 2000 talk of the
existence of the Great Indian Middle Class had considerably
subsided. However, after lying dormant for a while, the idea of
the Great Indian Middle Class is resurfacing—it always does
every time there is an upswing in the demand cycle or
when we have a shortfall in supply, leading to the illusion of
runaway consumerism.

The confusion continues. Pavan Varma, author of *The
Great Indian Middle Class*, has declared that the number of

people in the middle class has now swelled to 500 million. But there are others who differ and describe it as 'the fabled beast', 'the unicorn', or, in the inimitable words of Shashi Tharoor, 'something that is perhaps more sociological than logical'.

As someone who was part of the creation of the myth, I would like to be part of its clarification too. Here are the things to think about when the theory of the Great Indian Middle Class is presented as the basis for a business case or a strategic plan.

There Is No Unique or Universally Accepted Definition

In the book, *Guide to Indian Markets 2006*, Hansa Research (a leading market research agency in India that conducts the mammoth 200,000 + sample size survey, the Indian Readership Survey, for the Media Research Users Council [MRUC]) makes the following observation:

> The size of the middle class in India has been debated for the last 10 years. There are diverse estimates ranging from 100 million (20 million households) all the way to 400 million (80 million households) that have been floated by various individuals and institutions. In the last couple of months we have met a number of senior marketing professionals to understand what in their opinion is the real middle class. Every one of them had a unique definition. Some used parameters such as income and socio-economic class, while others defined it in terms of ownership of durables such as cars and televisions. A few held that the middle class are those who are participants in the consumer economy.

It sounds exactly like what they say about pornography:, 'I can't define it, but I will know it when I see it.'

Beauty (Size) Lies in the Eyes of the Beholder?

Hansa Research goes on to say that after all its interviews, it was forced to conclude, 'It soon became obvious that there is no common definition for the middle class. Nor is it something that has been accurately sized. In fact no one really has a fix on this nebulous entity called the middle class.' Any statement about the size of India's middle class, no matter how author-itative a source it emanates from, therefore, is a totally subjective number. One definition often used by multinationals is, 'those at the top end of the population (by income) who can afford to consume international products and brands as much as any global consumer'.

By this definition of 'those who can afford to consume . . .', through the lens of the US$50 branded jeans or the US$100 sports shoes or the US$60 Scotch whisky, the size of the Indian middle class is no more than 50 million people, maybe 100 million at the most. People talk a lot about the cell phone revolution in India as an indicator of the swelling middle class. Actually speaking, there are under 20 million cell phones so far and even if they double in the next one year, that is still under 40 million owners of cell phones—a far cry from a 500 million middle class. Even at one cell phone being used by the entire family, that's an outside limit of still only 200 million users. However, through the lens of an FMCG marketer, the size of the middle class, defined as those who can afford to consume mid-priced or popular segment toothpaste or soap or skincare products, is about 250 million to 300 million.

However, in terms of the NCAER definitions that we examined in Chapter 4 ('Understanding Consumer India's demand structure') the 'consuming class' of 375 million (75 million households), defined as cost–benefit optimizers who account for the bulk of branded consumer goods purchases, would qualify to be called the middle class.

By the logical definition that the middle class is the middle majority of the market, the top 10 per cent of the population who account for 34 per cent of national income would not be 'middle class', nor would the bottom 60 per cent who account for another 30 per cent of the national income. The 30 per cent in the middle, who contribute 36 per cent of the national income, could qualify for the 'middle class' label. Therefore they would be 300 million in number.[1]

Much Poorer when Compared to the Middle Class in Developed Countries

What is hardly ever articulated—and perhaps not quite recognized—is that the Indian middle class, whichever way you define it, is still far less affluent than the middle class in other countries. Hence the surprise that people often feel at how little the Indian middle class consumes compared to the European, American or even Chinese middle classes!

The criterion the NCAER used in 2005–6 for the middle class was 'an annual household income of between US$1900 and US$2900 (approximately)'. On that basis, it estimated the size of the middle class to be 34 million households or 170 million people. By international standards, this does not really qualify as middle class.

If, however, we were to say that the label 'middle class' should stand for a certain amount of consuming power and that, based on the data from other countries, we believe this should be at least US$5000 or above per household, then the size of the middle class in 2005–6, according to NCAER data, was 21 million households or 105 million people. These people, whom we would like to term middle class, actually represent the top 10 per cent of India's population in terms of income.

Beware! Dangerously Limiting for Business Planning

Worse still, despite being notional and subjective, if treated as a gospel, it leads to non-exploitation of opportunity and lazy strategy. A.S. Ganguly, former chairman of Hindustan Lever and

---

[1] See Bijapurkar and Bhandari, 'Solving the Income Data Puzzle', *Businessworld Marketing White Book 2006*.

director of Unilever, later chairman of ICI India, had this rather sharp comment to make about the myth of the middle class that multinational entrants into India so deeply base their strategy on:

> One of the more prominent topics preoccupying corporate India as well as foreign investors is the real size and promise of the Indian consumer market. The most widely quoted estimates have put this number between 150 and 200 million consumers. Following some marketing disappointments, downward estimates have gained prominence and the view is that it could be as small as 20–25 million consumers.
>
> This shrinkage in estimates based on consumption and purchase of a certain class of goods represents a severely restricted sample. Such arbitrary downward estimates of numbers do not truly reflect a state of restricted opportunity, but rather non-exploration of opportunities that the rest represent, whose needs for purchase and consumption continue to remain unsatisfied.

And, I might add, who harbour purchasing power and may or may not qualify for an ambiguous label called the middle class.

How to Think About the Purchasing Power of Consumer India: From a Monolith to a Multi-tiered Cake

First, we must abandon this fruitless debate about the size and the affluence of the Indian middle class and change the mental model that most marketers have of Consumer India. Second, replace the model of a monolithic middle class of large numbers of people with approximately equal purchasing power with a model of many layers of people (a multi-tiered cake, perhaps) of uneven size and with different levels of affluence in each layer.

To quote from Hansa Research again. 'A good understanding of these layers would be more pertinent (to understand the purchasing power of India) than trying to determine the size of the middle class.'

The rest of this chapter is devoted to doing precisely that. It describes different ways of slicing or stratifying Consumer India based on different definitions of affluence, and sizing and profiling these layers or strata in different ways. Is a detailed tour of methodology and numbers from various sources really necessary, particularly if the data will be outdated as soon as the book is published? Why confuse the issue further with different definitions of affluence? Isn't there one 'best' way to work with? The answer, regrettably, is no. All sources of data do not provide exactly the same kind of information, and in order for a comprehensive picture to emerge, several of them need to be pieced together. To complicate matters further, there is (and will continue to be) a lot of opinion based on partial facts, using some favourite databases and ignoring others that tell a different story. Therefore, the answer to the question of Consumer India's purchasing power will constantly be subjected to the same confusion as in the story of the blind men of Hindoostan who were asked to describe an elephant. Some said the elephant was like a rope. Others likened it to a wall and also to a pillar. And while these answers are all contradictory, they are also all true.

The purpose of this discussion is to enable strategy developers to do a one-time examination of all the facts, piece them all together to visualize the whole beast and then come to their own judgements about whether it is attractive or not! Further, since different people are comfortable thinking about market opportunity using different criteria (the classic 'glass is half full –half empty' debate), what follows would also enable them to develop their own point of view. Finally, since pluralism always prevails in India, and different (though equally respected) data sources will be prevalent at all points of time and there's no knowing which one will be quoted to you when, it makes sense to see for yourself the extent to which they all converge as well as diverge.

Stratifying Consumer India Based on Income

The most obvious metric to use to define layers or strata of affluence is income. However, income data in India has always been a contentious issue. Income data needs to be obtained from household surveys and there are some unique problems with getting people to report their income truthfully. Income is almost always underreported, especially at the higher end of the income spectrum. This has nothing to do with weak survey design methodology, but more with cultural issues. I have had years of discomfort trying to explain to understandably puzzled overseas business people when they pose the question, 'how can someone who earns so little afford to buy so much and still manage living expenses for a family of five? What's not adding up?' The fact is that there is some logic to the illogical income data obtained from surveys, some consistency in the underreporting. For now, here is a simple survival guide for intelligently using household income distribution data in India.

- Do not use it literally. It (income) is always under-reported. The most rigorous survey, the National Data Survey on Savings Patterns in India (NSSDP),[2] accounts for only 59.6 per cent of the total disposable personal income in the country, as put out by the National Accounting Statistics of the Government of India.
- Do not try to reconcile in order to compare across different surveys—it is frustrating and fruitless, because they all report differently defined income classes, elicit income data using different questions, index current survey income, for comparison, to different base years. All things considered, it's a Tower of Babel out there.
- Income data has proved over the years to be what statisticians would call reliable but not valid—each reports a certain

---

[2] Survey conducted in 2004–5 for the Ministry of Finance, Government of India, by India Economic Foundation and AC Nielsen.

kind of income construct—and if you repeat the survey again and again using the same questions, you do get exactly the same answers. So while income is understated and does not measure the real thing, it is perfectly usable for grading the population based on its relative purchasing power and for comparing the growths and declines of various income groups over time. Therefore a household earning Rs 50,000 according to survey data will definitely be earning much more; however, it will be twice as rich as households earning Rs 25,000 from the same survey. Further, comparing the number of households that earn a certain amount today, compared to ten years ago (after adjusting for inflation), is accurate.

Consumption Data vs. Income Data

Let me narrate an incident to illustrate the confusion that income data can cause in explaining purchasing power. I received a call one day from the CEO of one of India's big business houses. He was on a trip abroad to give a talk on business opportunities in India for the automotive sector. The supply side facts about the industry looked great—turnovers, growth in sales, margins, Deming prizes, cost positions, technology, etc. Then came the demand analysis. He needed a few slides on the demand environment/market potential side to complete his talk. 'What is the definition of the high income household in NCAER reports?' he asked. I gave him the answer—this was in 2002, and the high income band was defined as a stated income of Rs 180,000 and above per year (about US$3830 per year). The estimated number of households having that income was about 14 million only. He gagged. Even on a PPP basis, it was less than US$2000 per month for a family of five, with education, healthcare, food and rent, all having to be met from this amount, leave alone buying cars. Yet, around that time, about 600,000 new cars were being sold per year in the country.

And if you removed all corporate and commercial purchases from that figure, that was still a lot of cars for such few people with so little income to buy.

However, when you look at the consumption levels revealed by the same survey, it did show that a lot of cars were purchased. Even at one level below the highest income group, that is at the level of households earning between Rs 135,000 and Rs 180,000 a year, as many as 60 per cent had two-wheelers and about 30 per cent had cars. If you calculated the total number of cars bought in the previous one year based on the household survey data number, it tallied reasonably well with sales data from car manufacturers.

Consumption data from surveys is accurate and tallies well with supply side information. Here's the mantra to remember—consumption is like maternity, a certainty. Income is like paternity—merely a matter of inference.

UNDERSTANDING THE AFFLUENCE OF THE INCOME STRATA: CALIBRATING INCOME NUMBERS IN TERMS OF CONSUMPTION

When considering survey income data from India, it is advisable not to worry about exactly what the right level of income should be to justify labels like high, medium or low-income. Since data from income survey is understated, labels like Rs 25,000–50,000 ought not to be taken literally. The best way to make sense of the income layers and of what affluence they actually harbour is to work with income percentiles. Further, to get a concrete fix on the purchasing power that goes with stated income labels you need to study what people in each income label bracket actually consume.

To take an illustration, NCAER data (2002) (Table 5.1) describes the different layers of consumers, labelled by income and by words like 'seekers' and 'strivers', and calibrates their

Table 5.1: Affluence Layers Based on Income (NCAER)

Income classes	Annual household income (Rs '000)	% of Indian house-holds in each income class	No. of durables per 100 house-holds in each income class				
			Two-wheeler	CTV	Refrigerator	Air conditioner	Car
Deprived	<90	71.90	7	5	4	0	0
Aspirers	90–200	21.90	47	40	34	2	4
Seekers	200–500	4.80	70	74	62	13	29
Strivers	500–1000	0.91	75	69	64	28	54
Near rich	1000–2000	0.29	66	89	68	32	66
Clear rich	2000–5000	0.11	77	113	81	40	69
Sheer rich	5000–10,000	0.02	91	117	100	38	77

purchasing power in terms of what durables they consume. For example, the 'seekers', about 10 million in number, have a stated household income between Rs 200,000–500,000 per year. On this income, 70 per cent of them have basic durables like televisions and refrigerators, and a little less than one-third have entry level cars and 13 per cent have air conditioners. On the other hand, the 'deprived', which comprise 70 per cent of India's population, own virtually none of the items that are considered basic necessities for consumers around the world—personal motorized transport, a colour television or a refrigerator.

Table 5.2 gives a stratification scheme (a special analysis done by Hansa Research using IRS data) where affluence tiers are constructed based on income percentiles, and calibrated in terms of their purchasing power (defined as what durables they own and what FMCG products they use regularly). This needs to be done separately for rural and for urban India, since they are two different worlds, about ten years apart in terms of consumption behaviour. This gives a far better fix on purchasing

Table 5.2: Affluence Layers Based on Income Percentiles (IRS)

Urban India

		Tier 1 Top 10%	Tier 2 Next 14%	Tier 3 Next 24%	Tier 4 Next 33%	Tier 5 Last 18%
Est. Households (million)		6	8	15	20	11
Durables owned						
Colour TV	(% of tier)	91.1	78.2	60.9	32.5	14.6
Refrigerator	(% of tier)	82.6	59.0	35.3	11.0	3.3
Two-wheeler	(% of tier)	66.3	50.2	31.5	11.3	3.6
Car	(% of tier)	22.4	5.0	1.2	0.2	0.0
Own telephone	(% of tier)	76.4	47.8	24.8	8.1	2.6
Washing machine	(% of tier)	47.7	21.6	8.8	1.7	0.5
Own PC	(% of tier)	18.3	5.0	1.3	0.2	0.0

Rural India

		Tier 1 Top 4%	Tier 2 Next 10%	Tier 3 Next 35%	Tier 4 Last 50%
Households (million)		6	15	51	74
Durables owned					
Two-Wheelers	(% of tier)	43.1	24.6	8.3	2.2
Car	(% of tier)	3.5	0.8	0.1	0.0
Colour TV	(% of tier)	40.1	27.7	12.3	4.5
Telephone	(% of tier)	33.3	19.4	6.6	1.7
Refrigerator	(% of tier)	24.9	14.3	3.6	0.9
Washing Machine	(% of tier)	3.8	1.7	0.3	0.0
P C	(% of tier)	1.2	0.3	0.0	0.0

power than an income number in isolation. From Table 5.2 it is clear that 85 per cent of rural India does not have the power to consume very much at the prices that currently prevail in the market. This does not however mean that they (a) collectively have no money or (b) have no desire to consume. It just means that no one has managed to innovate a 'value right' (i.e. a 'right benefit, right price') set of products for them.

Table 5.3 provides another scheme for stratifying Consumer India into affluence layers based on consumption intensity. This is similar in concept to the NCAER framework of rich–consuming class–climbers–aspirants–destitute discussed in Chapter 4. However, it is more transparently constructed and, hence, better to use. In Table 5.3, the rows describe the strata or layers, the columns profile each layer in terms of size, the consumption intensity index of the layer based on the penetration of 50 consumer durables and FMCG products, the urban–rural composition of the layer, and finally the aggregate of consumption intensity of the layer and the population size or thickness of the layer, which is the total consumption weight of the layer.

The last column of Table 5.3 provides yet another startling view of the structure of purchasing power, thanks to the Indian rope trick of numbers. The lowest consumption stratum has less than 1 per cent of the consumption intensity of the topmost consumption stratum; however, by virtue of being 83 times its population size, it accounts for 62 per cent of its total consumption (and hence purchasing power). Similarly, the consumption layer of the 'strivers', which accounts for 35 per cent of Consumer India's population, has more total consumption than the highest consuming layer of the rich, which is a minuscule 0.5 per cent of the population—despite having 60 times higher consumption intensity.

Table 5.4 provides some of the base data on which the consumption index has been computed. For each consumption intensity stratum, it provides the penetration of different durables. Therefore it is easy to see that even for the minuscule top two layers, accounting for 1 per cent of Consumer India, the penetration of cars, air conditioners, PCs and even modern packaged food is limited to 50–70 per cent and far from universal.

The remaining six layers of consumers who account for the balance 25 per cent of Consumer India are consumption enabled to varying degrees. However, even the lowest of these, the 9 per cent thick layer labelled *Unmukha* or upward looking,

Table 5.3: Affluence Layers Based on Consumption Intensity
(IRS Consumption Pyramid)

Layer name	% of population	Households (million)/ Population	Relative Consumption Intensity Index (million)	Profile % Urban-Rural	Consumption index x population*
Samriddha 1 (Prosperous)	0.5%	1/5	1997=100	96–4	100
Samriddha 2 (Prosperous)	0.5%	1/5	199=100	93–7	100
Sampanna (Well off, not wealthy)	2%	4/20	484=24	89–11	96
Siddha (Achieving, just entering upper classes)	3%	6/30	235=11	76–24	70
Unmukha (Upward looking, aspiring, moving beyond average)	9%	19/95	119=6	60–40	113
Saamaanya (Average, ordinary)	10%	21/105	65=3.2	45–55	68
Sangharshi (Strivers)	35%	71/355	32=1.6	30–70	113
Nirdhana (Poor)	40%	83/415	15=0.75	11–89	62

* (Consumption index x population) is the basis on which the total purchasing power index of the strata has been computed.
Source: Guide to Indian Markets 2006, MRUC, Hansa Research.

Table 5.4: Consumption Profile of Layers in Consumption Pyramid (IRS)

Layer name	Household/Population (Mn)	% of households in each layer consuming/having								
		TVs	Cars	PCs (Internet)	AC	Was m/c	2W	Modern foods *	Shampoo	Bank A/c
Samriddha I (Prosperous)	1/5	100	71	59 (42)	48	81	65	55	93	94
Samriddha II (Prosperous)	1/5	100	44	42 (24)	26	76	72	39	91	93
Sampanna (Well off, not wealthy)	4/20	98	24	18 (3)	5	53	69	25	89	87
Siddha (Achieving)	6/30	94	10	4	–	30	62	9	85	80
Unmukha (Upward looking, aspiring, moving beyond average)	19/95	92	2	–	–	8	50	1	79	69
Saamaanya (Ordinary, average)	21/105	79	–	–	–	–	30	–	70	54
Sangharshi (Strivers)	71/355	51	–	–	–	–	6	–	69	33
Nirdhana (Poor)	83/415	6	–	–	–	–	–	–	38	8

* 3 out of 5 of the following products consumed = Jams, cheese, ketchup, instant noodles, soups.

Source: *Guide to Indian Markets 2006*, MRUC, Hansa Research.

are firmly on the road to consumption—80 per cent use shampoo, 70 per cent have bank accounts, 50 per cent have two-wheelers. There are no about-turns on the road to consumption, and as consumption confidence grows so does consumption. Therefore, despite current consumption indices being low, one would count all 25 per cent of Consumer India as offering the potential for a vibrant, growing consumer market.

A whopping 40 per cent of Consumer India, the lowest consumer layer of the 'impoverished', has no purchasing power for any consumer durables at all and only 8 per cent of them even have a bank account. The next layer, the 'strivers', has 35 per cent of the population of which 50 per cent own television sets and about one-third have bank accounts. It is easy to see how it will serve as a springboard to further consumption. Television provides the informational resources and aspirational images to strive for a better life and banking is the first step to thinking about earning, spending, borrowing and saving in a planned manner.

However, even though the lowest consumption layer has no durable ownership to speak of, its FMCG usage is quite impressive according to the IRS data. If any proof were needed that purchasing power is a function of the supplier's drive to value innovate and not intrinsic consumer wealth, this is it. Thanks to Hindustan Unilever's efforts at lowering the price per unit, 75 per cent of this layer has purchasing power for shampoo, detergent and tea (available in sachets) and edible oil (available loose). About half of this layer has the purchasing power for dentifrices, but only 16 per cent use toothpaste. The penetration of pain relieving rubs and balms is also pretty impressive in this layer.

If we were to go strictly by the conventional, globally understood mental picture of middle class consumers and what their consumption ought to be, then, based on current consumption behaviour, the top four layers of Consumer India (Table 5.4) comprising 60 million consumers would qualify.

And that number would increase to 95–100 million by the reckoning of a low to mid-priced FMCG marketer.

SUMMING UP ACROSS SURVEYS: THE VERDICT ON PURCHASING POWER

The judgement across all surveys and data is that, as of today, 70 to 75 per cent of Consumer India cannot be counted as healthy consumers: NCAER puts the figure at 70 per cent (Table 5.1); the IRS consumption pyramid puts this figure at 75 per cent (Table 5.3); and the income–consumption calibration puts the not-very-healthy consumer group at 70 per cent too (tier 5 of urban India and tiers 3 and 4 of rural India) (Table 5.2).

In sum, the top 30 per cent of Consumer India can be divided into a 50 to 60 million people creamy layer of high purchasing power, a 100 million layer below it, who are well on the road to consumption, and another layer below that, again of 100 to 150 million consumers, who have just begun their consumption journey.

However, we have learnt that consumption growth happens very quickly thanks to consumption confidence that grows with every unit increase of penetration in a given layer, accelerating consumption further (more 'people like me are buying this or that. . . if they can, maybe so can I'). Table 5.5 gives an idea of consumption increase in a five-year period in rural India, 85 per cent of which we have written off as not having consumption power.

Translating this into GDP per capita

The underestimation of income from survey income data, and the fact that GDP per capita is a universally prevalent basis for thinking about income leads to the obvious need to stratify Consumer India based on GDP per capita. Using a methodology

Table 5.5: Penetration of Consumer Goods in Rural India

Item	% of rural households owning/consuming	
	2000	**2005**
Colour TV	3.7	11.1
Refrigerator	3.2	4.2*
Packaged biscuits	39.1	54.2
Soft drinks	9.8	12.2
Shampoo	13.3	31.9 **

* While a 1 per cent increase does not appear to be much, on the massive base of rural India of about 140 million households, this accounts for 1.4 million refrigerators. The CTV penetration increases by 10 million, which is the size of Sweden's population or half the size of Australia's population.

** This massive increase in shampoo consumption is the effect of packaging innovation lowering price points and unit sizes enabling regular occasional consumption.

that is described in the paper 'Solving the Income Data Puzzle',[3] income distributions from survey data have been applied to total GDP in US$ and a GDP distribution and a per capita GDP distribution generated as shown in Tables 5.6, 5.7 and 5.8.

To put it in a perspective that makes international comparisons easier:

- The top 10 per cent of India is a little more than 100 million people, who account for about 35 per cent of India's income, 45 per cent of its household savings, and 30 per cent of its expenditure. The figure of 100 million makes them three times the size of Canada, five times the size of Australia, a bit less than the double of France and about 80 per cent of the population of Brazil. They have a per capita income of about 60 per cent of Malaysia's level and about 80 per cent of Brazil's.
- The top 30 per cent of India is equivalent to a country that would be a quarter of the size of China and has an equivalent GDP per capita.

[3] Bijapurkar and Bhandari, 'Solving the Income Data Puzzle', *Businessworld Marketing White Book 2006*.

Table 5.6: Affluence Layers Based on GDP and GDP Per Capita (2003–4)

Deciles in terms of income	GDP (US$ billion)	Population (million)	GDP per capita (US$)
1 (lowest)	12.0	108.8	110.2
2	19.2	108.8	176.3
3	24.8	108.8	225.8
4	32.3	108.8	296.6
5	37.1	108.8	340.7
6	47.9	108.8	439.9
7	50.3	108.8	461.7
8	71.3	108.8	654.7
9	94.6	108.8	868.7
10 (highest)	204.3	108.8	1876.0
Total	599.0	108.8	550.0

Table 5.7: Summary of GDP Distribution (2003–4)

Income percentile	Population (million)	GDP (US$ billion)	GDP per capita (US$)	GDP per capita of other BRIC countries (US$)
Top 1	10.9	51.5	4733	Brazil 2700
Top 5	54.4	136.0	2500	Russia 2610
Top 10	108.8	204.3	1876	China 1100
Top 20	217.6	298.9	1374	
Top 30	326.4	370.2	1136	
Bottom 70	761.6	228.8	300	

Is There a Magic Number Above Which 'Consumption Take-off' Happens?

It is correct that the top 30 per cent of India, who have been classified as those with consuming power based on their proven consumption behaviour, have a per capita GDP of US$1136 (2003–4). So there is some sanctity to the number of US$1000 per capita that is often touted as the 'consumption take-off' point.

**Table 5.8: GDP Distribution in Class, Mass, Bottom
of Pyramid India (2003–4)**

Percentile of income	Population (million)	% of income	GDP per capita (US$)	Total GDP (US$ billion)
Class India Top 10%	109	34.1	1878	204.6
Mass India Next 30%	326	36.1	662	216.6
Bottom of Pyramid India Last 60%	653	29.7	265	178.2

However, at the category level, the consumption data for certain FMCG items with a history of aggressive value innovation (detergents, tea, shampoo) show that consumption can take off well below the US$1000 GDP per capita mark.

Is There a Fortune at the Bottom of the Pyramid?

The simplest way to think about Consumer India's purchasing power is to split it into three layers of approximately equal *aggregate* purchasing power, as shown in Table 5.8.

Clearly, at the bottom of the pyramid, there are 600 million people who earn less than a dollar a day. However, collectively, they account for a market opportunity of US$178.2 billion (in 2003–4), which is approximately double that of Singapore or Malaysia.

Can this fortune be profitably retrieved? Yes, if innovative, low-cost–right-benefit business models can be created for tapping it. No, if cost structures from richer country business models are mechanically transplanted.

POSTSCRIPT

I had asked in the beginning of this chapter if a detailed, academic, exhausting tour of methodology and numbers from various sources was really necessary. Yes, such a tour of methodology and sources was necessary, because I have seen far too many CEOs and strategists picking any one income number a consultant puts in front of them, without any idea of what that really means, and making investment decisions based on that. I have seen presentations from big name consulting firms, one of whom arbitrarily moved the income data slab upwards by 30 per cent, stating 'team analysis' as the source, alongside NCAER.

The purpose of this chapter was also to provide a framework (illustrated with 2003–4 data) for conceptually and analytically thinking about Consumer India's purchasing power and about how to blend the available data sources into more customized pointers for different businesses, as well as to enable interpretation and integration of all the numbers that exist aplenty in India.

Prognosis: What Will Happen to Each Purchasing Power Layer in the Future?

It is a no-brainer that as India's economy continues to post 8 plus per cent GDP growth each year, the purchasing power will increase. At the aggregate level, the BRIC report of Goldman Sachs forecasts that in 2010, India's GDP per capita will be over US$800 and in 2015, it will be US$1149, that it, equal to the per capita income of the top 30 per cent of Consumer India today, the layer that we have examined and classified as healthy consumers or 'soon-to-be consumers'.

Technopak, an Indian retail consultancy, says that by 2011, an additional US$122 billion will be added in terms of consumer spending.

However, as we have seen from all the data discussed above, the layers of purchasing power reflect the true worth of Consumer India more than an average number.

At different points of India's economic growth, different layers of income grow or decline, resulting in periods of strong growth for certain kinds of products.

In the period 1995–6 to 2001–2, it was the high income layers that grew the most (see Table 5.9). The highest income group grew the most in terms of its numbers, followed by the upper middle in both urban and rural India. The lowest income group declined, more sharply in urban India, while the middle group grew modestly everywhere. It was therefore not surprising that the expected middle class boom did not happen.

In the period 2001–2 to 2005–6 (see Table 5.9), the uppermost income layers continued to grow the most, but there was also a sharp increase in the middle layer of rural India, which has led to strong growth in mid-priced consumer durables

Table 5.9: Growth in Number of Households in Each Income Group

Annual household income*	% AAGR 1995–6 to 2001–2			% AAGR 2001–2 to 2005–6		
	U	R	Total	U	R	Total
Low	−8.5	−2.7	−3.5	−5.8	−5.1	−5.2
Lower middle	0.7	7.6	5.6	0.2	4.1	3.2
Middle	4.8	4.9	4.9	3.1	9.7	6.6
Upper middle	8.4	7.0	7.8	5.7	6.8	6.2
High	17.3	12.1	15.3	12.5	11.5	12.2

* at constant prices   AAGR = average annual growth rate
Source: NCAER, MISH Surveys, 2002.

The prognosis for the period 2005–6 to 2009–10 is shown in Table 5.10.

In the next four years, the rich households will continue to increase equally in both urban and rural areas. Alongside this, a rural middle income boom is also forecast. This 'middle income' is really between tiers 2 and 3 of rural India, characterized by modest consumption and 20–25 per cent penetration of most durables.

Concurrent with this predicted rise in economic growth is a predicted fall in population growth rate. This will be prevalent more sharply in rich households than in poor ones, making the rich even richer in terms of disposable income.

**Table 5.10: Projected Growth in Number of Households
in Each Income Group**

Annual house-hold income*	% AAGR (2005–6 to 2009–10)		
	Urban	Rural	Total
Low	−14.3	−9.4	-9.9
Lower middle	−3.6	1.0	0
Middle	1.4	14.8	9.7
Upper middle	5.5	8.4	6.8
High	14.7	13.4	14.2

*constant prices   AAGR = average annual growth rate
Source: NCAER, MISH Surveys, 2002.

Finally, if this increase in consumer income is also accompanied by a substantial drop in price thresholds, then there will be substantial market growth for products and services across the board. This phenomenon can already be been seen in categories like cell phones and colour televisions.

6

schizophrenic India

MANY INDIAS, EVOLVING DIFFERENTLY

For years, businesses have been trying to come up with a singular and definitive point of view of India and the Indian market. Lately, however, most of them have begun to realize that finding the Holy Grail of the Indian market lies in understanding its plurality; and that in order to extract the maximum value from the Indian market, they need to develop the mindset, the strategy and the competencies to manage that plurality. India's plurality goes far beyond the heterogeneity of a consumer base of sixty-two socio-cultural regions, twenty-three languages, and diverse food habits, climatic conditions and cultural orientations. Managing plurality is also not about operational marketing stuff—about executing programmes and policies and tweaking products and pack sizes and communication for socio-cultural diversity.

Understanding plurality in the context of the Indian market is about recognizing that the 'big monolith' mental model we have of *one* India and *one* Indian market should actually be replaced by a mental model for a *schizophrenic India*. The key here is to think of India as being a collection of many discrete islands—each with its distinctive economy, consumer character, demography as well as distinctive demand drivers and consumption patterns. It is also about recognizing that the many discrete islands will evolve in different ways, depending on where they are and what forces affect them. These changes end up creating many more discrete islands or little Indias, in the future.

THE LOGIC OF THE DEMAND SEGMENTS

Market analysts and businesses operating in India have all too often been done in by what they describe as the fickle and capricious behaviour of consumer demand in India. For no apparent reason, sales patterns suddenly shift and sales volumes start zooming upwards or suddenly slow down. It is not unusual for several quarters of steady growth of the premium segment of the market to be suddenly followed by equally healthy growth of the discount segment. The usual factors, such as a slowdown in GDP growth, environmental shocks that shake consumer confidence or new entrants into the market, etc., cannot always explain this erratic behaviour. It is not unusual for poor monsoons to be followed by a spurt in motorcycle sales but a decline in the sales of toilet soap.

However, when all this is viewed through the lens of the 'many Indias', which are, in effect, many distinctive demand segments, it becomes clear that there is a logic behind all the erratic and capricious consumer demand in India. The key to understanding and forecasting the behaviour of the Indian market is to recognize its schizophrenic nature and know that the overall demand patterns that we see are actually merely the aggregate of these individual demand segments. And each of these individual demand segments is subjected to a different set of forces, and responds differently to the same environmental forces. Hence, each has its own pace of demand growth and consumer evolution.

The IT India and agricultural India are examples of two totally different small Indias or demand segments. The first is rich, relatively small, very young and well educated. It has a little over 1.5 million people directly employed in it; counting all their dependants, IT would have about 10 million people and account for about 5 per cent of India's GDP. In sharp contrast, agricultural India has fifty times more population than IT, but accounts for only five times as much in terms of its share in India's GDP. It is older and is very low on education. One is global in outlook and benefits hugely from the forces of globalization that are flattening the world. The other is extremely local in outlook and highly vulnerable to the forces of globalization and the WTO regime as they are today. IT India's consumer confidence hinges on the behaviour of the US economy, while agricultural India's consumer confidence depends largely on the behaviour of the local rain god. To see the two as being on a continuum of modernity to backwardness would be totally simplistic. Interestingly, IT India has many young people from very small towns who are experiencing the bright city lights for the first time and are struggling with culture shock, while agricultural India embraces cell phones, television and the Internet and other technologies with ease.

Rural India has two distinctive demand segments within it, of which agricultural India is just one. The non-agricultural rural India comprises half the population of agricultural rural India, but it is an equivalent-sized economy. This segment comprises the non-agricultural entrepreneurs of rural India and this explains why motorcycle sales in rural India are not well correlated with the agricultural cycles. Motorcycles are the basic business enablers for these entrepreneurs, enabling them to widen their footprint of operation and transactions between the rural hinterland and the nearby towns.

A bad monsoon, which has the power to swing India's GDP growth rate by over 1 per cent, does not affect IT India at all. And the US immigration law has no effect on agricultural India though it can make or break IT India.

Government employees form another interesting mini India or demand segment. The government economy comprises about 20 million people employed in government and quasi-government jobs—including families and direct dependants. By my reckoning, the government economy demand segment harbours anywhere between 150 and 200 million people. They account for more than two-thirds of the organized sector employment, although they are just 20 per cent of the total population of the country. They are, however, mercifully, a shrinking segment. The hallmark of this entire group is cautious, regular and planned spending and surges in spending when special bonuses with arrears of pay are received all at once by this entire group.

In the 1990s, the durables market in India suddenly boomed. Some unfortunate companies assumed it was the beginning of the rise of the middle class. Then the growth died out and the market returned to its original levels. The reason for the one-time starburst of demand was this interesting demand segment called government employees. Twenty million in number, they are well paid and with a high degree of bargaining power over their employers. They had been accorded a pay hike with retrospective effect and resultantly at least US$4 billion was pumped into the disposable income of this demand segment. This is just one of the many illustrations of how environmental factors can affect just one demand segment and create significant distortions in the overall market. Today as the government contemplates privatization of some of the larger government-owned businesses, a large part of this demand segment, which stands to lose its jobs, has become savings oriented and cautious, and this can be a boom for mutual funds and pension schemes.

In sharp contrast to government employees is self-employed India, whose growth is matched by the decrease in formal employment in the government sector and the transition of the manufacturing sector from the old small scale labour intensive factories to modern, large scale, capital intensive ones. On the other hand, since labour laws in India have not been liberalized and the threat of highly political trade unions still looms large, almost all of the organized sector, including the government has moved to outsourcing services to small sized satellite vendors who also tend to have far lower overheads as compared to the organized sector. This set of forces has provided lots of opportunities for self-employment. Today, almost half of the urban Indian male workforce is self-employed. Rural India has always been self-employed, in the sense that they have been agriculturists or freelance agricultural labour. However, as discussed in Chapter 2, with over half of rural India's GDP coming from non-agricultural activities, over one-third of rural families are engaged in some form of self-employment or work in micro scale enterprises. Since the services sector requires virtually no capital, especially if done on a very modest scale, it is the logical activity for most self-employed people.

The dependence of the self-employed mostly on the services sector, where there is intense competition and low customer loyalty, gives them exceptionally fragile consumer confidence. The business people among them (as contrasted with professionals) have a fair amount of black money or undeclared income and will spend on 'invisible' or hidden assets. At a time when the economy is booming and confidence is high, they spend freely. They go into a non-spending shell at the first signs of interest rate hikes or stock market hiccups.

LIBERALIZATION'S IMPACT ON INDIA'S SCHIZOPHRENIA

When it began the journey into consumerism, Consumer India was relatively simple. It was widely believed that there were two Indias, one rich and urban; the other, poor, rural and agrarian. We called them India and Bharat, the ancient historical name for India, which is still used in Indian languages and is also constitutionally recognized. We thought that with liberalization and the resultant economic growth, we would see the arrival of a huge and homogeneous mass of the 'have some', the so-called middle class. The belief was that with this rapidly evolving homogeneous consuming mass, the rural–urban divide would be blurred and a uniform 'western' cultural outlook would emerge. As far as marketers were concerned, one mainstream size ought to have fitted most of the market.

In actual fact, of course, this did not happen. It was almost as if the laser beam of liberalization fell with varying intensities and varying characteristics on different parts of Consumer India, which were at different points of socio-economic development. The result was many different patterns of change resulting in many Indias—an even more schizophrenic India than when the journey began (see Figure 6.1).

- Before liberalization, there was the minuscule rich India and the poor India: the 'haves' and the 'have nots'. With liberalization came the 'have somes' and the 'have some mores' and the 'poor but not so poor', as the national income growth trickled down in varying degrees to different segments of people.

The Changing Face of Consumer India	
From →	To
Two Indias	Many Indias
Rich and poor India (five consuming classes)	Many shades of rich, not so rich, not so poor, poor Indias
Urban India and rural Bharat	Many oases and deserts within India as well as Bharat
Two age cohorts with uniform consumption ideologies—all brought up in a socialist ethos	Four age cohorts with two distinct consumption ideologies, and shades in between
Three economies—agriculture, manufacturing, government	Five economies—agriculture, manufacturing, government, services, IT

Figure 6.1: The Changing Face of Consumer India

- After liberalization, different states in India have grown at varying pace. Given more freedom to operate, different private companies and banks, by themselves or in partnerships with governments, started making an impact in pockets of rural India. The result? No longer two uniform blocks of India and Bharat, but many oases of development in a desert.

- At the start of liberalization, there were two age cohorts in the country—the pre-Independence generation and the first post-Independence generation. While there were the usual generational differences between them, they were still very similar in the socialistic ideology that they were brought up on and they saw only a crawling change in their lives. Following liberalization, we now have two new-age cohorts, the first ever generation of liberalization children and the next generation who will grow up in an India that is confident about its new path and has found its moorings.

- At the time of liberalization, India had three broad occupational groups. The government was the most sought after employer. If you weren't lucky enough to get a government job which was guaranteed and came with other benefits like healthcare and a pension, then you looked for a factory job, Failing which you were self-employed or an agriculturalist. Post-liberalization, several new occupation economies emerged—the most prominent and transforming one being the IT sector. Referring to the impressive increase in Indian women winning international beauty pageants and to the equally impressive increase in Indian IT companies winning large overseas contracts, a wag famously commented that the reason why they bloomed so soon and so well was that India had neither a Ministry of Beauty nor (at that time) a Ministry of IT!

IT was India's first export-oriented sector, uncontrolled, manned by professionals, enormously accretive, and one that shared its wealth with its employees. It created a totally new mini India, a far cry from the days of stringent foreign exchange controls, when going abroad was the preserve of the rich and the sophisticated. It enabled lots of unsophisticated, middle class engineers to go abroad and bring back stories of the world beyond. This was a huge step in cultural exposure. With the advent of call centres, this new India is going to get even larger and spread its tentacles even deeper into the average Indian home.

The service sector is another occupational segment that was born post-liberalization. It is the mainstay of the self-employed individual or the micro entrepreneur. It has a unique character, and though the fastest growing sector of the Indian economy, it will remain largely a collection of individuals and very small firms who work for themselves.

Newer occupation-led economic sectors will continue to emerge, driving greater plurality, and creating more interesting demand segments and mini Indias each different in character from what we have known so far.

FUTURE VIEW

In the future, this pattern of many Indias becoming many more Indias will continue. The genesis of each of these Indias is so different as is their people composition. The economic, political and social forces at work on each of them are also different and the resulting impact will also differ. Consequently, each of these Indias will not converge to make a homogeneous singular consumer India in the foreseeable future. Regional diversity continues to grow, with regional parties in power in most states and with each choosing to pursue different kinds of economic and social policies.

Sunil Khilnani in his brilliant book, *The Idea of India,* tells the story of an Irishman who was asked if trousers were singular or plural. His reply was that they were singular at the top and plural at the bottom. Khilnani goes on to say that India is like its national dress, the *dhoti*—plural at the top with endless folds below. This plurality is schizophrenia because there is no saying which of these many Indias nestled within is the real one, if there is one such India. There is also no saying how many more personalities will emerge over time.

The Idea of 'My Target India': Implications for Business Strategy

In Chapter 1, we had endorsed the idea that India is an idea, not a geographical entity, and suggested that every business needs to define its own 'my target India' and not expend too much energy on trying to find the Holy Grail of one India.

Hindustan Unilever has decided that growth for its utensil and fabric care business will come from the 'least developed India'—deeply rural, media-dark, low on literacy, poor, using traditional products like ash and mud for cleaning. The company has a unique capability, born out of its history, of converting the heathens, so to speak, and has the infrastructure and operational capability to undertake a genuinely pioneering market creation effort, at a reasonable cost, by leveraging its already existing, geographically well-spread infrastructure and dealer network. This pioneering effort starts even with the locating and listing of these villages all over India, pinpointing them on a map, reaching them in the absence of good roads, carrying out promotional activity, gathering crowds and organizing product and education demonstrations through village fairs etc. Between 2005 and 2006, they did this for 30,000 villages personally, contact 13.6 million women in eight states of India, for their detergent business alone.

ICICI Bank, on the other hand, has decided that the developed and well-off rural India is its India to focus on for the next round of growth—an India which has the aspiration, the exposure and the need, but not enough supply of sophisticated, urban top-end services including wealth management for high net worth individuals.

Many a Fortune 500 MNC narrowly, and usually by default, defines its target India as the rich, urban, educated 'like anywhere in the world consumer who happens to be in India'. The size of this India is minuscule in population, maybe the top 5 per cent, which collectively represent an India that has about 20 per cent of the country's total GDP. It is easy to serve, but there is too much competition for it. The size of ICICI Bank's new target India is the top 1 per cent of this rural India perhaps, which probably has 5 per cent of the GDP; it is easy to serve by ICICI which is already a big urban winner since it represents a quick way to mop up a pool of ready and waiting demand at far lower incremental costs than the benefits received. Hindustan Unilever's next target India is the 20 per cent band at the bottom, which has about 5 per cent of the GDP and is upwardly mobile, creating a guaranteed loyal new consumer pool, with virtually no competitor wanting to target them.

So 'my target India' could be the self-employed India, who might be offered a whole slew of specially tailored products and services with innovative pricing and delivery systems. An aggregator model could offer financial services, and sell real estate, as well as organize broad-based preventive healthcare (since staying well, and earning a living are so closely correlated for people who have no fixed paychecks), as well as offer a whole range of 'work mate' productivity tools and services. In fact, offering grid computing based 'pay as you use' services and simple, ready-to-use software business solutions for the self-employed sector is a very interesting proposition—it automatically creates the backbone of infrastructure for a growing community that has none of the traditional support systems.

However, as pointed out earlier, this group has an exceptionally fragile consumer confidence and is likely to overreact to sudden shifts or temporary downturns and is likely to create 'bubble' markets that marketers have to watch out for.

Different target Indias have different levels of pain and gain and different levels of attractiveness and competitiveness. The interesting thing, though, is that you can actually do a lot of customization in defining 'my target India', and do not need to use cookie cutter templates of the many Indias available (though if you are keen there are many pre-defined mini India's available to choose from). It is a bit like a kaleidoscope. There are many individual pieces that can come together in myriad ways to make a myriad of patterns—you just have to manipulate them until you find a combination that works for you, given your strategic objectives, your pain–gain profile and your competencies. As India evolves further, more pieces will be added to the kaleidoscope, enabling the definition of even more customized target Indias.

VARIABLES FOR DEFINING 'MY TARGET INDIA'

Let us now examine the individual pieces in this kaleidoscope— the variables around which the demand segments or the small Indias can be built, so that strategists can piece them together to define 'my India'. At the more operational level, this will help business managers and market analysts construct forecasting and analytical models to throw light on the apparently illogical demand patterns that they see. Figure 6.2 provides a picture of the main drivers of the schizophrenia of Consumer India.

- *Consumer classes*: Consumer India has five consumer classes with different value orientations. There are 'benefit maximizers' who are willing to pay money for the desired level of value; 'cost-benefit optimizers' who balance value

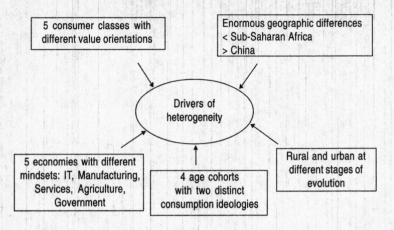

Figure 6.2: Schizophrenic (getting worse)

and money to find the appropriate level of value for money; 'benefit point constrained cash minimizers', cash constrained benefit maximizers who have a fixed price point they are willing to pay and shop for the maximum benefit available and the destitute who form the fund of future consumers.

- *Urban–Rural*: Urban and rural India are different worlds evolving at different speeds. While it is generally correct to say that on an average rural India is ten years behind urban India in terms of assets and amenities and has half the per capita income of urban India, it isn't universally true. Some parts of rural India could end up getting even more developed and advanced than urban India as they leap-frog with new and better infrastructure, technology and retail environment. An observant chief executive once made the insightful comment that rural India shops the way urban America does at factory outlets—travelling long distances to a very large one-stop 'stocks everything' shop and buying in large quantities. Rural India is far more fertile ground for a viable range of mega-superstores than urban India will ever be. Within rural India there are about 150 districts which are urban-like in assets and amenities and have a mindset that someone once described as 'ural'—urban-rural.

- **States**: The twenty-eight states are totally different from one another—some growing at the pace of China and others growing at the pace of sub-Saharan Africa; some with progressive, modern governments that encourage private enterprise and others with repressive, old fashioned ideologies and inefficient state systems. The term *Bimaru*, or 'sick', is used to describe a contiguous belt of north Indian states that perform poorly on all economic and human development indicators.

Literacy in states varies from 91 per cent in Kerala to about 75 to 80 per cent in large states like Maharashtra and Tamil Nadu, to less than 50 per cent in Bihar. Given that the starting point of most states in terms of per capita income and level of economic and social development is so varied, and that their economic growth rates are so different and will continue to be so, state level disparities are bound to grow. The large scale emergence of state level political parties often creates a situation where it is not unusual to see a party in power at the Centre that controls very few states. Some states are business and investment friendly and this is reflected in how much FDI they attract and whether they receive large loans from donors such as the World Bank or Asian Development Bank (ADB). There is a story, hopefully apocryphal, about how a large prestigious business school, promoted by prominent members of India's diaspora and Indian industry in partnership with two Ivy League American schools, eventually found its home. The story goes that they first decided to set up in Mumbai, since it is India's business capital. The government of Maharashtra, known for its parochial ideology, immediately demanded reservation of seats for students from the state. The delegation then went to Bangalore, India's Silicon Valley. The government of

Karnataka invited the delegation to meet the chief minister who did everything that Indian politicians are known to do—he was late for the meeting, distracted, said yes, yes, yes of course, but did not offer free land or any other benefit that should normally accompany such an initiative. They then moved on to Chennai and met the regional party in power in the state. They were met at the airport by people with garlands and then told that these garlands were for them to garland the chief minister of the state whom they were to meet for breakfast. The delegation then moved to Hyderabad. They were met at the airport with garlands—meant for them—and, hold your breath, received by the chief minister himself, who came with offers of free land and an agreement which would insulate them from all froms of bureaucratic interference from the department of education. The Indian state can often leave you completely befuddled. A case in point is the communist government of West Bengal which has been aggressive in its wooing of investment, besides being the only state in India to have implemented land reforms whereby the small farmer gets to own the land he tills. The result? An interesting amalgam of urban and rural development.

- *Age cohorts*: India has two distinctive age cohorts that have been raised with totally different worldviews and ideologies, not the least of which is their consumption ideology. Children born after liberalization are India's first free market capitalist generation and their parents are India's first post-Independence generation, brought up with a socialistic, xenophobic outlook. With liberalization children now coming of age and entering the workforce, and soon going on to set up their own homes, we are seeing distinctly new patterns emerging in the mosaic of consumer India.

- *Five economies*: It is interesting to see how the combination of the service economy and the non-agricultural rural economy in advanced and progressive states is an ideal example of a newly emerging 'my target India'. Such a definition reveals the opportunity for a whole new generation of businesses which can offer a whole set of new solutions to new needs ranging from low-cost grid computing and mobile Wi-Fi-based Internet access for small rural entrepreneurs, to digital pathology and X-ray labs with appropriate technology to enable the data to be digitally transmitted to doctors in cities, to hub and spoke models of micro banks linked to larger banks, etc.

POPULATION STRATUM-BASED DEFINITION OF 'MY TARGET INDIA'

Conventional wisdom had it that market potential and consumption sophistication were correlated with population strata. Metropolitan India, small town India, semi-urban India, and rural India are some of the phrases that are often heard to define 'my target India'. However, as explained earlier, with so many forces at work there is no predictable order of things. Towns with smaller population (tier 2 towns as they are called) have been a source of significant growth that consumer durable manufacturers and retailers are recognizing and now nurturing. Rural India too has several segments of varying quality within it and the many forces of development at work have created oases that no longer follow the logic of population strata or town size. Hence, blanket, population stratum-wise or state-wise definitions of 'my target India', or any combinations of these, are no longer wise.

The Pain (or Pleasure) of Strategic Business Segmentation

It is true that doing business in India demands a strategy complexity that is way ahead of its present market worth. There are several markets, including China, where the strategy complexity needed is far less for a market that is worth a lot more. The best articulation of this was from an exasperated American CEO who was attending a business strategy presentation and demanded to know: 'Why do we need a Rolls-Royce approach to segmentation for a market so small'?

His business was the manufacture of polyurethane which has applications in several industries. He was told that each industry vertical that was an end user (footwear, mattresses, refrigerators, mining boots, construction, etc.) had to be sub-segmented further into three or four customer types. The requirements and cost structures, and in turn the polyurethane purchase behaviour of each customer, were shaped by which end consumer segment they were serving. So there were footwear manufacturers who used recycled old tyres to make rubber footwear and were ready to make a mass shift to low- grade polyurethane, provided the price was low enough. There were also top-of-the-line footwear exporters who often had orders but not the expertise to fulfil those orders and who would seek technical expertise from the polyurethane vendor to save costs and meet specifications as a value added service and so on. Similarly, the construction segment had equally diverse requirements as it consisted of both fly-by-night contractors and international construction companies. It was entirely possible to have created a business which was geared towards the belly of the market, gradually upgrading as the market did and getting in on the ground floor of a mega long-term opportunity. What one needed was patience and a steady investment in marketing and R&D of products, processes as well as the overall business system, to get the costs right. It was also possible to build a nicely profitable but small business, targetted entirely at international companies operating in India, desiring global suppliers offering world-class standards of quality at global prices. In short, play the global game for the limited scope and size of global India—a few LNG pipeline projects with international majors, top-end models and brands being offered by global car, appliance and footwear companies, where indigenization of specifications is not being contemplated. Though profitable, this would be a slow burn approach, which could miss the evolving opportunities of the Indian market altogether. A plural approach would be to pursue multiple strategies and have different strategic business units (SBUs) based on strategy (mass and class/global relationships and local development), organized appropriately in terms of individual systems, structures, skills and costs and investment–return profiles.

However, there is, regrettably, no way out of this. India is plural (schizophrenic) to a degree that makes the European Union look totally homogeneous in comparison. Many mini Indias make up the larger India. The kaleidoscope has new pieces added every day and, with every turn, creates a new picture. The good news, however, is that there is plenty of choice for creating competitive advantage by defining 'my target India' innovatively.

7

demographic,
psychographic and
social determinants
of consumption

'MY TARGET INDIA'

What do we need to know about the caste system in order to do business in India?' I was recently asked this while addressing a group of CEOs of US companies who wanted to understand India and China better. My answer was 'nothing'. One of them persisted: 'And in order to understand Indian consumers?' My answer again was a flat 'nothing'; I added that caste influenced voting behaviour but not consumption behaviour and that it is impossible to tell a person's caste from a person's brand buying behaviour or his or her home. However, factors that do significantly influence consumption are social class (as opposed to caste), ethnic diversity which impacts just about every aspect of consumption from worldviews to food habits—and psychographic diversity. Style clans and tribes are increasingly being created with the forces of liberalization impacting different people in different ways and allowing for different ways of self-expression through the products and services that they consume.

We know by now India is not one entity but actually a kaleidoscope of culturally diverse, ethnically varied and linguistically distinct different Indias. Each of them is a mini country in its own right, existing in many eras. As writer Arundhati Roy puts it, India lives simultaneously across 400 years.

However, there is a further twist to this tale. Within the confines (and the broad consumption paradigms) of each of these mini Indias live many different segments of Indians. They differ in terms of socio-cultural, ethnic and 'life mindset' variables, which cause them to consume in different ways. Therefore 'my target India' needs to be defined one level further, keeping some segments of people in each of the mini Indias, discarding others, to carve out a final 'my target India'. So how do we define the next level of 'my target India'?

Demographic Determinants of Consumption

Socio-economic Classification (SEC) of Consumer India[1]

The socio-economic classification (SEC) system is perhaps the most widely preferred consumer classification system, since it combines social and economic factors through intelligent use of the demographics of occupation and education, both of which majorly influence consumption patterns in India. SEC is a special favourite because through it we are able to identify consumer segments not just in terms of how much they consume but also in terms of what they will and will not prefer to consume. Moreover, as it is closely correlated to income as well, SEC is intuitively easy to understand—just as income is—yet, in terms of its predictive power, it goes well beyond income.

The SEC system was developed in the early 1980s by the Market Research Society of India, which was looking for an alternative measure to income that was easier to collect, but was closely correlated to income and based on which Consumer India could be segmented in terms of its consumption potential. This search led to the SEC system for urban India based on the occupation and education of the head of the household, defined as the chief wage earner (CWE).

It is a fact that in India, occupation and education shape not just an individual's earning capacity but also family self-image

[1] All data for this section has been drawn from the Indian Readership Survey (IRS) study of Hansa Research, done for MRUC, 2005 data.

and social status and set the tone and tenor of how they live. The 'people like us'–'people not like us' differentiation is very strong in everybody's mind and governs behaviour.

Thus, a junior executive with a professional qualification working in a firm will live differently from a shopkeeper with a similar income. What each of them spends on will also vary greatly. The executive may think that the soft, gentle, Johnson's baby powder costing three times as much as the normal talcum powder is worth spending on, while the shopkeeper may rather put that money into dry fruits. The executive shopkeeper may think that fancy bed linen is a necessity; the other that it is a total waste and may think that fancy tiles at the entrance of the home make more sense.

This difference is more marked when it comes to selecting products and services that require a certain social and cultural capital and not just economic capital. Examples of these are newspapers, laptops or computers at home, overseas holidays and so on. Television buying is more income driven, but the programmes watched are SEC driven.

The marketing director of one of India's largest hotel chains narrates what happened when he offered a discounted package at one of his luxury hotels, where the room charge was discounted and food from the hotel was optional. The kind of people who came, he said, did not know how to use a shower and a western toilet properly and were far more 'down market' than he would have liked for his brand. He concluded, after some thought and investigation, that the willingness to pay for food at five-star hotel rates (even though discounted) was a function of social class and had he bundled food into the package as well, he would have got the right profile of clientele!

Spending on books, computers and other knowledge resources, especially for children, is also determined by social class. A family from a lower social class, even with income comparable to that of a family from an upper social class, may spend a lot of money on clothes and shoes and more visible accessories for their kids rather than on computers. Cell phones have transcended social classes, and are driven almost totally by income, as they have moved from being an indulgence, or an option, to a necessity.

The rural SEC system is based on two variables, education of the CWE and type of structure (*pucca* or *kuchcha*) that the household lives in. These two variables have been found to be most closely correlated with income, as also to be the best determinants of what people consume or are likely to consume.

The SEC system is now a standard industry framework used by all consumer goods and services, including financial services. I personally prefer SEC to income because its framework is more akin to the mental models in marketers' heads of the consumers they are targeting. It often happens that marketers assign an income label to the target consumer they are developing strategy for, but when they come face to face with a randomly selected sample of members of that income group at a focus group, they find there is absolutely no resemblance between their mental model and the reality. This happens much less with SEC classification.

The urban SEC system: It is an ordinal scale that goes down from A (the highest social class) to E, with shades in between of A1, A2 and B1, B2 and E1, E2. There is a minuscule top end called SEC A1+, but it is usually used to refer to 'not in our orbit'—as in 'well, I think this will work only with A1+'. The grid in Table 7.1 provides details of the classification.

In urban India, SEC A are households where the head is very well educated—a graduate or postgraduate who is either self-employed or in a middle or senior level position if employed.

SEC A represents the top 10 per cent of the urban population, and under 5 per cent of all of Consumer India. In size, it is about 6 million households or 30 million population. SEC A1, a rich subset of SEC A, is just 2 million households and 10 million in population. This is the minuscule group that all international lifestyle, luxury brands target. They mostly live in the large metros, and are discerning, sophisticated consumers.

Table 7.1: Urban SEC

Education → Occupation ↓		Illiterate	School up to 4th/literate but no formal schooling	School Classes 5th–9th	SSC/HSC	Some college but not graduate	Graduate/Post-graduate general	Graduate/Post-graduate professional
		1	(2/3)	4	5	6	(7, 9)	(8,10)
1. Unskilled workers		E2	E2	E1	D	D	D	D
2. Skilled workers		E2	E1	D	C	C	B2	B2
3. Petty traders		E2	D	D	C	C	B2	B2
4. Shop owners		D	D	C	B2	B1	A2	A2
5. Businessmen/industrialists with number of employees	None	D	C	B2	B1	A2	A2	A1
	1–9	C	B2	B2	B1	A2	A1	A1
	10 +	B1	B1	A2	A2	A1	A1	A1
6. Self-employed professional		D	D	D	B2	B1	A2	A1
7. Clerical/Salesman		D	D	D	C	B2	B1	B1
8. Supervisory level		D	D	C	C	B2	B1	A2
9. Officers/Executives Junior		C	C	C	B2	B1	A2	A2
10. Officers/Executives Middle/Senior		B1	B1	B1	B1	A2	A1	A1

SSC: Senior Secondary Certifiers
HSC: Higher Secondary Certifiers
Source: Market Research Society of India.

SEC B represents those who have a high level of one or the other factor—education or occupation—but not both. In SEC B1, for example, the CWE could be a college graduate but in a lower level job than a CWE in SEC A, or could have the same high level job as a CWE in SEC A, but not the same education.

SEC B is double the size of SEC A, numbering about 11 million households, compared to 6 million SEC A households. It exists between the 11th and 30th income percentile of urban India. SEC B is what people usually mean when they talk of the 'middle class' that is desirous of consuming more and more. They are the social class that comprises the 'wannabes', struggling very hard to arrive and conspicuous consumers of everything they can afford. If you get SEC B on your side, then you pretty much have your future growth ensured. They are geographically a little more widespread than SEC A.

I would be SEC A1, my realtor would be SEC A 2 (he is a graduate and has his own business). My contractor, who has two or three employees and no college education, would be SEC B1. He recently bought my Honda City car for his family (he couldn't afford a new one); he also has a Maruti van, which he uses for all his work-related errands.

SEC C has modest education—the CWE is typically '10th class plass' or 'school final', that is, he has 10 to 12 years of schooling or maybe even a few years of college education. He may be in a very junior level position as a skilled or unskilled worker in a small or large enterprise or may own a small business—owner of the corner store or a business with 0–5 employees.

Numbering 12 million households (about 60 million people), SEC C is double the size of SEC A, and slightly larger than or the same size as SEC B. It is the core consumer of products in the price band that is at the border of popular and discount segments. Almost 80 per cent of them have television sets (70 per cent colour), 40 per cent have refrigerators and an equal number have personal transport.

SEC D are those households where the CWE has not finished school, though he or she has five to nine years of schooling, and is typically self-employed or works as a clerk or a supervisor in a small store or factory—a classical lower-end blue collar worker. SEC D households are about 14 million in number, roughly equivalent to those in SEC C. They are the aspiring urban poor, who experience great upward mobility in and through their children, who make do with necessities and unbranded products, but aspire for more. Seventy per cent have television sets (half of them colour), 20 per cent have refrigerators, 20 per cent have personal transport.

Neeta, the masseuse who works at a health club and earns Rs 5000 per month, is typical SEC D. She spends Rs 2500 on food, owns a small one-room tenement in a *chawl* (a housing community with common toilets and basic facilities). She sends her children to study in an English medium school and spends Rs 1500 on it. She uses LPG, pays Rs 150 to the cable TV operator so that the family can have cheap entertainment, owns a second-hand cell phone with a prepaid card for her customers to call her and schedule appointments. Her lifestyle has lots of paradoxes. She has a refrigerator, her clothes are hip, yet there are open gutters in front of her house; and when rats enter her house and family members sometimes get bitten, they are rushed to the local doctor for tetanus shots. Her children speak English and will definitely become at least SEC C when they start out in life.

SEC E is the extreme poor of urban India. SEC C, D and E are spread all over urban India, in the big cities as well as the small towns.

The rural SEC system: The rural SEC is on a scale of R1 to R4. It is based on the education level of the CWE and the kind of house the family lives in (permanent, semi-permanent or permanent). (See Table 7.2 for classification scheme.)

R1 and R2 are the major consuming classes in rural India, while R3 and R4 are the very poor. A little under 5 per cent

Table 7.2: Rural SEC

Education	Type of House		
	Pucca	Semi-pucca	Kuchcha
Illiterate	R4	R4	R4
Literate but no formal schooling	R3	R4	R4
Upto 4th standard	R3	R3	R4
5th to 9th standard	R3	R3	R4
SSC/HSC	R2	R3	R3
Some college but not graduate	R1	R2	R3
Graduate/Postgraduate (General)	R1	R2	R3
Graduate/Postgraduate (Professional)	R1	R2	R3

SSC/HSC: Senior Secondary Certifiers/Higher Secondary Certifiers
Source: Market Research Society of India.

of all rural households are R1 (college educated CWE and living in a permanent structure) and a little over 10 per cent are R2. Together they account for about 22 million households or about 110 million people. In terms of scale, they are equivalent to one-third the population of urban India, despite being only 15 per cent of rural India. Nearly half of rural India is R4 while R3 and R4 together constitute a whopping 85 per cent of rural India. However, rural India is different in different states. In certain states, where R4 is actually far smaller in size than R3 and upward mobility has set in.

About 60 per cent of R1 and R2 would own a television of which half would be black and white. About one-fourth of R4 households would also have a television set. Television is a major source of exposure to the world as also a source of aspiration. Therefore, the fact that 30 million R3 and R4 households have television sets is in itself a significant indicator of this group awareness and the desire to consume—should the right supply come along.

The fact that 80–90 per cent of R3 and R4 households use detergents in some form or another is a tribute to the pioneering efforts of Hindustan Unilever, and demonstrates how value-right products and a marketing juggernaut can work in creating markets out of the poor. In contrast, only 12 per cent use mosquito repellants, for which there is a definite need though not the same level of marketing effort. The difference between R1 and R2 and R3 and R4 is best illustrated by the fact that almost 70 per cent of R1 and R2 rural households use toothpaste, while only a little over 30 per cent of R3 and R4 use it. The gradual and inevitable rise of R3 and R4 incomes is the real massive growth story of the future.

Relative Purchasing Power Across SECs

The SEC groups are well correlated with income, in that the mean or modal value of income in SEC A1 will be greater than A2, which will be greater than B and so on. There will, of course, be individuals in SEC B, especially those who could have more income than those in SEC A. This is a result of growing entrepreneurial opportunities and high rewards for most skills. So the invaluable plumber-cum-electrician, with a few years of schooling and five assistants, could earn more than an executive in a public sector bank. However, the purpose of the SEC systems is to establish the fact that he will spend less on home furnishings, newspapers or non-stick cookware even though he may go on a package tour to Europe.

In order to arrive at an objective measure of the relative purchasing power of each SEC, Hansa Research, using IRS data, has computed a measure for each social class, based on consumption, not income.[2] They call it the 'household premiumness index' (HPI). This measure is based on the penetration of fifty items in each social class. These were: eighteen consumer durables, twenty-two packaged consumer goods (FMCGs), four services and six demographic variables.

The graphic representation of HPI based on these variables is is given in Figure 7.1

---

[2] Indian Readership Survey, 2005 data, all-India sample of 242,118 households.

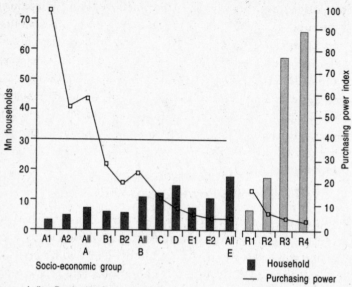

Source: Indian Readership Survey, 2005 data.

Figure 7.1: Relative Purchasing Power Across SECs

The steep drop in consuming power between social classes is self-evident and often the increase in the number of households does not make up for it. Even between SEC A1 and A2 the purchasing power, or, to be more precise, the consumption power, falls to half. SEC C has double the number of households compared to SEC A and one-fifth the consuming power. SEC A, which is just 1 per cent of all households, clearly has disproportionately high consumption potential. The richest rural social class, R1, which is just 6 million households, has consumption potential somewhere between urban SEC C and B2.

DEFINING 'MY TARGET INDIA' IN TERMS OF SEC

The frequently used definitions of 'my target India' by luxury brands, which want to target people who are 'anywhere in the world consumers who happen to be in India', with their lower end offerings, would be SEC A1, numbering 10 million people, the tip of the India iceberg.

SEC A+B form a greatly favoured 'my target India' definition. It encompasses the 'prospering and spending' India comprising the A and B social classes—about 17 million households or around 85 million consumers. High-end Indian brands and upper-end international brands, who can locally manufacture and reduce costs, define their target India as A and B. Their strategy is to get higher per capita consumption from these two classes rather than to drive large volumes.

SEC C+R1 form a nice continuum of the 'middle India' market based on their consumption patterns—numbering about 18 million households or over 90 million people. Between 70 and 80 per cent of this group have television sets, 30–40 per cent have refrigerators, 40 per cent have two-wheelers. This is where urban and rural meet each other, and it would be the target India for budget brands and value stores.

SEC D+E1+R2 together form 'mass market' India, because they are similar in terms of consumption power. Comprising about 37 million households or 185 million people, 60–70 per cent of them have television sets, though about half of these are black and white, 15–20 per cent have refrigerators and as many as 30 per cent of rural R2 have personal transport, as compared to less than 20 per cent of D and E. Given the poor state of public transport in rural India, a two-wheeler is a high priority purchase which is much coveted because it substantially increases mobility and hence earning capacity.

Finally, there is SEC E2 + R3, that is the 'poor but consuming' India, which has been discovered by committed FMCG companies and is catered to with micro-pack-size offerings for consumption. This is a market of about 70 million households and about 300 million consumers 37 per cent of this group have television sets, more than one-third of those being colour, 10 per cent have motorized two-wheelers. About 80 per cent use and buy dental hygiene products—either toothpowder or toothpaste. There is near universal penetration of toilet soap and detergent in some form or other, about 19 per cent of these households use some bazaar-bought skin care product.

THE SELF-EMPLOYED AS A DISTINCT CONSUMER CLASS

Self-employed people in India have distinct needs that drive their consumption behaviour. These-self-employed are different from employed people anywhere else in the world because in India most formal support systems like healthcare, pensions or even easy access to rented apartments has been typically built around employers. Consequently, the self-employed have no access to them. In a robust and confident economic environment this group provides a demand kicker for popular FMCGs and durables. Cell phones, workhorse-sturdy motorcycles (especially in rural India) and low-end vans are special favourites with them. It puzzles many a market observer as to why otherwise low socio-economic class folk like plumbers, carpenters and auto-rickshaw drivers so heavily drive the growth of these items. The answer is that this consumer group sees them as work partner productivity tools, and though expensive are valuable to them in order to significantly increase income. However, their consumption is not all about pragmatism and good sense. Their ego need is very strong too.

I once did an assignment with a motorcycle brand. The motorcycle had an ugly design by conventional standards; bulky, showy and visually startling. Though it had a core constituency of buyers, it failed to appeal to a wider audience no matter what attempts were made to market it. The explanation was found in its buyer profile—it appealed only to self-made businessmen, mainly small traders and shopkeepers.

Growing up as they did in an environment where either you were from a business family or you had to be employed in a proper government or private company job, they wanted to signal their economic arrival. Hence their preference for this motorcycle design. A follow-up benefit segmentation study on the motorcycle category showed that 23 per cent of the two-wheeler buyers were 'dominators'—people with big egos, money but searching for social approval. They wanted power, pick-up and visual dominance in a motorcycle. They were mainly traders. In fact cell phones, sturdy motorcycles and low-end vans are part of the 'work partner productivity tools' value space that the self- employed spend money on, especially in rural India.

Offering grid computing-based 'pay as you use' services for the self-employed sector is a very interesting proposition. It automatically creates the backbone of infrastructure for a community that has none of the traditional support systems but is growing.

PSYCHOGRAPHIC DETERMINANTS OF CONSUMPTION

'Arrived, Aspiring, Striving and Escapist' Consumer India

Kishore Biyani, the founder of India's most progressive retailing business, The Future Group, defines his company's target India as the 'aspirational class'. According to him, anyone who does not feel the yearning for a better life, despite living in these heady times is not worth losing too much sleep over. To explore his target group further, we once did some market research in Dharavi, Asia's largest slum in the middle of Mumbai city. Dharavi houses people all the way from SEC B to E, with a smattering of SEC A households as well. We interviewed young educated people, with good jobs and enough money to be able to move to better localities in the suburbs but who continued to live in Dharavi despite the numerous inconveniences and the lower status it signalled to the outside world.

Despite their protestations that they were saving up to eventually move to their dream house nearly in the heart of the city, Biyani defines them as dreamers but not aspirers. The aspirational class definitely demonstrates upward mobility even if in small steps.

Himanchal, a twenty-seven-year-old driver who works for a limousine service in Mumbai, has bought an Indica that he runs as a taxi in his village in Orissa, employing his distant cousin to drive it. He prides himself on having used a cell phone since 1998, flashes his ATM card and wonders how to set up an 'electronics showroom' in his village, since someone else has already beaten him in setting up a petrol pump on the highway near his village. He is a typical aspirer that the new India will see more and more of.

Several years ago, Rediffusion DY&R Advertising, the Indian affiliates of Young and Rubicam (Y&R), showcased a cross-cultural classification system developed by it, which resonates well with the Consumer India of today. According to this system, Consumer India can be divided into the 'resigned', the 'strivers', the 'mainstreamers', the 'aspirers' and the 'successful'.

The 'resigned' are the really poor who are struggling for survival and have pretty much given up on life. They exist at a subsistence level.

The 'strivers' are those whose goal is improvement and escape from hardship. They value hope and luck and especially look for 'escape velocity' (a term used in physics to define the minimum speed an object must have in order to escape the gravitational pull of the earth) for their children into a better orbit of life. Micro credit-based retail models and discount brands of FMCGs are aimed at this segment. Often you find that they do not have enough money for food but will pay for basic FMCGs and send their children to an English medium school.

The 'mainstreamers' are the middle majority who seek security, value and social acceptance. Their motivation is familial responsibility and their behaviour is marked by conformity. The young here are typically the children of the strivers. To this consumer group, brands signal belonging to a group and are not about self-expression. Blending in is fine. Sticking out is not. This is the target group for whom brands like Hero Honda's Splendor, the market leader among motorcycles in India, have been built. In both product and brand value, Splendor defies all western conventional wisdom of how flamboyant a motorcycle should be! The 'aspirers', the wannabes, are those who want to be perceived as successful, and for whom status and envy are important. A leading brand of television with the tag line 'neighbor's envy, owner's pride' and a mid-priced detergent bar that portrays envy inspiring success with the tag line 'wonder how his shirt is whiter than mine' are examples of targeting this segment.

The 'successful' want material success and control, achievement and recognition. The aspirers eventually evolve into the successful. Most modern retail and high functionality premium brands are targeted at this group.

It is not just people, but cities also that have mindsets. Consumer researchers say that each town has its 'mindset'. They identify three types of mindsets—arrived, striving and escapist. Bangalore, India's Silicon Valley and home of the IT revolution, typifies the 'arrived' mindset. The assurance of guaranteed progress, the balance and harmony between cultural capital and economic capital. Hyderabad, another equivalent town in size, is not yet there but is well on its way to becoming another Silicon Valley. Nagpur, Ludhiana, Madurai, Surat, all tier 2 towns, are examples of the strivers—totally focussed on improving lifestyle, maximizing earning and enjoyment, the impatience of those who have heard the epiphany, and have much catching up to do. Varanasi in one of the poor performing states (Uttar Pradesh) and, to a lesser extent, perhaps Vijayawada are examples of the escapist mindset—wanting to do better but still feeling weighted down with problems, aware of possible opportunities but not knowledgeable or energetic enough to work towards them. Consumer goods sales and acceptance of modern retailing and entertainment venues correlate well with these mindsets.

Age Cohorts

Virgina Valentine, founding partner Semiotic Solutions, a UK-based cultural analysis and market research firm, describes an age cohort as

> comprising a group of people born at roughly the same time in the same place or country. Consequently, they have experienced the same major economic, political and social upheavals at about the same age. Their lives are punctuated by the same crises. They share the same nation—memories of music, film, entertainers, public figures, fashions and fads. And they encounter every new decade, each with its own particular flavour, at similar stages in their lives.

In Chapter 6 ('Schizophrenic India') we discussed the age cohorts that exist in India today, and the ethos each of them comes from. First, there are the young who are under twenty-five years of age and are termed, 'liberalization children'. The oldest of them were just about eight or nine years old when India's liberalization process began. Then there are the parents of liberalization children, who can be called 'midnight's children', a term used by Salman Rushdie to describe India's first post-Independence generation. This cohort actually encompasses two sets of people. The first set comprises those who were born between about 1940 and 1970 and who are today between about 35–40 and 60–65 years of age. The second set comprises those who were born between about 1970 and 1980 or 1985 (specifically, this set can be called 'midway children'). They are today about 22–36 years old. Lastly, there is the pre-Independence generation.

The pre-Independence generation accounts for less than 10 per cent of India's population and the post-liberalization generation accounts for about 35 per cent. Midnight's children account for 26 per cent of the population and the balance 30 per cent are those born in the twilight years, between Indira Gandhi's heyday of the 1970s and liberalization.

These age cohorts are particularly relevant to a discussion on consumption, because each of them has been raised with totally different worldviews that have naturally influenced and shaped their consumption ideology and hence their consumption behaviour.

The pre-Independence generation's worldview, maybe its very consciousness, was shaped by the Gandhian values of simplicity, honesty, abstemiousness, self-reliance and frugality.

Midnight's children and midway children, the latter perhaps to a lesser extent, bore the brunt of post-Independence nation building. They saw wars, famine and food rationing and coped with an identity that was either a badge of sufferance or a cross to bear. Many from this generation fled to America and England, and later to West Asia, and swore never to come back to penury. While both these generations are products of the same post-Independence socialistic ethos, only the midway children were young enough at the time of liberalization to be able to adopt a new worldview.

I call the midway children, the 'Rajiv Gandhi age cohort', because it was he who first fired their imagination with his clarion call, 'Let's take India into the twenty-first century.' His persona and policies epitomized the changing face of India in the mid-and late 1980s, as did his attire—home-spun khadi pyjama-kurta, teamed up with modern and stylish westernized accessories.

If those from the pre-Independence generation are unhappy consumers, the midnight's children are guilty consumers. My mother, who is seventy-five years old, bemoans the fact that she needs to use air-conditioning to survive the 45°C summer heat. 'I have become soft,' she says with genuine pain. Midnight's children and the midway children consume, but are always justifying and rationalizing their consumption, saying that they can walk away from all this any time! A hangover from earlier life values and experiences.

Each of the age cohorts has a different set of attitudes to 'foreign' anything, for instance to, say to big international brands. The pre-Independence generation, of course, was told to boycott foreign goods during Mahatma Gandhi's Quit India movement and was made to feel quite guilty about using anything foreign. Midnight's children as well as midway children grew up in splendid isolation, listening to discourses on self-reliance and the constant admonition that the country's precious foreign exchange resources were not to be frittered away. Yet they could not help but see the difference in quality between the shoddy swadeshi products that the inefficient domestic industry produced and the few smuggled foreign goods, far superior in quality and design, that made their way into the country. Further, because such few people travelled abroad, a pair of Levi's jeans was a very proud possession indeed for any teenager then. Today, like liberalization, things foreign are a sensible, pragmatic choice, but primarily if their purchase can be justified on the grounds of their functionality rather than their brand or badge value. This is because with liberalization, one of the important things that happened to this age cohort was an enormous surge of the slogan 'proud to be Indian—India is as important for the world as vice-versa'.

This age cohort, of midnight and midway children, which is today's mainstream 'ruling' cohort, has experienced life both before and after liberalization and seen the enormous progress after liberalization, so they enthusiastically push their children to avail of all the opportunities 'we never had'. The higher social classes amongst them are at the peak of their earning careers and consume, almost in a childlike manner, by themselves and through their children, to make up for all the years of childhood deprivation. I often say that the youth market in India is found amongst the adults in their forties and fifties. Yet, this cohort is still very value-conscious, does not like to waste money, is perennially guilty about consuming and needs a rational and function-based reason to part with the big bucks.

For the liberalization generation, of course, having been born or at least brought up in a consumption-friendly environment, consumption is a positive thing. Growing up as they do in a 'getting richer' ethos, they are a materialistic cohort. Having or getting all the goodies that life has to offer at such an early age is obviously and naturally very important for them. And it almost goes without saying that for them the labels 'foreign' or 'Indian' or even the cultural overtones of 'is this imported' do not exist.

Today, most households are run by either midnight's children or midway children. The early liberalization generation is just beginning to enter adulthood and we are at the point in time when liberalization children are about to begin setting up their own homes. Whether this will change things dramatically or marginally is yet to be seen. However, statistics indicate that even in 2025, about half the households will still be run by midway children. The coexistence of various shades and grades of consumption ideologies will continue to be an irrefutable fact in Consumer India for some time.

ETHNICITY

Consumer India is a federation of different cultures that just happen to be sharing the same geography and, to some extent, the same history. The situation is analogous to the European Union, where countries differ vastly from each other. And yet, just as there is a shared and clear European ethnicity that is different from, say, the American identity, there is a shared Indian ethnicity. Is there such a thing as 'pan Indian'? Or is that also merely a geographic expression like the equator, as Winston Churchill once said? The answer, as always in India, is yes and no, depending on the category, and the proposition.

There are many levels at which businesses in India have dealt with ethnicity and made it work for them.

In the area of media and entertainment, there is no single channel or film producer or film star that enjoys pan-Indian popularity. Even Bollywood, the Hindi film industry, is not popular in south India where regional language films prevail. It isn't just an issue of language but of cultural identification. Ekta Kapoor is a very successful producer of television soap operas and her programmes command the highest viewership ratings right across the country, much to the envy and bafflement of her competitors. Her story lines are seen to be regressive and ordinary by many critics, but yet she notches up loyal viewer ship. Her formula lies in executing programmes around different ethnic groups, because she knows the extent to which ethnic identity influences consumer preferences. Anyone else would have chosen to go with a pan-Indian set of characters and dub the content in different languages. But that would not have released the full potential that identification with roots could provide.

Several companies have chosen to consider ethnicity as one of the many variables in their operational marketing strategy, but not as a major decider of their business market strategy. Product formulations are suitably changed to suit ethnic preferences, while keeping the brand proposition the same. For example, a brand of tea called 'Taaza', popular in the 1990s, was positioned across India on the same platform of freshness (the literal meaning of the name in Hindi), but contained high-flavour Darjeeling or strong Assam tea, depending on which part of the country it was available in. The cooking oil category also tends to maintain the same brand across India with the same consumer proposition, but with different types of oil (mustard, sesame, coconut, etc.) to cater to different culinary requirements, in different parts of the country. Advertising often has a singular concept, but is executed for different cultures, in exactly the way global advertising is. An enormous amount of original effort is needed to ensure that the communication retains its flavour in all languages and is not translated literally. Market research, especially qualitative research, is another area which needs an enormous amount of process and skill to synthesize findings drawn from culturally and linguistically diverse groups. Distribution strategies have also been altered by region. A tap-attached drinking water purifier discovered to its chagrin that a singular distribution strategy across the country did not work because in the hygiene conscious south India, consumers expected to find the product in modern chemist stores, while in the gadget-collecting north Indian market, it needed to be distributed through mom-and-pop household utensil shops. Of course in regions of the country where water was short, the product itself was not suitable and had to be modified to a tablet that could be added to a bin of stored water.

The popular notion was that as the Indian market evolved, it would get more homogeneous and 'pan-Indian' brands and one product would work for all. In fact, some believed that even global products and brands directly transplanted would work. Now we know that exactly the opposite is true. With modern retailing chains making it easier to tweak merchandising to suit a locality, the big national, pan-Indian brand is now being given a run for its money. The big national FMCG brands from large companies are increasingly under attack from small but sharply targetted brands that operate in narrow, localized geographies. Addressing the highest common factor of the market has been the way to play for big consumer companies so far. Until about a decade ago, they had the big advantage of being national—most of the media was national too and it was suboptimal and very wastefully expensive to use national media for a regional brand. Now, however, media, especially television, has become strongly local. Regional language, ethnic, state-level television has firmly entrenched itself, regional political parties are here to rule and national political parties perforce have to ally themselves with a whole host of regional *satrap*s (leaders) in order to be able to form a government at the centre. With the strong emergence of regional media and identity, perhaps it is time to think about the ethnic factor as a strategic variable.

Biyani believes that every community in India has a cultural DNA and it is possible to configure business propositions around these. The Gujarati community, for example, is the one that owns most of the motels in the US. They have a strong entrepreneurial gene, the women are *au fait* with the stock market despite having very little formal education and they will travel all over the world with their own cooks so that they get their own vegetarian food exactly the way they like it. Food is a very important thing for them, and the queues outside many a Gujarati restaurant bear testimony to this. They continue to buy and store, in bulk, commodities like oil and rice and while they will spend in the kitchen, they are not so ready to spend on house beautification. The north Indian, on the other hand, is flamboyant. The food and family living quarters may be spartan but the food served to guests and the drawing room décor always make a statement. Yet they are adept at achieving high show-off value at minimal cost. After one particularly difficult market research assignment for a paint company, we discovered that the reason our user and volume estimates were not tallying was that the living room walls were painted with plastic emulsion, while the ceilings, where guests were unlikely to look, were painted with distemper. Similarly, the bedrooms, where guests do not go, were painted with cheap distemper.

North Indian weddings are often an extreme display of wealth, where even the bridal trousseau is displayed for all to see. I remember a study done on how different ethnic groups were responding to a generally inflationary environment. It was called 'tightrope walking on a shoestring budget', and the findings showed that certain communities had cut out the high-priced Johnson's baby soap and were bathing their child with cheaper soap but ensuring that guests were served cashew nut biscuits. In contrast, other communities were keeping the child's portfolio of products unchanged but were moving to money saving home-made pickles and jams and saving money there.

The Emergence of New Culture Classes and Consumption Tribes

In an interview with the *Times of India*, V.S. Naipaul said that he did not believe that the future strife in India would be between the rich and the poor. He said that it would be a 'clash of civilizations' within India. And maybe we are beginning to see that. He refers to a particular emerging group as 'green card wallahs', saying that they aspire to and emulate an American lifestyle even if they don't live there. I have a friend who calls them RNIs or Resident Non-Indians (a twist on the word NRI or non-resident Indian). In contrast to this is another group that is 'proud to be Indian'. Ethnic men's wear, ethnic homes and minimalist living are fast emerging as trends. The Indian trader or bania community is an interesting mix of the old and the new—he will take his wife to Bangkok for an expensive holiday and buy his children an expensive video game, but his shop will be dusty, run down and exactly the way his grandfather ran it.

The uninitiated westerner may be tempted to dismiss all this as a whole lot of stereotypes peddled by storytellers. However, those familiar with marketing to Consumer India know that this diversity is for real and cannot be ignored.

It may be too early to say that 'my target India' can be defined as a collection of tribes or culture classes or ethnic communities. Nevertheless, this space definitely needs to be watched, especially if you are a retailer or a financial services or food company.

8

how to read and
predict change in
Consumer India

THE FORCE OF CHANGE

India changes in very insidious, hard-to-see ways. Sometimes, it appears like everything is changing; at other times it appears like nothing ever changes! Executives who work on that annual ritual called the 'strat plan' confess that year after year, they watch with an eagle eye and a wide-angle lens for signs of changes that will reshape their markets and usher in new threats and opportunities for their business—and report not having found any changes worth mentioning. Yet, five years later, they invariably discover that their market is starting to look distinctly different, causing them to ask in bewilderment, 'When did we blink and not see this happening?' The answer lies in understanding the process of change in India.

To experienced market watchers, change is about acceleration. As any high school physics textbook will tell you, Force=Mass×Acceleration. However, we automatically assume that the only way to generate a significant force of change is to have a large acceleration. But in India it works the other way around. Conventional wisdom, that 'doesn't everybody know' authoritative piece of knowledge, tends to forget that if Force=Mass×Acceleration, then a small acceleration (small changes over long periods of time) can also unleash a large force of change, if the mass that is changing is very large. That's how change comes about in Consumer India—a large mass of people moving with a very small acceleration unleashes a large force of change. It is a bit like a gigantic iceberg. Even if the centre of gravity shifts marginally, a whole lot of water is displaced. A slight change in the income of rural India brings in its wake a huge new market. Similarly, the popularity of western cuisine or western clothes of a few creates a quick growing market and, of course, an illusion that everyone is changing. However, this change is not visible through the usual run of the mill 'usage and attitude' type surveys that most companies ritualistically engage in.

The language of high acceleration change is about megatrends, discontinuities and key drivers of change, all very testosterone laden statements! The language of low acceleration change is more subtle. It is about almost invisible, below-the-surface change caused by change confluences (i.e. a collection of small changes that occur simultaneously), that lead to slowly swelling change waves, creeping trends and resultant ripple effects. This chapter provides a framework to read and recognize the changes in Consumer India.

CHANGE CONFLUENCES

The reason why change confluences are easy to miss is because they are caused by the coming together of several seemingly insignificant little changes. Individually, each appears unimportant. However, when they occur together, they cause a change confluence or a change wave, unleashing significant changes in markets. Consumer India excels at this—it changes a little bit on several dimensions at the same time, thus collectively resulting in a changed market and consumer landscape over the medium term. These changes occur not only to the consumer-intrinsic world (economic, demographic, resultant lifestyle and worldview), but also on the supply side—where any given market space can get significantly impacted even by small increases in sophistication and evolution of apparently unconnected market spaces, each moving at a different speed.

An example of such a change confluence is what adversely affected the FMCG industry in 2000, leading to a puzzling decline in demand and consumer 'downtrading' (that is, switching to options in a lower price-performance band), despite incomes going up and an overall increase in consumer confidence. Most of the early exploration to understand what was going on was confined to the FMCG category and the conclusion was that nothing within the FMCG industry had changed dramatically. It was only a broader investigation that revealed that there was a change confluence outside the FMCG world that was to blame. There was a sudden boom in housing finance and consumer credit caused by a fall in interest rates. Also, there was the simultaneous blossoming of several categories of consumer durables, tempting consumers to buy their own homes and stock them with all kinds of consumer durables payable in equated monthly instalments. Because consumers had borrowed so much for these, they had committed a large part of their future income towards paying off loans and the residual amount had to be kept for food and FMCGs. Obviously, downtrading and careful spending were inevitable outcomes. As a consumer once explained, if status signalling was to be done, then spending on a brand new car did it far better than spending on a premium brand of shampoo or aftershave.

Another example is the premium hotel industry that was hit by another change confluence in the first decade after liberalization. Air travel had just got privatized and, after decades of suffering an indifferent government airline monopoly, consumers at least had a choice in the form of the many new private airlines. Suddenly, from two flights a day from Mumbai to Delhi, there were fourteen. Since there was not enough traffic to sustain all of them, they vied with one another to pamper the business traveller. The car industry also came into its own at exactly that time, and the bumpy pieces of non-air-conditioned metal that passed for cars earlier were replaced by modern cars. The business traveller could do a comfortable day trip and avoid overnight stays altogether. At the same time, cell phone penetration had started to grow rapidly, changing the norms of business communication, reducing the need to travel. Earlier, hotel economics was based on the assumption that one day's work for an out of town visitor resulted in two nights of stay and since travel was expensive and cumbersome, people also tended to stay longer on each trip, and spent more therefore on services like laundry. These assumptions lead to creation of appropriate services, and a pricing and check out system that was configured for longer stays, but was not as profitable for shorter stays. Moreover, premium hotels spent a lot of effort and money in creating facilities and fine dining experiences for older clientele, and were almost one generation behind the new power men and women. Thanks to the aggressive growth in the economy and the rise of service businesses, especially financial services, there was a shortage of people and senior management got younger. Younger managers had younger kids and wanted to spend as many nights as they could at home. Suddenly, the basis of competition and perceptions of what constituted features and price value delivered by hotel rooms changed quite dramatically.

I once did some work for a bicycle company whose market share was beginning to decline. Nobody paid much attention to it, dismissing it as statistical aberrations in market share measurement. However, when it was clear that it was a downward trend, albeit slow, a detailed market analysis was done. Historically, buyers of bicycles mostly comprised poor villagers who wanted the cheapest piece of metal with two tyres, and were not willing to pay more for something better. There were no obviously visible signs of change in the market and each year, at strategy review time, no changes were recommended. However, when we finally looked more closely, we noticed that over the past five years, several small changes had been taking place, which collectively had reshaped the market.

We noticed that although bicycle buyers still comprised the lower income villagers, the average income had risen, equivalent

to what would have been classified as lower middle income, five
years ago. Also the age profile had got younger and the school
and college going proportion had increased. The mindset was
not about the cheapest possible bike to buy, but about getting
better quality for a slightly higher price with more functionality
built in, in terms of brakes and stability. The startled CEO
suddenly said, 'You mean we are youth marketers?' He also said
in a worried tone, 'We have to overhaul our entire R&D
department. They can do value-engineering and provide less
or the same benefit for less money. But now we need to look
at value addition.' The fact is that the entire market had been
reshaped by a combination of a number of little demographic,
economic and supply-side forces. First, thanks to liberalization
and the pattern of economic growth in that period, the lowest
income group in rural India had declined sharply, leaving only
the ultra poor there, who could not afford anything much. The
erstwhile lowest income had moved one rung up the income
ladder, but since the price gap between two-wheelers and
bicycles was so large, they perforce remained bicycle buyers,
but now had higher standards of living and higher expectations.
More neighbourhood schools had come up and more young
people were going to nearby schools and college. Simultaneously
some of the older folk were choosing to opt out of the bicycle
market and switch to public transport which had improved
marginally. Thanks to better communication, the area of activity
or the geographc footprint of the average skilled worker in a
village like the carpenter, tile workers and small door-to-door
salesmen had also widened, making the present bicycle far too
humble, both in style and in utility, for the new consumer. A
whole new category of bicycles had to be invented, which were
not quite the sports or mountain bikes popular in the rest of
the world, but were roadsters with higher functionality and
sporty looks, but priced affordably low. Several attempts have
been made with limited success so far, and it appears that the
traditional bicycle has had its day, and the new one has not yet
been innovated to everyone's satisfaction.

MORPHING CHANGE VS. MOLTING CHANGE

There are two ways in which change can happen. The one that most people know well is molting change—like the snake which sheds its old skin overnight, to reveal a brand new one. But that is not the way change happens in India. Change in India is of the morphing kind—slow but definite. This transformation is from within, like an amoeba which, with every tiny particle it ingests, infinitesimally changes shape. Over a period of time, almost without us noticing, we end up having a totally different looking amoeba.

Many people look for evidence of molting change in India and almost inevitably end up being frustrated by two common phenomena called 'mixed verdicts' and 'continuity with change', both of which are typical of morphing change. India continues to flag off space satellites by breaking an auspicious coconut at the launch site, a new computer is welcomed into the office with the auspicious vermillion mark on its 'forehead' (the monitor!). At the same time, poor fishermen in the coastal state of Kerala use cell phones to check the prices of fish in different markets, in order to decide which jetty to land their catch on. And young people continue to want to have weddings with all the traditional rituals; yet the henna that was traditionally applied on palms of hands now also serves as tattoo, either on the arm or on the shoulder. Wedding outfits have since got more revealing and the traditional song and dance now has a distinct Bollywood movie flavour to it!

MIXED VERDICTS

Anyone wanting to read change in India must be prepared for mixed verdicts, which are the hallmark of everything Indian, be it India's economy, polity or markets and consumers. The best illustration of this is in India's voting behaviour and nuances of government formation based on the 'first past the post' system that we have. After a general election, it is not unusual to find that the party qualified to rule at the centre could have a majority of the seats but a minority of the vote share. Does this reflect the nuances of electoral arithmetic or the people's preference in a democracy? Increasingly, no single party at the centre is getting the clear majority needed to form a government and pre-or post-poll alliances with popular regional parties are common. Incorrect choices of regional partners can result in even the largest single party at the centre (in terms of people's vote share) being unable to occupy the treasury benches in Parliament. The questions that cannot be unambiguously answered are: Is such a Parliament reflective of the people's mandate or is it the result of someone's genius in understanding the electoral arithmetic? Does this indicate the maturing of India's democracy? Do multi-party alliances reflect its plurality or the creation of fractious alliances between strange bedfellows?

Here's another example of mixed verdicts. Between 1996 and 2006, India had the highest continuous growth in national income ever, yet less than 20 per cent of Indian households would have enough spending power to qualify as mainstream consumers of normally priced consumer goods. However, there are sharp reductions in poverty levels, bringing large numbers into the consuming fold for the first time, with limited consumption of low-priced goods. Question: Does India qualify in the world FDI sweepstakes of 'attractive markets of the new millennium'?

Even in the top eight metro cities in India, we see that only 25 per cent of the population own cars and only 10 per cent own air conditioners—this too the topmost socio-economic class (SEC A). Yet in the top twenty-three urban centres, one out of two of the lowest SEC (SEC E) households has a television set, one in three has an audio system, and one in five has cooking gas and satellite TV access. Is this a vibrant consumer market, or is it not?

Continuity with Change

If confused verdicts leading to difficult judgements are one hallmark of morphing change, 'continuity with change' is the other. For example, young people tell me that they no longer want to have the traditional arranged marriages. But they don't want to move to love marriages either—too much of an effort to find your own partner. Instead they want 'engineered' marriages—a modernized version of the arranged marriage process. Insted of the boy's side descending with a vast retinue on the girl's home, only the boy and his immediate family meet the girl and her family at a mutually arranged hotel, club or friend's house. Instead of the usual expected instant 'yes or no' answer after just one meeting, it is now acceptable for the prospective partners to meet alone, or loosely chaperoned, a few times, and then make a decision. As Santosh Desai, one of India's best known cultural analysts and managing director, Future Brands, opines, the dating market isn't here, but the mating market has just got deregulated!

Modernity in India has often been likened to the loosening of a tight fist. Women are not moving en masse to western apparel, but the salwar kameez is giving the sari a run for its money, even in conservative small towns. At the same time, the traditional salwar kameez is getting more fusion in its look, and has spawned a new genre that is called 'east–west' outfits. The kurta is getting shorter and the salwar getting narrower and more like trousers. The dupattas considered mandatory for modesty have not disappeared but they have been reduced to thin wisps of chiffon. At the same time, tops worn over jeans are getting longer, so that even girls from conservative families can wear trousers or jeans without raising eyebrows!

Everyone wondered how the sari would morph, given that it has been an unchanging six yards of unstitched fabric, draped in just one way with minor variations. And of course while we were busy looking at how slowly the sari was changing, the traditional sari blouse is the one that has changed. It has got daring, halter-necked, off-shoulder, sequined, T-shirt like, and much more. This has given the garment a new lease of life for young women.

Joint families still exist, but they have loosened in some significant ways to accommodate individuality. The defining point of a joint family usually is a common kitchen, and modern joint families still have a main common kitchen. However, modern joint families now permit a mini kitchenette for the younger generation, so that even non-vegetarian food can be stored, heated and consumed in orthodox vegetarian households—as long as it is brought in from outside and not cooked at home!

In the cargo carrying truck market, it was automatically assumed that as the trucking market evolved, it would consolidate, and end up with a typical developed market structure. The current market structure of lots of small truck owners, owning one or two small trucks each would give way to larger trucks, and the small trucker would eventually get swallowed up by larger fleet owners. However, consolidation is happening, but in a morphing, 'continuity with change' kind of way. Several small truck owners are aligning as a constellation around a bigger trucker, forming a virtual fleet that is controlled, though not owned by the big trucker, who has the market access. The bigger trucker ensures that they all buy the same brand of truck in order to form a buying group that can get preferential treatment with suppliers, and encourages them to gradually add new trucks, sell the very old ones, and effect small net increases in the number of trucks each of them own. For the truck manufacturers, the market share risks are the same as if classical consolidation were occurring in the market, but the benefits of market consolidation in terms of having fewer, larger customers to serve do not accrue. The pain of servicing several small customers stays. Truck manufacturers who look for change in this market through molting lenses and through the lens of international analogies will end up betting heavily, at their own peril, on large trucks. Large international market leaders like Volvo who came in with only large trucks are now hastily adding smaller trucks to their portfolio.

Rural India is a classic case of morphing change. We will discuss its changing contours in detail later but here is a brief overview of how it morphs. Even as people continued to argue that over 70 per cent of the Indian population was being supported by 26 per cent of the GDP, comprising the agricultural sector, rural India had diversified beyond agriculture and had added another equivalent sized non-agricultural economy to itself. How did this happen? It happened in a hard to notice, creeping sort of way. Children of rural households went to nearby large towns for their education, realized that the farm was not large enough to support their aspirations or even occupy their time. Since government jobs were no longer easily available because of staff downsizing, they typically started doing some extra non-farm business to stay gainfully occupied. Initially, this was a small part of the household income but over time it started getting larger, and the tone and tenor of the household changed from that of a farmer's house (and lifestyle) to that of a small businessman or service provider—and with it came a new self-image and new consumption behaviour.

Creeping Trends and Ripple Effects

Looking for the mega trends or huge change waves that come and sweep society in their wake is a futile exercise in Consumer India. The things to look out for are the creeping trends. The creeping increase in income is one clear trend. On an average, the growth in national income doesn't look like it has enough acceleration to cause much of an impact. However, as income levels creep up over the years, the change in income levels and self-perception and hence aspiration becomes evident in less than one generation. The thought is no longer one of 'one day, my children and their children will have a better life', but rather, 'soon I myself will begin to live differently'. The mindset then also shifts from 'dreaming' about a better future to 'planning' for a better future.

The change in employment patterns is another example of creeping occupation trends. Occupation shifts have crept slowly and changed the face of Consumer India, without any fanfare. From a predominantly agricultural and government servant composition, Consumer India now has a large chunk of self-employed, especially in the service businesses, both urban and rural bringing with it a whole new set of opportunities, mostly untapped.

The blurring of boundaries between India and Bharat (urban–rural), the 'ural' mindset that we talked about earlier, is yet another morphing change. Caused by the exposure to television and decreasing 'power distance' (a construct developed by Dutch social psychologist Geert Hofstede, referring to the extent to which less powerful members of society accept and expect that power is distributed unequally). The changing attitude of the poor from demanding social justice to grabbing economic opportunity is yet another creeping trend, best portrayed in the electoral defeat of Laloo Prasad Yadav, former chief minister of Bihar. He asked his people why they wanted roads—did they have cars to drive on them? No? Well, then, if they still wanted roads, the rich man would drive by in a car and spit on them. So it was better not to have roads, he explained to his largely illiterate electorate. His sudden electoral defeat after several victories was caused by a hitherto subservient electorate deciding to cast its vote, instead of voting its caste. This is indicative of another creeping trend which certain sections of the media have labelled as a preference for 'development over dignity' (as in voting for a person of your own lower caste).

The increase in literacy in every successive generation is another example. Again, while the percentage of the population who have finished school or got a college degree does not increase at a rapid rate, the total number of years of formal education is slowly increasing, and when summed up over a large mass of people, the impact is quite significant. This is one of the factors that is driving another creeping trend—the rise of 'womanism'. Womanism is not the more overt and aggressive feminism, but a milder version of it that negotiates for more space and power within the broad framework of traditional gender equations.

PREDICTING FUTURE CHANGE: THE ANALOGY TRAP

During my brief stint with one of the 'Big Five' consulting firms, we did copious team analyses to plot multi-country data with GDP per capita on one axis and the per capita consumption of anything we were studying, on the other. The conclusion always was that, given the empirical evidence, as GDP per capita increased, the people of India would consume as much cola or beer or toilet soap or wet wipes or Viagra or whatever. This was a representative example of the thinking of the analogy school, a great favourite of many, especially the consulting fraternity, which assumes that all emerging markets will follow the same path as developed markets once did, and the world will, in its fully developed state, look exactly like America. As far as colas were concerned, I personally always thought that it was a bit of a shame to judge the state of development of an economy by how much coloured water it consumed per capita. Maybe Indian kidneys were different. Or maybe we would never have enough clean public toilets outside of home, and would always hesitate to give our kids a drink of cola outside, even as our GDP soared!

The truth is that analogies need to be thought through carefully. Global warming, health hazards from fast food, the latest research into the causes of cancer, are all available in real time and in as much graphic detail to nascent market consumers as they are to developed market consumers. How then can the former walk down the same beaten path that the latter traversed? And as Arun Adhikari, the former managing director of Unilever in India, once said to me, the very purpose of studying history is to learn from it and try to see if you can escape that fate. A lesson that Kishore Biyari has taken to heart. If Wal-Mart style hypermarkets is what modern and western is all about, then the consumer will go in that direction, as long as no one creates a modern Indian version of the same. 'We are chaotic people,' he points out. 'We do not like shopping in straight and neatly labelled aisles, or operate with checklists that are linear.' So he designs his hypermarkets the way trad-itional Indian bazaar shopping is done—with islands rather than aisles.

Actually this lack of relevance of analogous markets in whose footsteps new markets will follow, is not so difficult to comprehend, if one were to shed corporate imperialism for a while. Americans do not text message or use cell phones as much as the average Indian, especially in small towns. They are well served by the extensive landline network and are far more Internet penetrated, using a variety of hand-held devices. It is exactly the reverse for several poor Indians for whom the landline is inaccessible and the Internet not widespread, but cell rates are affordable, and text messaging is cheap, and available in regional languages too.

How then does one predict the future cultural contexts of Consumer India? The only way to do it is to painstakingly construct it from first principles, by studying age cohorts, by looking at cultural drivers of change and by understanding the process of change and the DNA of the society which is changing.

THE DNA OF INDIAN SOCIETY: *THIS* AS WELL AS *THAT*

In retrospect, the expectation in the early years of liberalization by market analysts that we would see an India overrun with the western way of living, eating and thinking, was naïve. The mental model that all of us had was that there would be a short sharp battle between tradition and modernity (read Indian and western) and the winner would be modernity, with tradition falling by the wayside, eventually buried in history. The dominant logic was that it was a zero sum game and that there could be only one winner. This OR that! But Consumer India surprised us yet again, by adopting a '*this* as well as *that*' approach.

Engineered marriages, computerized horoscope casting, cyber *aarti* (screen savers with pictures of favourite gods, enabling the traditional *aarti* offering to be done with a click of the mouse) abounded. In fact, even as the traditional fundamentalists loudly voiced their disapproval of the celebration of Valentine's Day and the 'westernization' of Indian culture, in just a couple of years, aided by television soaps, Karva Chauth has become the new home grown Valentine's Day! Karva Chauth is an old north Indian ritual, where the wife fasts all day for the well-being of her husband; when the moon rises, she looks at the moon and her husband's face and he feeds her the first morsel of food that breaks her fast.

Another example is from the chocolate market. Ever since I can remember, chocolate companies have been asking how they can get a share of the traditional Indian sweets market, especially during festival time. How could they get chocolates into the traditional exchange of sweets during Diwali, the festival of lights, when people send each other boxes of Indian sweets? They tried advertising but with no success; they tried special chocolate flavours and special gift boxes printed with traditional Indian motifs, but that didn't work too well either. Eventually, the small players of the market innovated the right 'this as well as that' combination, which took off—a set of individually wrapped chocolate mounds of uneven shape, packed in traditional decorated clay lamps used for the traditional lighting up of the house that is done by everyone on Diwali.

The evolution of the food market is another example of the 'this as well as that' hybrid solutions that Consumer India revels in. The batter for making idli and dosa became available in plastic packets, made every day by a host of housewives and distributed through local grocers. Such solutions, followed for other foods, have succeeded in pre-empting the entry of ready-to-eat processed food. As lives get busier and women have less time to spend in the kitchen, cooking at home is bound to decline. However, the solution has not been the adoption of packaged food or change of food habits, as the analogy school would have thought or imagined, but the rise of a cottage sector 'kitchen outsourcing' industry. There are more and more women supplying 'tiffin boxes' of home made food in each of the big cities. Their consumers are not just the bachelors and hostel dwellers but urban homes as well. So the cook who cooked in your kitchen has been replaced by the cook who cooks in a professional kitchen and supplies the food to you (the mental model here is that of a 'community kitchen', not a restaurant).

If home-made food is warm, wonderful and fresh, and its factory-made alternative is cold, clinical and preserved, then the above solution is actually the best of both worlds—made on a micro scale, as if at home, by other housewives; ready to cook (all negative labour outsourced!) but homemade (the positive labour retained!).

And McDonald's now offers varieties for the vegetarian and the Indian palate, enabling the impeccable fast food experience of McDonald's brought in the comfortingly familiar form of the *aloo tikki*. Not to be outdone, a chain called Jumbo King has taken the *vada pav* and offers it the McDonald's way.

Generally, we find that change outside the precincts of the home is quite revolutionary, while change within the home is evolutionary. Automatically, you deal with the same individual living in two different and sometimes contradictory worlds. The western mind is conditioned to think in terms of 'this or that'. This gives rise to inner contradictions, causing great dissonance. The Indian mind can happily cope with these real contradictions, and not feel hypocritical or misaligned. Oriental societies generally have far less dissonance than occidental ones, and they do not find too much tension between the different facets of life—the westernized version of them in the world outside, and the Indianized version in the world at home. Some call it hypocritical and two faced; but actually it is just high tolerance of ambiguity. I know of young wives who are virtually unrecognizable when on trips abroad—they change at airports from traditional clothing to western clothing usually forbidden at home and do the reverse when they come back. Far from feeling pressured, they pride themselves on their adaptability, and their husbands admire them all the more for it!

Anyone familiar with the history of India would actually have known that this is the way India would respond to new influences that liberalization would bring. It would bear repetition to say that societies change around their DNA. And plurality or 'this as well as that' is the DNA of Indian society. Think of the stories from the Hindu pantheon that every child in India grows up with, irrespective of religion. The concept of the avatars creates many dramatically different manifestations of the same god they all are but different facets of the same. So Ram, the ever good, dutiful, obedient son who deferred to public opinion and made his wife publicly undergo tests to prove her chastity, finally abandoning her when she was pregnant, is actually an incarnation of the same god as Krishna, the playboy cowherd sharpshooter whose deeds have inspired some of the finest romantic poetry and music. He is a brilliant manipulator, had many women in his life, and manoeuvared his way out of trouble often. Equally, most Indian men have no trouble believing that the bloodthirsty Kali, the patient wife Parvati, and the strong, ten armed, multi-skilled and tough Durga are all but different forms of the same divine feminine power.

The moral relativism of the Hindu way of life is often startling to those encountering it for the first time. You can cross the seven seas and eat and drink forbidden foods but you can come back home, take a dip in the Ganga and be morally purified and as good as new! In the days of the British Raj it was not unusual to see clerks in government offices wearing shirts and ties on top and dhotis and sandals below, because as they sat at their desks, the top part of their bodies was all that the British officer saw. On a similar note, Brahmins in almost all parts of India are forbidden from eating non-vegetarian food but Brahmins in Bengal are allowed to eat fish, because, in Bengal, fish is considered a vegetable of the sea!

The economy also is clearly a hybrid model of 'this as well as that'—socialism in some form coexists with free market economics. The future of Consumer India, therefore, must be thought of in terms of coexistence, fusion, loosening of rigid structures and new ways of doing old things. And what does that mean? Maggi noodles made of whole wheat with sambaar flavouring, Punjabi Chinese food, ready-to-wear pre-stitched saris, herbal cosmetics coexisting with glycol peels, and the Gayatri mantra available for download as a ring-tone, if you are hip enough for that!

THE CONTRADICTORY INDIAN

At an MTV conference many years ago, a youth market observer called the younger generation of India the 'dual passport' generation, to signify how they were a contradictory blend of western modernity and Indian tradition. Author Pavan Varma in a media interview about his book *Being Indian: The Truth About Why the 21st Century Will be India's,* says that we Indians are a bundle of contradictions. 'We are focussed and will work towards a goal despite formidable obstacles. So we are resilient, ingenuous, ever hopeful'. Anyone who sees the epic proportions to which we take the saga of class X, XII and college admission exams with an entire nation, rich and poor, coming to a standstill will not doubt our single-mindedness or sense of purpose.

Yet Indians are very relaxed in their acceptance of dug up roads, mounds of uncleared garbage, eternal traffic jams, and abysmal services from public utilities for which they pay good money. They are also relaxed about the way they litter, spit and relieve themselves in public spaces. The poor will borrow to go to a rural private practitioner for their child's illness, but not demand better from a government clinic.

The increase in the number of women working outside the home was widely expected to trigger large-scale changes in the way the home was managed and in a surge in the use of convenience products. However, the neglected detail was that the Indian female identity is just as contradictory. Outside the home, a woman is her own person, the confident, 'in control' working woman, but inside the home, she is the role-bound wife and mother. So while there is an increase in personal products purchases, there is no surge in the use of convenience foods or disposable diapers within the home.

9

cultural foundations
of Consumer India

The Cultural Meaning of Liberalization

Of the three foundations of consumer behaviour—psychological, social and cultural—the last one is the hardest to see and to decode. It is often unfathomable and changes slowly, yet wields considerable power. As Virginia Valentine, founding partner of Semiotic Solutions says repeatedly: 'Culture isn't inert. Its pretty "ert". If it isn't working for you, then it is probably working against you.'

The complexity of understanding the cultural foundations of consumer behaviour increases significantly in markets where age-old cultures are ruptured by sudden and sharp events that cause ideological, political, economic and even technological discontinuity. Though cultures are embedded to varying degrees and slow to change, yet events may be forceful (e.g. the fall of the Berlin Wall, the collapse of the Soviet Union, the opening up of China, the liberalization of India), inevitably resulting in some sort of redrawing of the cultural map of the market. This also bring some unusual opportunities and unforeseen threats in its wake. An understanding of the cultural future of such a market transitioning is critical for CEOs and strategists who need to gear up their organizations to compete in that probable future.

The contours of India's cultural future are still unclear because everyday evidence of the surprising ways in which India is changing comes to light and the old theories about inevitable westernization sound simplistic. We can easily see from the evidence at hand the emergence of an Indian culture which is an amalgam of the old and new and on which the traditional labels of 'western' or 'oriental' do not sit comfortably. To attempt a forecast in matters as complicated as this would be hazardous—as they say, if you want to gaze into a crystal ball, then you have to be prepared to eat ground glass! So instead of dramatic forecasts, let us examine the forces that are driving cultural change in India. We know so far how they work. This work-in-progress snapshot will also provide some pretty good hypotheses about the new culture of Consumer India, and what it could mean for consumer markets.

The force of liberalization and its cultural meanings: All major events in a nation's life are loaded with cultural meaning, and have an impact on popular and consumer culture. So too has been the case with liberalization in India.

The cultural meaning of liberalization and the consequent cultural shifts are best described in Table 9.1.

Table 9.1: Liberalization's Impact on India's Culture

From ⟶		Towards
1.a. Genteel poverty	to	Learning to earn more
b. Contentment and stability (e.g., Hindu rate of growth)	to	Striving to keep up with others (e.g., If China/Korea/even Indonesia can, why can't we?)
2. Swadeshi	to	International (e.g., Striving to make 'world class' goods, which can find export markets)
3. Self-reliance (no matter what the price to be paid)	to	Efficiency (if it's cheaper to buy, don't make it)
4. Isolation/Aloofness	to	Exposure to/Interaction with the rest of the world
5. Ideology/Emotion	to	Pragmatism/Rationality
6. Soft options (doing the popular thing)	to	Biting the bullet (doing what has to be done)
7. Obeying authority (e.g., government dictates)	to	Freedom of choice (e.g., a free market economy)

(contd...)

(contd...)

8.	Punishment/Guilt/Control (e.g., Curbing consumption through massive taxes on 'luxury goods')	to	Motivation/Positive incentivization (e.g., Stimulating demand by cutting duties and lowering interest rates)
9.	Aiming for the lowest common denominator (e.g., 'Garibi Hatao')	to	Aiming for the highest factor (e.g., 'Take India to the twenty-first century'—Rajiv Gandhi's signature tune)
10.	Protection (of the weak)	to	Enabling people to become more competitive
11.	Scepticism about technology ('may not be suitable to our conditions')	to	Seeking and embracing technology ('We can lead the world')

THE END OF CONTENTMENT AND ABSTEMIOUSNESS

The most important cultural shift is the emergence of discontentment with the incorrectness of continuing to be content with whatever little you have. As a country, we now have an obsession with China comparisons. The chief minister of Maharashtra coined a slogan about wanting to make Mumbai another Shanghai, and an Indian soldier on duty high up in the Himalayas informed me that I should not be impressed with the good quality of Indian border roads, because the Chinese had built a double road to the border. Indians today are completely preoccupied with what the GDP growth rate is each year, and the extreme competitiveness of the society is now shown in the epidemic of awards that have cropped up in every aspect of life. It would be an understatement to say that both the rich and the poor in post-liberalization India are engaged in a crazy scramble to maximize their earnings. Liberalization has certainly meant the death of the acceptance of Gandhian living in genteel poverty and being content with the 'Hindu rate of growth'. It is this shift that now drives consumerism at the national, institutional and individual levels.

Even the different states of the country are getting increasingly competitive about attracting investment. A bright, young executive said to me that I didn't appreciate how stressed his generation was, because they had so many options, so few constraints, and they were all constantly worried that there was a better deal somewhere around the corner that they were not seeing or not going after!

Clearly, as Santosh Desai says, there is a new view of life today. 'Life is not a condition, but a product. It is a blank that WE need to fill with achievement, enjoyment and meaning. Time is a real construct. Therefore it is a canvas that needs to be filled.'

Pragmatism Replaces Nationalism

Public and private life in India is now marked with opportunity and pragmatism. Hardline ideological positions are on their way out and increasingly we see the strong emergence of the middle path on several issues. Student union and trade union activity that marked the 1970s is virtually unheard of today. Political parties also have very little ideology; most of them hold centrist positions—some leaning a bit to the left, others a bit to the right. As the commerce minister said in a recent speech, since 1991, India has had five governments and six prime ministers but only one policy and point of view on liberalization. The communists practise some form of ideological protest in their role as minority coalition partners in the central government. However, in their home state of West Bengal, which is the seat and source of their power, they are now unabashedly capitalist!

Independent India was built on the Gandhian and Nehruvian values of swadeshi and self-reliance (be Indian, buy Indian, as the popular old slogan went). Out of this philosophy came a lot of excellent homegrown strongholds, whether elite educational institutions that could hold their own in the world—such as the Indian Institutes of Technology (IITs) and the Indian Institutes of Management (IIMs)—or the capability to build nuclear reactors, cars, computers and much more. But there also came an era of splendid isolation, and an attitude of accepting status quo. Interestingly, even as liberalization has replaced swadeshi and self-reliance with 'international and efficiency', India's competitiveness in the international arena has come by leveraging the very same capabilities built as a result of the 'self-sufficiency' ideology that now many dismiss as unfashionable.

This change in values from self-reliance to efficiency is most palpable in the way women across social classes think about how to run their homes. Equally, and ironically, the abolition of swadeshi has also decreased the lure of the opposite pole, *videshi* or foreign goods. Nowadays, Indian products are considered to match up to world standards and in some cases, viewed to be as international as those from anywhere else.

The best view of the changing cultural mores emerges by contrasting the younger generation with their parents. As early as 1994, an article in *India Today*, based on an opinion poll of over a thousand 18 to 22-year-olds, pointed out presciently,

> The new generation is playing by a fresh set of rules:
> Rule 1: It's a war out there. Choose your weapons and make sure you are fast on the draw.
> Rule 2: You've got only yourself to bank on, so watch your back.
> Rule 3: Idealism is a drag. Rebellion (and non-conformity) is a bum trip, and no one has time for a loser.
> Rule 4: If you've got it, flaunt it.

> There has rarely been a generation so competitive (68 per cent have set their eyes on zooming careers and outrageous wealth). Pragmatism, that once shameful word, is more than just a slogan; it's a conviction. (63 per cent will play the game and network to get ahead; 65 per cent would not change their religion even if it came in the way of marrying someone they loved).

In fact, marriage, an institution considered to be a pillar of Indian society, is seen to be a pragmatic partnership, an event that brings economies of scale. Living with parents is not such a bad deal either as it saves on the rent. There is not much talk of changing the system—the majority focuses on improved coping and working the system better. The goodies that life almost assures at this point in the country's growth overcome any desire to rebel.

THE FORCE OF THE 'ICE' WAVE: TECHNOLOGY-DRIVEN CULTURAL CHANGE

In the 1960s and 1970s all talk of technology used to be around the idea of 'relevant technology'. The notion was that poor countries need low-cost technology, and that they must compromise efficiency, speed and even quality in order to be able to offer 'right price' products. The discourse was that advanced technology was for the rich and basic for the poor, and India had to peg its technology levels somewhere in between. In contrast, today we see a clamour for world class technology. The rush is on to catch up with the rest of the world and make up for lost time and lost money. High-tech is seen to be the solution to create low-cost, wide-scale high-quality products and services that will enable businesses to get a share of the Indian as well as global market. Technology is viewed as the new money-spinner. It is perceived as the solution to a lot of problems and also viewed as an enabler of democracy and social development, the new definer of Indian identity—both as perceived by Indians themselves and the outside world.

ICE is the acronym for Information Technology (I), Communication (C) and Entertainment (E), the three converging to create products and services that are slowly, yet definitively, shaping a new India. Impacting the lives of the average Indian across socio-economic or regional boundaries, it is perhaps the single most potent force that distinguishes emerging markets. The significance of this point merits repetition—never before in the history of humanity have we had so many poor people subjected to so much technology, getting exposed in real time to issues that affect the rest of the world.

The less informed view of ICE is that it is about the Internet, cell phone ownership and conventional education, and hence limited to the top of the Consumer India iceberg. However, the actual ICE wave that has swept the country and is still sweeping it with ever-increasing force is something that I call the I $C^2=E^2$ wave.

Appreciating the Ubiquitousness of I $C^2 = E^2$

I stands for IT power. The power of job opportunities that are available to any qualified person, where qualification is all you need to get the job, given the huge demand and the short supply of such people. The power of services that were not available earlier and which significantly improve the quality of life or reduce the pain of everyday living—whether it is about computerized railway information and booking or about distance healthcare.

C^2 stands for the communication revolution and the connectivity leap, thanks to the extensive reach of television and the spread of telecom services, which are now touching remote villages as well. Often people look at the metric of ownership and penetration, and get deceived and are consequently dismissive about the low numbers. However, Consumer India is about community consumption, which is a number several times larger than penetration. Also the benefits of access go well beyond the individuals who have physical access to a television or a phone. There is a lot of virtual benefit or a 'by hearsay or osmosis' benefit when someone in one's extended family or circle of friends has access.

E^2 stands for the result of the connectivity leap and the communication revolution—an explosion of 'exposure to the world', and a rising demand for education of the practical and vocational kind. Private consumption expenditure data points to an increase in the share of communication and education expenditure. A taxi driver told me that his daughter, who lives in the village, paid Rs 4000 for a computer course, which he said was 'something called Windows after which she would have to do something called Words, and while I don't know what all this is, once she does both, she would have a job'. The National Association for Computer Training is looking at a Rs 50 billion market size in the next few years. The demand for education is extremely high, because it is now well established in the new Indian psyche that education enables more access to information and knowledge, which, in turn, enables someone to make more money. Computer education is seen to be the manna from heaven because it enables your child to participate in the big wealth creation and growth opportunity that the country is seeing. IT parks, even in communist-run states, have become the symbols of the wealth that the new democratic and merit-based India can create.

Awareness of IT and its power in solving problems/improving living conditions and creating employment has now sunk in and trickled down to the lowest social classes and to much of the rural population. There are just so many instruments of trickle down that even the poorest now talk of an IT education for their children. In other words it is an idea whose time has come. Television and the telephone are clearly the most ubiquitous drivers of change and their enormous reach and impact make the e-revolution feel like a minor ripple in a large pond. ORG-MARG market research data showed that 75 per cent of urban India watches television and the majority of them watch satellite and cable channels. In developed states, one out of two rural Indians watch television and in developing states the number is still one out of three. Even by the most conservative estimates, we are talking about over 500 million people whose lives are being impacted by television. Television which was once state controlled, has over a hundred channels available at affordable tariffs. It has exposed and educated the Indian mind like never before. It has widened points of reference and provided windows to other worlds, and in this process, created new information sources.

Further, the per capita consumption is 100 minutes on weekdays and 150 minutes on weekends—that is, around 10 per cent of waking hours. The viewership is skewed towards women and children and is greater in the lower social classes. While purists might insist that television is not an interactive medium, all research points to the fact that it is indeed interacting deeply with the brain of Indian viewers, impacting their worldview, shaping their identity, enabling expression, affirming rights and providing hope. The most interesting aspect of television is that it can access your mind even if you are uneducated. A fascinating research study, *Satellite in South Asia*, by the Institute of Development Studies, Sussex, has this to say:

> Far from passive viewing of television, people have tended to take up messages of self-improvement, self-confidence, egalitarianism, participation. It has shattered the myth of the 'good Indian woman', replacing it with a bolder version and led to the unbottling of women's feelings [even though many are too conservative to approve of the changed image]. It has produced a perceptible modernization in the usage of language among middle and lower middle income [groups and] created a popular culture of western style consumerism with that of Bollywood [and] reinforcing regional culture.

The connectivity leap is quite significant, too. Most of the 600,000 plus villages have telephone connectivity, and it is only a matter of time before everyone has access to a telephone. The issue isn't about telephone density. It is about the ability of connectivity to enable people in living better lives and broadening their scope of activity. Qualitative research often picks up views of villagers expressed in group discussions, that with telephones they can now leverage their contacts in cities and get help and resources to get their work done.

RESULTANT CULTURAL CHANGES IN CONSUMER INDIA

In a nutshell, increased social mobility, reducing 'power distance', hunger for information, and an even greater move from demanding social justice to grabbing economic opportunity are the new markers of the changes in consumer India. While earlier people waited for the 'messiah of the masses', what we now see is the search for the new 'messiah with the Midas touch'.

Tech-led democracy, reducing power distance: Perhaps the most powerful impact of IT has been in reducing the perceived gap in power between the educated and the uneducated, and those in positions of power and those out of it. Narayana Murthy, Infosys founder and chairman, once told a wonderful story of how he found his low-income colleague, the peon in his office, going to an ATM to withdraw money. When he asked the peon why he chose the ATM over the teller, he replied that the ATM did not care if he withdrew Rs 20 or Rs 2000, or whether he was well dressed or not. The teller, on the other hand, did care. I once witnessed something quite similar at a vegetable vendor. As I stood at the shop making up my mind about what I wanted, I noticed a scruffy little child from the neighbouring slum ask the shopkeeper for Re 1 worth of tomatoes, and quickly. The vendor mocked him—one whole rupee worth of tomatoes, and that too quickly? Get lost! I remember thinking that at a vegetable kiosk with automatic vending, this would not have happened. People discriminate, machines don't! These two stories force a rethink of the commonly held assumption around the world that advanced technology is for the rich and literate, while basic technology is for the poor and illiterate.

The Government of Karnataka's Bhoomi project is another example of tech-led democracy. It computerized all the land ownership records in the state and for a small fee of Rs 2. This allowed anyone to access them to check what the ownership status was, thus liberating the illiterate or the powerless from corrupt government official. Similarly, online ticket reservations has liberated the railways and passengers from the corrupt booking clerk and tout.

With the arrival of the Internet, even poor people understand that there is a way for your idea to get seen and heard, even if you do not have connections, and that there are opportunities that do come into the public domain.

The cultural impact of this is a reduction in the power distance, increased bargaining power, and hence instances of bargaining from various sections of society, and a general move from accepting status quo to demanding rights.

The cultural labels and mythology of social mobility of IT and IT-relevant education are dramatic. *Outlook* magazine refers to it as 'silicon moksha'. If you know computers, you can create the escape velocity to break free and get to the world outside, or at least to the nearby big city. IT education is 'the ceiling breaker' and the manner in which it provides access to information that can lead to more money.

It is, then, not at all surprising that the poor embrace technology and have a hunger for education and access to information, far more than the rich.

OTHER BIG CULTURAL THEMES THAT ARE HERE TO STAY

Empowerment and enablement: There are two major themes or threads that are running through India today. One is about the good life—the rising incomes, easy credit, significant increases in consumption, rising aspirations, rising respect from the world outside and so on. Of course, as is typical of middle-class thinking the world over, this is accompanied by a minimal concern or empathy for the rest of society or any desire to improve social structures. This is the theme that large sections of the popular press and television media play on. Their reportage of social issues is sensationalized, making it suitable only for entertaining the upper and upper middle class viewers rather than having an impact on the issue itself. Telling a story to entirely suit the tastes of this audience is not confined to the media alone. The Bharatiya Janata Party (BJP), in its last election campaign, used the slogan 'India Shining' to highlight its five-year term at the centre. This resulted in a close defeat in terms of percentage of votes for the BJP, because obviously all of India was not shining. As a newspaper article pointed out, even the semiotics of 'India Shining' were very interesting. Both the words, 'India' and 'Shining' were in a modern western idiom that only the urban educated would empathize with.

The much more populous heartland of India, Bharat as it is called, did not vibe with either the line or the sentiment it embodied. It was excluding rather than being inclusive. Wags added another line to the slogan: 'India Shining, Bharat whining'. Is Bharat whining? It was, for what is called 'bijli, sadak, pani' (electricity, roads, water). And once they started seeing the general improvement around them, their patience levels sank. Alongside this is the second major cultural theme. A large section of India today is gradually demanding empowerment and a fair share in the growth and prosperity that is sweeping the country.

Foreigners often ask me if there is not a real risk of severe social unrest in a country where the gap between the haves and have nots is so wide. It is a question for which one does not have a clear answer. Perhaps there is no one answer to it. On the one hand, the Indian way of life is accepting of God's script and hence, accepting of the fact that someone else can have a better script. Yet on the other hand, the rise of rampant aspiration always makes one wonder how long it will take for aspiration to overcome acceptance. But then again, India has shown that it has a unique way of resolving social contradictions.

This new demand for empowerment is different from the earlier socialist discourse of protection of the weak, and offering hand-outs to the poor by taxing the rich. It is a demand for strengthening the poor to effectively compete for opportunities, by giving them education, institutional interventions, etc. The focus on enabling is also seen in the changed discourse of NGOs, who are no longer in search of philanthropy but in search of partnerships that will enable them to have financially self-sustaining business models. This is also manifest in the election victories of Dalit leaders and political leaders of the backward classes whose constitutents expect them to carry their voices into Parliament and influence legislation.

Negotiation: The theme of negotiation is very dominant in India's culture. Modernity, as we discussed earlier, is nothing but negotiated tradition. A senior civil servant once remarked that if we just stepped back and looked at the country, we would see that it had become a massive negotiating table with every institution negotiating with every other group constantly. The left and the non-left political parties are negotiating hard, the backward classes and the forward classes are negotiating via the politicians for a fair reservation policy in education and even the supreme court and Parliament have been locked in an unhappy battle on several counts. In business the profit and no-profit sectors are painfully learning to negotiate partnerships with each other, as is the government and the private sector. Within the home, negotiation is furiously happening on issues of gender and generational disparaties. Themes related to negotiation are adjustability, adaptability, 'this as well as that', synthesis, hybrid models. Maybe in negotiation lies the answer to the question what shape social tension will take, as wealth gets more visible and the have nots get more aspiring.

Hybrid models: These themes are reflected in the way life works for an average Indian business or an average Indian home. The emphasis is always to make do, cobble together, and somehow manage, to create the appropriate solution at an affordable price. For example: buy a two-wheeler and a car— use them according to the need of the hour and optimize on petrol costs and status signals. Another common practice among housewives is to buy an expensive and a cheap detergent, one for your husband's office shirt and your child's school uniform, and the other for bedsheets and home-wear. And while at it, buy a liquid detergent for silk saris that you choose to wash at home in order to save money by not getting them dry-cleaned. Similarly, when shopping buy a mix of branded and non-branded apparel to bulk up your wardrobe. Inform yourself on the latest trends by browsing and then hunt for cheaper knock-offs on the high street. It always reminds me of Ogden Nash's rhyme 'Tell me octopus I begs, is those things arms or is they legs?' The theories of marketing that require people to be categorized in one way or another are far too restrictive, and even dangerous, to use for developing marketing strategy for India.

Contextual morality and ideology: When the negotiation theme plays out, the solutions are all-round accommodation, adjustment and collusion with detachment. It is not unusual for political parties to be partners in the central government and electoral enemies at the state level, nor is it unusual for a political party to ally with one party for one election, and a polar opposite in the next. The electorate understands that ideology is about electoral arithmetic and pragmatism and each time gamely evaluates the new combination depending on the demands of the new situation. Therefore adoption of new ideas is not a problem at all, but not allowing room for negotiated solutions is a problem.

Social legitimacy of aspiration: Santosh Desai talks about the 'unlocking of the social and economic fixedness of life'. He says that the earlier thinking of 'know your place, this is our place in the world, this is who we are not', which was something we took great care to teach our children, is now no longer valid. The idea of following your dreams and taking a chance, or aiming for a station way beyond where anyone you know has gone, are entirely legitimized. Stories of rags-to-riches entrepreneurs are celebrated, even if some of them have used doubtful methods to get to where they have. Earlier, education alone was a legitimate aspiration. Today, a whole range of aspirations are socially legitimate, whether it is about becoming Miss Universe or a movie star or wanting your child to win a *Boogie Woogie* dance show on television or anything else that can make you rich and/or famous.

Child-centricity: India and China represent totally child-centric cultures. While in China child-centricity may have been driven by the one-child policy in existence for so many years, in India child-centricity is because of the hope and expectation that children need to be indulged today so that they can take care of their parents in their old age. Also driving this obsessive child focus is the fact that there are far more kids than ready-made opportunities, including school and college seats, and aspiration levels of parents for their children have jumped.

FAQs About Consumer India's Culture

No discussion on the cultural aspects of Consumer India is complete without answering the following questions (a) Are Indian values and western values really different, and if so, then in what way? (b) How much of ancient India's culture will flow into modern India? and (c) What exactly is the Indian cultural discourse on money, and is it changing?

Is There a Real Western–Indian Values Divide?

It is extremely difficult to figure out the answer to this question. A key reason for this is the morphing way in which India changes, coupled with the hybrid mix of western and Indian behaviour that we observe. What one can safely conclude is that there is a 'this as well as that' sort of negotiated settlement that Indians have had with modernity and with western influences.

However, if we were to go beyond behaviour to values, which are either general guiding principles that govern behaviour or broad tendencies to prefer certain states of affairs or feelings, then there are real differences between India and the West, as can be seen as in Table 9.2.

Table 9.2: Indian and Western Values

Indian Values	Western Values
• Patriarchy	• Egalitarianism
• Ambiguity, adaptability, low dissonance	• Clarity, linearity, need for resolution of contradictions, of choosing between opposite positions
• Socially defined roles, dharma (translated in today's age as 'know what your DNA is and what type you are and play accordingly, or you will be unhappy')	• Individually chosen roles (you can become anything you want to be)
• Patience, passivity and Vairagya, (Sanskrit word for renunciation—especially of sexual pleasure—being the ultimate prescription for happiness)	• Impatience, assertion and a never give up attitude (Viagra—the western view of managing impotence and ensuring the continuance of sexual pleasure)
• Continuing with tradition (in some hybrid or morphed form)	• Constantly seeking novelty and change
• Happiness=Self-harmony	• Happiness=Wealth accumulation
• Respect for age	• Respect for youth

How Much of the Past and How Much of the Present?

Now that we have observed the several hybrid and fusion customer solutions which exist at the core of Consumer India, it is apparent that the past is being shed actively with regard to some aspects. Perhaps the most important one is in terms of the personal construction of identity. Santosh Desai describes the earlier Indian identity as being rooted in the collective past and about 'where we came from'. Even Hindu prayer and rituals demand that you give the names of the past seven generations of your family so that the Lord knows who exactly it is that is praying to him. In contrast, modern Indian identity is determined by the personal present and by the promise of the future.

However, the more interesting question that has been arising of late is how much of modern India's culture is a return to its pre-British roots. Were the Gandhian and the equally rigid Victorian eras, which happened to follow one another, actually an aberration? Will we understand consumer and people culture a lot more if we go back to pre-British India? Perhaps this may be the case. But that's another matter for historical investigation.

Cultural Discourse on Money

In the past, abstemiousness was a much lauded virtue. This was primarily a result of uncertainty, inflation and lack of economic growth; it was also deeply rooted in the Gandhian ideology of simple living, even if you were rich. Businessmen were frowned upon and wealth accumulation was seen as going against the very grain of what a good Indian should be doing. Now, of course, things are different. Sixty-five per cent of India's incremental GDP growth is driven by private consumption. Government ministers who now regularly confer with businesses have told businessmen in many forums, 'you have been legitimized. Please use your new-found power for the larger good.' All speeches laud the growth rate of consumer markets and we celebrate each new cell phone, each new car, and each new television set that is sold.

The idea of an ascetic, abstemious culture not into enjoyment or creation of wealth is actually perhaps a detour caused by the Gandhian and then the Nehruvian way of life. Hindu India is probably the only culture in the world that prays so blatantly and fervently to the goddess of wealth for prosperity. Diwali, the big festival of lights, is all about decorating your home with light so that it is inviting enough for Lakshmi, the goddess of wealth, to step in. Nowhere in the Hindu scriptures is it written that enjoyment is not good. They offer far more pragmatic advice and always say 'enjoy but do not get attached'. Indian mythology is replete with stories around money, not just money bringing sorrow but money bringing a great deal of joy to the virtuous as well.

As Santosh Desai says, money is about energy (and I add that it has always been so ever in the pre-Gandhian days). There is a far more liberated view of money, from something that has to be static and held in the bank locker to something that is integrated into the flow of life.

I am often asked why are Indians so value-conscious then? Will they be willing to pay more for brands? Why will they not spend more to get more 'feel good' benefits? The answer is partly in the fact that the Indian consumer is far from satiated with the 'do good' products that he/she owns, and it will take some time before the 'feel good' products find their place in his/her purchase priorities.

10
young India, woman
India: a closer look

LEVERS OF GROWTH AND TRANSFORMATION

Popular theories about the Indian market say that there are three things that will drive the growth and transform the character of the Indian consumer market—the coming of age of liberalization children, the changing Indian woman, and the rising income and consumption and the eventual transformation of rural India into a mega market, several times the size of urban India.

The rise of 'generation next' has been written about with unbridled optimism and enthusiasm, based on the coming of age of liberalization children. This close to 250-million-strong contingent of young people between the ages of fifteen and twenty-five is India's first non-socialistic generation. Global in their worldview, they have been exposed to enormous information and, unlike their parents, raised amidst a consumption-friendly and consumption-encouraging social discourse. They are expected to be at the forefront of creating a new, modern, west-embracing consumer society, as well as yield the demographic dividend that will drive economic growth.

The second growth and transformation lever is a slightly less dramatic one though a great favourite with the Indian media. It is based on the expected changes in homes as a result of 'the new, emerging Indian woman'. As more and more Indian women are beginning to work outside their home, they are becoming increasingly independent and assertive. This is expected to bring widespread changes in the old-fashioned, labour-intensive ways in which homes are managed and children are raised.

The third lever that is frequently discussed, but with a greater degree of scepticism, is the expected increase in consumption and consumption sophistication of rural India as both its income and exposure increase.

There is no consensus on whether rural India is a big pot of gold available to companies with the appropriate market strategies or a declining monsoon-dependent economy, rather like the proverbial quicksand that sucks unsuspecting businesses and destroys their profitability.

Like everything else about Consumer India, there is some truth in every point of view and every piece of data, no matter how conflicting. Directionally speaking, each of these levers does contribute to the change confluence that is happening in Consumer India today. However, like everything about Consumer India, god is in the detail, and in order to understand the big picture, looking at the detailed stories is very necessary. This chapter examines both the young and women in India providing data, discussion, health warnings, little noticed changes and points of inflection.

YOUNG CONSUMER INDIA

A Youth Market Still Waiting to Happen

One would imagine that a country with about half a billion people below the age of twenty-five and with its first non-socialistic generation just coming of age, would have a very vibrant youth market and culture shaped by a whole host of youth brands. One would also imagine that given such a huge virgin opportunity to shape a new market space, most youth brand marketers, old and new, would be here in very high gear and with lots of visible success.

Yet again, Consumer India has responded in a way contrary to expectations, given the experience in other emerging markets. The fascination for the US exists but only in terms of migrating to or studying or working in the promised land, and not in terms of aspiring for American brands. Coke, Pepsi, Levis and Wrangler, to name a few, did not have the success they thought they would.

Part of the reason was their incorrect assumption that they had a brand-aware and consumption-obsessed market awaiting them. This is based on the premise that the magic of the US is all-pervading. The truth, however, is that some countries are deeply exposed and influenced by America and some are not. India never was, in the way that the Philippines or Russia or even China was—the former because it was an American military base for a long time, and the latter two because they defined their own power and influence in the world in relation to America.

Another error of judgement on the part of overseas youth marketers was that they assumed that youth the world over are similar in terms of their values and desires, hopes and dreams. They did not realize that different generations in different countries might have been subjected to different economic-political and social forces that shaped their view of the world. Young India can never be like young America—in the last fifteen years there have been different forces at work in India and America. GDP growth and per capita income alone do not define how exactly a section of humanity will behave.

And, finally, because the mental model was not one of market creation, there has been no critical mass of youth marketers, each spending any significant amount of money, reinforcing one another, in defining a modern Indian youth culture with appropriate rituals, symbols and role models. Those that did spend the money spent it trying to project an alien youth culture that did not resonate in this country.

Why did such a youth culture not evolve on its own, given that the two most important ingredients were there already—large numbers of young people and tumultuous change in the environment? Perhaps because Indian society is more about affiliation and family and less about individualism. So the young do assert themselves, but within the framework of the family, and hence with far fewer degrees of freedom. Nevertheless there still exists a huge opportunity to shape the outside-the-home space for young people, which is their own, and quite different from what they do within their families. In the upper income groups, we now see a distinctive pattern of return-to-roots on the one hand and adopting international, western lifestyles on the other.

UNDERSTANDING YOUTH DEMOGRAPHICS

Teenage Market Structure: Income/SEC

The most important health warning that Young Consumer India comes with is the fact that its demographics are disappointing.

Let us examine the teens market. Of the 187 million or so twelve- to nineteen-year-olds that exist, 110 million or close to 60 per cent are rural and poor. They belong equally to the SEC R3 and R4. R3 means that they come from homes that are typically semi-pucca and the father has usually studied between standards 4 and 9; at best, he has finished high school. R4 means that they come from homes that are typically kuchcha where the chief wage earner is either illiterate or with some education. An almost identical pattern exists for the twenty- to twenty-five-year-olds. Of the 121 million of them, close to 60 per cent are rural R3 and R4 and about 3 per cent are urban social class A.

Table 10.1, profiling the twelve- to nineteen-year-old population, is what I send to editors of magazines in response to their cover stories on Indian Youth. Based on sample surveys of the highest social classes in just four or five big cities, they say that Indian youth are prolific consumers of everything from wire to ipods and make sweeping statements about 'gen next' attitudes to voting, family and the workplace. In reality, such

Table 10.1: Profile of twelve- to nineteen-year-olds in India

Label of attractiveness to marketers	SEC	Size of town/ city lived in	No. in millions/ % of total
Rich Brats	A1	Top 23 cities	0.9/0.5
Creamy Layer	A	Top 23 cities	2.2/1
Consuming Class	A, B	Top 23 cities	5.1/3
'Stretch-a-bit'	A, B	All urban	12.0/7
Urban Lower-Middle	C	All urban	11.0/6
Urban Poor	D, E	All urban	33.0/18
Rural Consuming Class	R1	Rural	4.5/3
Rural Marginal Consumers	R2 to R4	Rural	132/70

Source: Indian Readership Survey, 2006.

surveys represent, at worst, less than 1 per cent of the youth in India, and at best, about 3 per cent. Therefore, the entire talk based on survey evidence of how the consumption will explode and attitudes will change with the passing of the baton to the new generation, is a bit far-fetched.

It would be equally suicidal to project market sizes based on this supposedly leading edge segment even though they are the fastest growing in number. Thanks to the media they seem a large overpowering segment. In truth, they are a disconnected minority, about 1 million-strong, who have grown by 80 per cent in the past eight years.

The creamy layer (including rich brats): This is the segment that premium youth brand marketers target with a fair degree of hype. This would be the heartland for Levis or Wrangler. Their limited number—in all, a little over 2 million—explains the limited success of these brands in the Indian market. This group is also fast growing, and has grown 50 per cent in the past eight years.

The consuming class: This 5 million-strong group are the 'big city well-off kids'. Social Classes A and B are both high desire consumers, and the big city exposes them to all the things that fuel teenage consumption—hangout places, tempting shop displays, fashion trends, from overseas as well as locally created, behaviour of their richer age cohorts and their own intensely consuming parents. This would be the core target group for a youth market that conforms to the mental model of youth consumption behaviour in other parts of the world—the MTV generation, so to speak. They have high aspirations and knowledge of brands they want to possess, a fairly high penetration, but they disappoint marketers with their less-than-desirable quantum of consumption, whether it is jeans or music or gadgets.

'Stretch-a-bit' consumers: The term 'stretch-a-bit' is used here in the context of supplier effort. A market more than double the size of the consuming class of 5 million—12 million more young people—is available to the marketers of premium-priced product range. However, they need patience to sustain an all-urban India distribution network across 500 cities and spend on the development of a 'slow burn but definite to happen' market.

The rest of the urban teens, a staggering 44 million in number, are served mostly by the unorganized sector, be it pirated music or low-priced clothes. They are a high effort segment for any business because they know what is available from the movies, from television, and from watching their richer peers. Hence they will only accept cheaper versions of the same look, style and basic functionality. They are not willing to settle for less at a lower price especially on aesthetics. It could be worse quality fabric and trims, or have less of the frills.

Rural Teens are a large and underserved market, which does not exist for several marketers.

Such an income/exposure market structure is reflected in the jeans market structure—a category that epitomizes youth the world over. Seventy per cent of jeans are low priced, sold on the footpath, or in small jeaneries, which are one-person mom-

and-pop tailoring shops. They are typically priced at Rs 400 or below a pair, i.e. under US$10. Another 25 per cent are in the price range of Rs 500 to 900 or US$12 to 20 and comprise a whole host of local labels, private labels of mom-and-pop stores or low-end department stores, who buy from small scale manufacturers, and charge a usurious 40 per cent mark-up for distributing them. The premium brands, despite being present with their cheapest models, are a mere 5 per cent of the market, priced as they are between US$20 and US$35. There is, however, joy in special high-end designer labels for the 1 to 2 million creamy layer, who are looking for uniqueness, differentiation and 'beyond the usual' embellished jeans. And there is obviously a market waiting to happen for a high volume, low margin, low-priced, retailer—is this a market waiting for Wal-Mart?

Recently a fund manager sent me the business plan of a small branded apparel manufacturer-cum-retailer, with a request to spot the catch. It seemed too good to be true. The price points were very low, under Rs 500 a garment, inexpensive media-like billboards were used to build brand awareness and reassurance about quality as well as the perception of status that comes with a label that other people recognize—even if the label has no image or badge value attached to it. It was retailed in its own and franchised single-brand stores, which were tiny, 700 square foot spaces in residential neighbourhoods and the net margin per store was positive. The conventional wisdom about retailing, which doesn't work for the Indian market, is that large stores drive profitability, as does premium pricing. Actually, the structure of the market is quite the opposite. The key driver of continued profitable growth of this business would be energy, more than capital. Locating thousands of franchisees, who can bring the minimalist real estate needed, and managing the large armies of them through low cost processes made possible with a judicious use of technology is the real challenge. The model, however, is basically far more viable than a Gap clone or a Levis or Wrangler exclusive stores model.

Education, Literacy, Affinity for English

Only 7 per cent of the 121.4 million twenty- to twenty-five-year-olds are college graduates. This 7 per cent is a weighted average of a much worse 4 per cent of rural youth and a much better, though still dismal, 15 per cent of urban youth of this age who are college graduates.

Yet English reading is widespread. Thirty-four per cent of urban youth read English (double the number of those with a college degree) as do 13 per cent of rural youth, that is, three times the number of those who have a college degree. The same goes for the teenagers (12–19), where 37 per cent of urban teens and 15 per cent of rural teens read English. However, the story, as always, takes twists and turns. Even in SEC A1, the topmost social class where English medium college education is a given, only 43 per cent that is less than half, say they prefer watching English programmes on television, a number that drops to just 28 per cent in SEC A2.

That there is rapid progress in literacy in India even in a five-year period is evident not just from government statistics, but from survey data as well. In the twenty- to twenty-five-year-old age group, 24 per cent are illiterate. In the twelve to nineteen age group, only 13 per cent are illiterate. The percentage of illiterates drops by half between the twenty to twenty-five age group and the twelve to nineteen age group in rural India. In urban India, the drop in illiteracy is actually sharper—it is 16 per cent in the twelve to nineteen age group and 7 per cent in the twenty to twenty-five age group.

If a gender perspective were taken on all the data in this section, it would perhaps look far better for the men. The young women are far worse off, and the data that we have just seen is an aggregate of both.

Family Orientation

While much is written about 'gen next', especially the women opting to stay single, it is probably most applicable to the upper social classes. On an aggregate, 9 per cent of the teenagers and 65 per cent of the twenty- to twenty-five-year-olds are already married. This aggregate of 65 per cent translates into 70 per cent of rural youth and 50 per cent of urban youth being married. If 65 per cent of this age group is already married, 40 per cent say they have been married for four years or more. Since the majority of families in India are nuclear, especially at the middle and lower income levels, this means that there is a huge, yet untapped, opportunity to shape the way the new generation lives and runs its homes.

Psychographics and Cultural Drivers of Behaviour

Contexts of existence determine youth psychographics: Youth marketers of global youth brands always tell me that 'teenagers are teenagers the world over'. When we compare notes, we do find that my teenager in Mumbai is pretty much the same as theirs in Boston or Buenos Aires. Untidy rooms, rebellious, television and telephone obsessed, late sleepers, etc. However, the similarity stops at such surface behaviour. Scratch the surface and they are different—because every generation in every country is brought up in different cultural contexts, which shape their collective character, and in turn their individual behaviour.

Various proprietary studies done by global marketers in BRIC countries show some stark differences between the youth in each country and provide some clues about which direction they are moving in. These are best expressed using the IMPSYS consumer behaviour mapping concept of Paul Heylen (Figure 10.1).

On the dimension of 'affiliative–assertive' (also interpretable as 'we oriented–me or ego oriented') both Chinese and Indian young people map closer to 'affiliative', while Russian youth are more 'me' oriented, with Brazilian youth being in between, not being family centric but very peer group oriented. Brazilian youth have a very strong street culture and a very strong peer

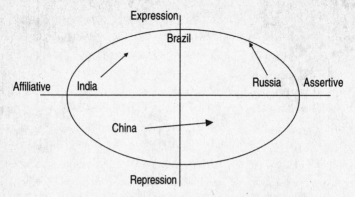

Figure 10.1: Youth Map for Different BRIC Countries

orientation where peer group approval is fundamentally important. Indian youth, in contrast, are very family centric, the cultural codes amongst Indian youth are about kinship of an extended family, about family obligation, and the home as a shared space.

Further, even though Chinese and Indian youth are both from cultures that are very affiliative, there are differences in the tone and the strength of these affiliative bonds. Unlike the Indian teenager who has grown up with a profusion of siblings and other relatives, the Chinese teenager has grown up in a milieu where generations have been following a one-child policy and where, consequently, the larger community is the family. With the sociological changes occurring in new China, the affiliative nature of society is gradually getting replaced by individuality. In India, technologies like cell phones and text messaging and cheaper air travel have actually extended the connected family circle even more.

On the 'expression–repression' dimension, Russian youth are midway, but moving fast in the direction of being expressive. Highly individualistic by nature and constantly asserting individual autonomy, they cherish the ability to have an opinion. Indian youth are also midway on this dimension, and moving towards becoming far more expressive. However, what makes them different from Russian youth is that they are very affiliative. They have socially codified norms of behaviour and even their rebellion is within the parameters of social approval. Brazilian youth are the most expressive of all while Chinese youth map the closest to the repression end of the scale. They exist in an environment that is relatively far more repressive, rule-bound, and with high control from powerful authorities, though not from nagging parents. They are moving in the direction of greater individualism, but not necessarily in a more expressive way, presumably explaining their easier adoption role for products to enable self-expression.

Achievement orientation is very high in Chinese society, as it is in Indian society. However, in the rambunctious democracy that is India, there is more chaos than order in the process of getting ahead. Russian youth are also very achievement oriented, but in a very individualistic way, while achievement in India is strongly connected with making one's family proud.

A Pressure-cooked Generation

I once consulted for a gaming company, which had the licence for an online multimedia game that was very successful in many markets, especially the Philippines, Taiwan and Brazil. Their assumption was that once the game was introduced through cyber cafes where the bulk of Internet penetration lay, it would explode. However, it did not. 'What do young people do for relaxation,' the puzzled non–Indian managing director of the company asked. 'They study, go for tuitions and try to get ahead,' was the response he got from his Indian team. Incredulous, he needed some explaining about what the key social drivers of this gen next actually are—'achievement and getting ahead' and making your family proud by doing better than your peers.

Young India lives in a world of unbelievable competition. There are more young people than there are opportunities, and everyone has been indoctrinated from childhood to study really hard, make their parents proud and pay them back by being successful. As many as 9.3 million young people want to go to college for the only 3 million or so available college seats. For admission to the premier engineering college, the IITs, there are 7,000 kids at each mark point in the entrance exam. My daughter got 92 per cent in her school final exam but did not qualify for the cut offs in the premier colleges for a subject of her choice. The list can go on. This is a 'grab any opportunity' self-made generation, who will conform and will not rebel or rock any boats for the rewards of success. They form a combat force, with their parents, school teachers and tuition teachers, to collectivaly conquer those elusive opportunities. The work market is equally competitive, but if you graduate from the right colleges, then 'life is made' as the popular Indian phrase goes.

Exam season, especially for families with children appearing for all-India board exams like standards X and XII, are near frenzy times and every household with a child appearing for these exams sinks into exam mode. Cable TV is cut off often, visitors are discouraged and tuitions are the norm—not just for the exam period but for the whole year. The Common Entrance Test (CET) for college admissions, the Common Admission Test (CAT) exam for management schools and the IIT entrance exam are national events where even the national news media telecast programmes on 'how to crack the exam'.

It is often argued that achievement orientation is very high in many other emerging markets as well. However, each of these societies has its own kind of spin on it, which is quite distinctive.

Pragmatism is the Key

Pragmatism and success seeking are the core of this new generation. A study presented at an MTV youth conference several years ago sums up this orientation.

1. Parents become democratic and friendly.
2. 'You get oranges, enjoy. You get lemons, learn to make lemonade.'

3. All things material are highly coveted.
4. No moral, sexual revolution here.
5. Youth icons are gilt-edged heroes.
6. Brand conscious but very value sensitive.
7. 'Pubs aren't second homes; drugs are absurd.'

They aren't adamant on finding themselves spouses and are open to parents finding them spouses, with the final choice left to them, of course. This is their pragmatic solution for marriage, which they view as a life business partnership, marching together shoulder to shoulder, on the road to material success.

Indian, Not Wannabe Western

The old Hindi film song *'Mera joota hai Japani, yeh patlun Englistani, sar pe lal topi Rusi, phir bhi dil hai Hindustani'*, was very popular in the 1950s, 1960s and 1970s and while one may not hear the lyrics belted out in the market square any more, it still does appear to resonate with how liberalization children feel. In 2006, Euro RSCG, a leading advertising agency, polled over 2,000 young people in the top eight cities in India, fifteen to thirty years of age, whom they call 'prosumers' or opinion spreaders, who are persuasive people, trusted by their peers, and who pick up ideas and spread them as they interact with their peers. The key finding was that they preferred Indian brands, Indian looks, and Indian environments to bring up their children. They actually believed that personal care products made for India worked better than the imported ones—a huge movement from the 1960s and 1970s, when there was a premium on imported goods. Nine out of ten young people said that they preferred taking up a job in India and being with their family rather than going abroad as long as they made enough money to travel abroad. Mixing the best of the west and the east is what they would like when it comes to music, and they believe that intellectually, Indians can hold their own against the best of elsewhere.

Young Indians have often been described as 'dual passport holders' (both ethnic and international in their outlook), and as being a cultural *khichadi*.

An article in the *Business Standard*, 30 March 2006, talks of how trendsetters feel about their Indian identity. They define trendsetters as the 9 million SEC A and B youth (twelve to twenty-five years) in the top thirty-five cities of India. 'The new young Indian is proud to be one, and is quite comfortable being one. He is as happy with Haldiram as he is with McDonald's, and Fab India and Esprit . . . Yet there is a global/western Indian emerging . . . some of the values they cherish (of the West) include the freedom to think, speak and act.'

How can they, despite exposure to far better lifestyles of other countries, still keep preferring India? While they recognize that India has serious problems, they make a real distinction between India and Indian. Indian is the brand they are proud to belong to and aspire to make it even better.

Optimism, success and aspiration: While their parents' generation had defined criteria of what success was, this generation recognizes that there are many routes to nirvana. Any form of self-employment including dog grooming parlours, adventure tourism, counselling, fitness instructors, DJs, is fine and respectable, as long as you are making money. In the India of the past, identity was based on caste, community and what your lineage was. Today, they see performance as something that can neutralize all these advantages (or lack of them) and their role models are first generation successful entrepreneurs, cricketers, newscasters, film stars and so on.

The small town India of Bunty and Babli: The 2005 blockbuster Hindi movie *Bunty Aur Babli* perfectly explains the worldview of India's small town young adults. What hits you hard in the movie is the force and nature of aspiration that drives small town India. It isn't about the old days of dreaming of being a famous film star and not knowing how to go about it.

Babli, the female protagonist, is a small town young girl who has decided that she wants to be a supermodel and that the route is the Miss India contest. She knows that trials are held in the bigger cities of Lucknow and Kanpur. Bunty, the male protagonist, is also from a small town and knows that a financial services business involving small depositors and finance companies could be a route to becoming rich. He is the quintessential small but innovative entrepreneur who thinks up business models like setting up a shower stall on his terrace for people in his neighbourhood to enjoy a better bathing experience for a small fee.

They are united by a severe hunger to escape the humdrum life of the good daughter turned into good wife and the good son with the modest, steady job with *izzat* and *imaandari* (honour and integrity). Rebellion is old-fashioned for the well-heeled, SEC A metro kids, who do not need or want to rock the boat, because the good life is at hand. But the rest are willing to run away and find their escape velocity into a newer and better orbit. In focus groups with young people, an oft-repeated refrain is: 'It isn't where you have been born but what you can do with yourself. There are so many opportunities for the bold and the smart who seize them, look at all the [role models] who have proved it.' There is no guilt about worrying the parents, no deep yearning for home and just the pragmatism of missing home-cooked food.

The duo are voyagers, who are happy to experiment with things that would earlier have been the preserve of the bad. Drinking doesn't make you a useless drunkard, and a cigarette is a useful accessory. They aren't one-way streets to hell, just harmless, occasional fun. The accent is on being street smart to get what you want, on working the system from the inside, on experiencing and enjoying the consumerist paradise when you can afford it.

The hip and happening clothes tell a story too. His 'Nik*ee*' T-shirt, jeans and sneakers are a good example of what the non-premium market is all about—not less style at a lower cost, but a more affordable, slightly less perfect clone. Her clothes are a good reflection of the broad spectrum that a modern young

Indian woman's wardrobe spans—both east and west and often somewhere in between (familiar in concept but totally morphed salwar-kameezs, for example).

The values described in the film and echoed in findings from consumer research studies show that values have not changed as rapidly as attitudes or lifestyles. Bunty and Babli are repeatedly shown as *shareef* (well-brought-up), well-mannered, and really good kids at heart, despite external appearances. Loud and clear in the movie are evergreen Indian values such as respect for elders, complete with the frequent ritual of touching elders' feet, and the family values of setting a good example for your child, and returning to live with your in-laws.

The wedding scene when Bunty and Babli get married echoes the theme of '*phir bhi dil hai Hindustani*'. They take the ritual seven steps around the fire but the vows that are traditionally taken with each step have been totally modernized. She is a virgin till her wedding day, despite living together before, and is not coy about the physicality, when it is permissible. The feminist statement about being an equal partner is a thread that runs right through, and the reasonable man is definitely taking over from the egoistic male.

However, the most telling part is in the end. They both agree that the dull life of disgusting domesticity is a very unhappy state to be in. And the 'this as well as that' resolution of their problem echoes what one hears from focus groups all the time. So they go back to the exciting life of scams and stings, but as good, establishment guys who are using their considerable dubious talent for creating a better world. We are like that only'!

LIBERALIZATION CHILDREN: A POWERFUL MARKET FORCE

Defined in the classical sense, liberalization children are a demographically disappointing market, yet to be shaped by

Table 10.2: Household Structure by Age Group

% of households who have a family member aged...								
0–2 yrs	3–4 yrs	5–12 yrs	13–15 yrs	16–19 yrs	20–24 yrs	25–34 yrs	35–54 yrs	55+ yrs
24	21	52	28	31	35	53	71	42

Source: Indian Readership Survey, 2006.

marketers. However, the importance of the liberalization children is obvious if one were to look at household structure by age group Table 10.2.

About six out of ten households have a liberalization child, who acts as a change agent in that household. They are not just a very attractive niche market opportunity but are also critical to the mainstream. The mainstream Indian market is a youth market.

THE WOMAN CONSUMER IN INDIA

Popular theory has it that changes in household consumption behaviour are happening rapidly because more women are now working outside the home. Hence, they are becoming more exposed and financially independent. They are also getting more assertive and they are all set to bring about a consumption revolution and explosion. The truth, like everything else about Consumer India, is not so simple and straightforward. Yes, it is true that women are changing and this change will create new and different opportunities. But to assume that they are changing only because of a huge surge in the number of women in the workforce might be a mistake.

Working Women Facts

To this day, only 23 per cent of housewives in urban India have a job outside the home. In comparison, this number is 42 per cent of housewives in rural India, where working in the fields

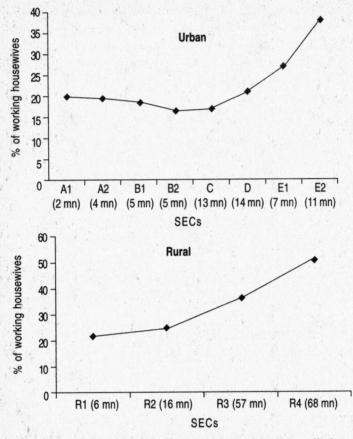

Figure 10.2: Comparison of the Working Status of the Housewife Across Various SECs (per cent Working Outside)

is common for women. (The term 'housewives' pretty much covers most adult women, since the age of marriage is still very low). What is more, as households get richer, the proportion of women in the workforce falls (see Figure 10.2).

The conservative working woman: Contrary to popular belief, more women working outside the home does not have the expected impact on consumption, since the 'this as well as that' working woman continues to play the traditional role at home, and in many ways is the last to change practices inside the home, even as she blazes new trails outside the home. Her personal spending and saving patterns on personal products will change quite dramatically, but not her household behaviour; at any rate, not in the same measure

The home entrepreneur: There is, however, a new category of working women just emerging, called micro-entrepreneurs, who run what they call a 'home businesses'. They stay mostly at home, refer to themselves as housewives and not as working women, but run some sort of business, typically tailoring, cooking, catering, giving tuition to children, beauty parlours, etc. A 2006 study conducted for TIE (a not-for-profit organization to promote entrepreneurship) in six cities among 1,200 women in the social classes B, C and D showed that 25 per cent were already doing some work from home and another 30 per cent intended to start a home business. The desire to be productive and to improve their self-worth by turning talent into money is huge, and this trend will only accelerate.

The changing housewife: Rena Bartos, an American demographer, pointed out in one of her books that the cookie cutter gender stereotypes of working and non-working women that marketers adopt is actually flawed. She pointed out way back in the 1980s that all working women are not the same— there are those for whom it is 'just a job' and there are those who are actually pursuing careers. Similarly, 'stay at home' women are of two types—those that want to work and see themselves as working women even though they do not work outside the home and those that are happy to be at home.

In India, the increasing number of working women is not driving change as much as the increasing number of housewives who have acquired the 'working woman' mindset.

Working from home or not, all women say they see themselves as chief executives of the household and primary coaches of children, ensuring their success in this ultra competitive world. Further, since around 60 per cent of families, both urban and rural, are nuclear, with no elders living with them, the housewife sees herself as having a very important role to play. This has resulted in the rise of what I call 'womanism', which is driving major change across households in Consumer India.

The Change Wave of Womanism

In India gender equations have always been skewed in favour of men. 'Your husband is your God, worship him' is the advice most brides were and often still are given. The Indian woman was always told, 'Yours is not to question why, yours is but to do . . . and die'. Slowly but surely, this discourse is changing.

Womanism is a gentler and less individualistic form of feminism. It is about women asserting themselves as their own person too, who want their space and place. They want to be productive/do something worthwhile and remunerative. Most importantly, they want their opinion to count, value their own time, and look after their own interests. They do not see any glory in self-denial. It marks a change in mindset of women rather than in behaviour—yet another example of morphing change that is the hallmark of Consumer India. It represents a change in the attitude of women towards themselves and their role in their world, and not just a change in how they dress or carry out their household chores. In fact, as one researcher put it, even for the most forward-looking Indian woman, the mental emancipation achieved in the past few years has been far greater than physical emancipation. Which is another reason why this change is not easy to see, but will drive sustainable behaviour change over the next few generations.

This is the slow but definite wave of change happening in India. Women are on the move, inching their way away from being doormats, away from the socially ordained straitjacket that Hindi movies of yesteryear so glorified.

I deliberately use the words inching their way away from being doormats rather than saying marching determinedly towards breaking free, to reflect the truth of the situation. So is this slow burn relevant to qualify as a change wave? It is relevant because, as mentioned in an earlier chapter, Force=Mass × Acceleration, and the force of change caused by a large mass of people moving even at a very slow speed is huge enough to qualify as a change wave

Various studies done by the advertising agency FCB ULKA and the Indian Market Research Bureau point out that urban women see their role as being a far more 'value added' one—that of the intellectual nurturer, helping her child to be competitive and achieving, and in being the CEO of the household.

Most women are re-evaluating the importance of each of their roles and activities, and are decreasing engagement with those that are high on effort and low on appreciation. Cooking continues to occupy an important place in the portfolio, as it is high on payoff even if it is high on effort. It ensures health and nourishment of the family enabling them to perform in this pressured world, and is a way of her self-expression and creativity. De-emphasizing certain traditional roles like cleaning or shopping does not bring with it the stereotypical old world mountains of guilt, because the time released thereby is going towards fulfilling other more productive roles. It is in this churn of women's portfolio of roles and activities that marketers will find huge opportunities.

A McCann Advertising study on rural India says that the biggest change that struck the researchers was the changing role of the woman in villages, and how she was beginning to get a mind of her own and express her own opinions. Village girls insist on going to school, and their mothers are letting them do so, sometimes against the wishes of the father. The experience of ICICI and Hindustan Unilever with self-help groups in states like Andhra Pradesh and Tamil Nadu shows that the networking benefits, along with the availability of finance, unleash a lot of woman power resulting in a definite rise in self-esteem and a demand for recognition from the rest of the family. While self-help groups often do not stay together after a time, they do throw up the occasional successful woman entrepreneur who serves as a role model for the rest.

Marketers who are busy tracking the metric of 'how many women work in offices outside the home', are perhaps missing the big changes inside the home. Some have got it, like two-wheeler marketers who have noticed the emergence of a whole new market for girls and women who want the freedom that comes with mobility.

There is a strong case for financial services companies to specifically create a 'women's business cell', and go beyond offering the odd add-on credit card to her husband. The home manager is ready to manage finances better, and wants to know how. In almost every category, there is the opportunity for forward-looking companies to actively encourage this movement and secure a lion's share of what will be an increasingly valuable target group as generations evolve.

The Many Shades of Modernity

According to Research International, a market research agency, the first step up the womanism ladder is when the traditional woman becomes 'less traditional'. She begins experimenting, seeks a better role for women, especially her girl child, starts negotiating with the male, albeit tactfully, not blindly accepting his dominance, but is still suspicious of excessive modernity.

The next and usually final step is for her to be 'forward looking'. That means that she is still family centred but individualistic, and her mental emancipation is far greater than her physical emancipation. She arrives at a balance of the modern and the traditional and there is no more movement after that.

The image that most of us have of western modernity is actually one that most Indian women do not aspire to. They call it 'ultra modern', which refers to the small group of young people who have broken away from tradition and custom and are free, unshackled and unfettered. It is certainly not the picture of the modern Indian woman, at least not for several decades to come.

Understanding the Forces of Change

Education: One of the forces driving this change wave is the increase in education amongst women of all social strata, especially urban women. At one level, the statistics on housewife education are dismal. Only 12 per cent of urban housewives are college graduates and another 20 per cent have completed school. Thirty per cent are illiterate and the remaining 40 per cent or so have studied up to a maximum of grade 9 in school. However on adding up the number of years of school and college in the total pool of women, it is easy to see that the total 'education capital' is definitely higher than before, and there are more years of schooling between them all, which collectively 'makes the worm turn'.

Outdoor work: This is the phrase used by Indian women to describe the chores that they are now increasingly beginning to do outside the home like visiting the bank or paying utility bills or going to school to meet the teacher or running around government offices for ration cards. With two-thirds of urban women living in nuclear families, the onus to do 'outdoor work', traditionally done by the men in the family, and to manage without the support of elders is giving them a new-found confidence.

Role models: The reservation of seats for women in the panchayats has brought them into the public decision making domain. A news report says that in Uttar Pradesh alone there are 20,000 women gram pradhans. If the figure is right, that's a lot of role models to show the way to the rest. Television, cinema, business and the arts now all offer women role models from bankers to pilots to beauty queens. Generations are growing up with a clear focus on education and future careers.

Television: The primordial force—television—has been the source of enormous change. Whatever may be the critical pronouncements of intellectuals on the retrograde stereotypes of women shown in serials, television has widened women's frame of reference and given them the information resources to imagine and aspire. While many people decry the soaps that are the staple of Indian television as regressive and brainless, the fact is that they all have a subversive feminist discourse. The protagonists are all women, good or bad, they all take charge of situations, and they all deal with them in different ways. The virtuous heroine can, when required, be the vamp and the vixen and the message is that all is fair in the game of life and women have the power, if they choose to wield it.

POSTSCRIPT

Women have more say at home today with families and in their own lives than they have had before. They are getting more educated, more entrepreneurial, and more gutsy about narrowing the gap between them and authority figures in their lives—more so spouses and in-laws than parents. This is going to keep increasing because once the worm turns, there is no stopping it.

While it is true, by women's own admissions, that mothers-in-law are more tolerant and husbands less repressive, and they have equal voting rights on family issues, it isn't social evolution that is driving this change as much as the state of the economy. In other words we have the phenomenon of the EMI to thank for driving this change. The concept of family has changed from a predominantly social unit to an economic unit. The new truth about Indian marriages is the old truth—that its business model is around a pragmatic life business partnership rather than around romance. Ask any young man, or woman, and you will know.

Taking a loan for whatever purpose is the new Indian way of life. The EMI is here to stay. And everyone has to do whatever they can in the family to enable family earnings to happen, so that the quality of living can be improved or the house can be owned or made liveable.

What is the role of the woman in this? In the lower social class, she must either earn and be a co-contributor or she must look after the housework and the children of the extended family so that the men and the women who are working outside the home can maximize their earnings.

In the middle and upper class households, she must take care of all home and outdoor work of the family so that she facilitates and insulates the man who is better qualified and who can earn big bucks, to do so with no distraction.

At the very top social class, if she can be an equal earning partner, she must contribute and do so. But only up to a point of 'adequacy', because the idea is to optimize the unit's earnings, not maximize the woman's earning. Therefore, predictably, 20 per cent of SEC A housewives work outside the home, sliding to 16 per cent through SEC B and C. And from SEC D as you make your way towards SEC E that number climbs up from 16 per cent to almost 40 per cent

Have no doubt about it—the beleaguered wife and mother is here to stay. But instead of being worried about stains on the rugs, kids' tiffin and husband's grumbling about the quality of dinner, she is alive and well, totally stressed out in her old role as nurturer and her new role as provider partner, either directly or indirectly contributing to the offering to Goddess EMI.

The good news is that as her economic role in the marriage becomes more and more important, she gets treated better and better, and she gets more and more freedom in terms of what she does when she is outside the house earning her living or doing 'outdoor' family work.

There is bad news though, as I saw from an analysis of matrimonial ads in a leading paper.

I first looked in the 'wanted brides' section, under the title 'cosmopolitan', 'well educated, beautiful, homely'/'convent educated, charming, extremely beautiful'. The emphasis on education is quite apparent. Because in her new role as provider/ facilitator, education helps for sure. Does that explain at least in part why girl enrolment in college, even in the smaller towns, is increasing? Then there are those seeking 'career oriented bride'/'working, very beautiful bride'/'beautiful professionally qualified girl'/'working girl preferred'. The ratio was 60 per cent of the latter and 40 per cent of the former. This clearly says a lot. Next I went to look at the Brahmin brides section because I thought maybe those hidebound enough to stick to caste may have a different worldview on this. I should have known better. 'Preferable engineering graduate'/'suitable medico girl'/'seeks engineer/doctor/MBA beautiful, fair slim girl from decent family'/'seeks qualified Maithil non Vatsa bride'. This list can go on as can the Indian English.

Truly, the times, they are a' changing. But not exactly in the way we think they are.

11

rural Consumer
India

A MARKET IN TRANSITION READY TO BE SHAPED

If there is any one part of Consumer India that epitomizes the line 'every truism about India can be contradicted by another truism', it is rural Consumer India. Therefore it is not surprising that despite masses of data available, it is not easy to form a clear picture of it. The view that rural Consumer India is large, poor, backward and made up of small farmers with handkerchief- sized farms of an acre or so each, that does not fulfil the needs—forget about the wants—of their families is quite accurate. It houses most of India's poor, and a large number of the world's poor. It is, therefore, a backward market but can be dragged into the twenty-first century, and become a sufficiently valuable market, with a lot of persistent effort, brute force and some innovation, as FMCG brands have shown

However, the story of rural India is how it is morphing under the cover of its poverty and backwardness, even as everyone watching it closely is missing the signals. Unfortunately, most people tend to look for the wrong metrics of change and, therefore, miss the big opportunities that it harbours. While large parts of rural India continue to be abjectly poor and dependent on an archaic, unprofitable agriculture business, there is a new and expanding rural India that has quietly emerged. This rural India is prosperous mostly self-employed and with fairly non-agricultural urban-like tastes. Though geographically scattered, it is ripe for market shaping.

Rural India is a potential market that is seeing significant income growth and employment diversity for the first time in its history. As it gets exposed, rural India will see enormous change in employment patterns, consumption patterns, spending power and aspirations. Almost by definition it offers enormous opportunity to be shaped. Rural India's per capita income growth rate is the same as urban India's but it is far more exciting as there are three times as many people and it represents a little over half of India's GDP. It is also exciting because it is generating tremendous forces of change as its large mass morphs, slowly changing from within.

What is needed is the opposite of the usual descriptive, deep dive consumer data on how rural India eats, breathes, lives and shops. Instead, a better bird's eye view understanding the structure and segments of rural India, of how it is morphing, and hence thinking about what the new business opportunities rural Consumer India can offer is required.

READY TO BE SHAPED, BUT WHY SO FEW TAKERS?

Rural India is vastly underserved today because most businesses do not recognize the opportunity to shape it. This is partly because their perspective of rural India is incorrect and hence businesses don't see the opportunity to shape it; partly because they do not have the capability or the vision to rise up to the challenge of creating whole new business streams to meet the needs of a low education, high exposure, low income, high aspirations, mostly young consumer base. As I explained to a senior management group at one of Europe's most respected electronics companies, 'If you are waiting for my government to electrify the villages so that you can come in with twenty varieties of light bulbs that conserve electricity, then you have a long wait in store for you before rural India becomes an attractive market. If, however, you can innovate and create, using solar power, LED displays and light bulb technology, a community lighting system that works, then rural India is exactly the place where you can create a long-term business with steady and profitable growth.'

Finding appropriately priced, smokeless, efficient and modern cooking fuel or cooking devices for rural India is a necessity. Rural consumers do know what cooking gas is—they see it on television all the time and women are getting more educated about health, grooming and home care. The cost of transportation of cylinders makes mini cylinders unviable from the manufacturer's point of view, and the unit cost makes large cylinders unaffordable from the consumer's point of view. The solution that some companies thought of was to innovate an efficient wood stove or a smokeless stove. That is one possibility, but the question is, 'why can't they have LPG cooking gas? Why must they have better candles when they want electric lights?' The solution was shaped by Hindustan Petroleum, an Indian public sector company. They established community kitchens with eight gas stove stations, a gas meter, and a 'pay as you use' system. Franchising this model to women entrepreneurs all over rural India would be the next step to complete this business model. Once conceptualized, it is easy to adapt this idea to local customs, caste and community idiosyncrasies and devise easy pay token systems or prepaid cards.

Another reason why rural markets are underserved is the assumption that as rural infrastructure improves, rural India will automatically adopt urban products and urban business systems and models. This assumption is not always true, because we find time and again that rural India is not following the same trajectory of evolution as urban India—any more than urban India is walking down the same path that the US walked down twenty years ago. It leapfrogs. To the illiterate person, a computer screen with icons is a far more basic (less advanced) device than a printed page. But to the literate, it is an advancement over the printed pages The most striking difference is that rural India is emerging as a growth market at a time when the government is stepping aside in favour of more efficient private players and when the Internet and wireless technology is now available, making hitherto unviable markets become very viable indeed.

For example, rural India used to be served by public sector banks, which were forced to set up offices in rural areas as part of the socialist government's diktat. These offices were unprofitable and there was no motivation for them to innovate, nor was there the benefit of technology which could lower the costs of serving a scattered and hard to reach population. Today, rural India can be served through state-of-the-art remote banking systems using business models of the hub-and-spoke kind, and the small local repesentative office kind, perhaps using manned machines—models that neither exist nor are useful in urban areas. Given the state of rural infrastructure, the cost and technology for ATMs will be different, and the specifications would also need to be different.

Similarly, rural healthcare needs can now be met through a distance healthcare system with mobile, state-of-the-art diagnostic equipment, with no doctors but manned by a number of local, not very well educated, paramedics—this would not be acceptable in urban areas.

Some version of e-commerce, perhaps combined bricks-and-clicks business models, will develop faster in rural areas than in urban areas, because, in contrast to the latter, such models would offer enormous value advantage compared to the current way of doing things in the rural areas.

It is important for companies to understand how best to segment it, define 'my target Rural India', and shape businesses for it.

The Changing Structure of the Rural Economy: Beyond Agriculture

The generally held, though erroneous, belief about rural India is that it is in the dark ages. This belief is based on a set of incorrect assumptions about the structure of the rural economy.

- Rural India is an economy comprising only agriculture and nothing else; therefore rural consumers=farmers, farm-related labour and other services.
- The agricultural sector in India is growing very slowly (at an annual rate of 1.9 per cent since 1995–6) and so is the rural economy. Hence there is no real improvement in rural per capita incomes.
- Since India's total GDP growth is much higher for this period, the urban economy is growing much faster at 7.3 per cent, and urban India's per capita income is rising steadily.
- Seventy per cent of India's population lives in rural areas and is supported by agriculture, which comprises only about 23 per cent of GDP and continues to grow slowly. In contrast, 30 per cent of India's population which is largely urban, controls the remaining 75 per cent of GDP, growing at 7.3 per cent.
- Obviously, therefore, the urban–rural income and lifestyle chasm is growing.

The conclusion is that the rural market must be approached with caution and that it will take a long while before it shows any real potential.

In reality, nothing could be further from the truth. The first hints of it appeared as early as the end of the 1990s, when data started showing that the occupational profile of consumer durables buyers in rural India was far more non-agricultural than the occupational profile of the rural population. Further, all anecdotal evidence of rural market behaviour contradicted commonly held beliefs about its backwardness.

In 2003, I was consulting with a leading Indian business house to develop its rural strategy. As a first step, we needed to get a few fundamental facts together about the rural economy and about rural Consumer India. It then emerged that India did not actually have an official number in the government statistics for rural GDP. I worked with Subir Gokarn, former chief economist of CRISIL (now with Standard and Poors), and based on a 1993–4 one-off report from the Central Statistical Organisation (CSO) which did a rural–urban classification of GDP, he constructed the rural GDP and its components for 2000–01. His numbers showed that 54 per cent of India's GDP was rural, and only 48 per cent of the rural GDP was agricultural, down from 56 per cent in 1993–4. It also showed that rural GDP had been growing at more or less the same pace as urban GDP. Since agriculture was growing slowly, it could only mean that the non-agricultural segment was growing much faster.

Omkar Goswami, economist and founder chairman of CERG Advisory, an economic research and consulting company, and I co-authored an article in the *Business Standard* in July 2005, refuting an article that had the usual fallacious logic on rural Indians being poor, and getting poorer:

> Our analysis shows that in 2000–01, out of India's NDP [net domestic product] of Rs 1,062,400 crore at constant 1993–4 prices, the share of rural India was 52 per cent. This is how its rural NDP played out in 2000–01: agriculture accounted for 46 per cent; industry took up another 21 per cent; and services was 33 per cent. Between 1993–4 and 2000–01, rural NDP at constant prices grew at an average of 6.2 per cent per year. Since agriculture grew at around 2 per cent during this period, it is obvious that the rural economy has been much more than just agriculture.
>
> Our second problem with it [this article that we are refuting] is that it doesn't look at other evidence, much of which demonstrates the growth of non-agricultural activities throughout rural India. According to the Annual Survey of Industries, even in 1993–4, rural India accounted for 29 per cent of the country's organised manufacturing units, 30 per cent of its employees, 32 per cent of its output and 30 per cent of its net value added. In 2000–01, over a rising base, rural India could speak of 36 per cent of organised manufacturing establishments, 38 per cent of its employees, 43 per cent of output and 41 per cent of net value added.
>
> Consider the Census of India 1991 and 2001. In 1991, 30.6 per cent of rural households had permanent houses (having roof and walls made of permanent material). By 2001, this had risen to 41 per cent,

over a base which was growing at 1.7 per cent per year. Between 1991 and 2001, households useing LPG for cooking rose from 1 per cent to almost 6 per cent, with Himachal Pradesh leading the pack at 22 per cent. In 2001, almost a fifth of rural households owned TV sets, and the rural regions of ten states were significantly above the national average. Between 1991 and 2001, the percentage of rural households with electricity connections at their homesteads rose from a little over 30 per cent to 43.5 per cent, with eleven states being placed well over the national rural average. In 2001, over 30 per cent of rural households kept their funds in banks or postal savings accounts. All this doesn't square up with the age-old dominant picture of rural India—that of highly indebted, underfed peasants ploughing their handkerchief-sized fields with emaciated bullocks under the blazing heat of the midday sun. That may still be true of the agricultural economy, but not of the rural economy.

We could inundate you with more evidence, but we won't. We want to make 3 points.

- First, rural is much more than agriculture; it has a thriving and growing manufacturing and services sector.
- Second, per capita rural income has grown at the same pace as that of urban between 1993–4 and 2000–01.
- Third, the top quartile of rural India have been discontinuously higher spenders than the average, spending at least Rs 179,450 crore (NSS, 55th round), with spending patterns that are similar to urban India.
- Finally, there is considerable pent-up demand for goods as well as services like education, communication and medical treatment—so maybe it is time for celebration for cell phone and durables manufacturers, with a large new market opportunity opening up.

COMPARISON OF SIZE AND PURCHASING POWER OF RURAL VS. URBAN CONSUMER INDIA

The NSS data of 2003–4 shows than 62 per cent of consumer expenditure in India comes from rural India and only 38 per cent from urban India. The NSS data also shows that while urban consumer expenditure grew at a rate of 8.3 per cent between

1993–4 and 2003–04, at 7 per cent, rural expenditure growth was not far behind.

Rural India's per capita income of around US$530 is far lower than urban India's of over US$1200 at current prices. Yet because rural India has three times as many people as urban India—750 million people as compared to 250 million in urban India—the rural market is larger than the urban market, for many categories.

According to data compiled by rural market expert, Pradeep Kashyap of MART, Life Insurance Corporation (LIC), India's largest life insurer, sells more than half of its policies in rural India. Around 41 million Kisan Credit Cards were issued to farmers, which is almost double the 22 million credit and debit cards issued in urban India. Forty-two million rural households availed of bank accounts, compared to 27 million urban households. These numbers sound very counter-intuitive, since we know that penetration of most products in rural India is actually very poor. However, as discussed earlier, the Great Indian Number Trick that usually surprises most marketers is that a small penetration of a large population results in a very large actual market size.

Another indicator of the attractiveness of rural India is provided by a simple metric based on NCAER data: While the percentage of middle income households (that is, those earning between Rs 45,000 and Rs 215,000 per annum) in rural India is about 18 per cent, the corresponding percentage for urban India is about 58 per cent. The number of middle income households in rural India, however, is around 27 million, while the number in urban India is just a shade more, at 29 million. Moreover, per capita income in rural India has grown at exactly the same rate as in urban India for the past ten years.

Indian Readership Survey data shows that between 2000 and 2005, there has a been a 5–7 per cent improvement in rural literacy and education levels, including those of women, and in television ownership and cable and satellite television access levels. There are also several pro-agriculture policy initiatives by the government and increasing acceptance of public–private partnerships in several states. Also emerging are several tech-based services that enable rural services like banking and telemedicine and e-governance to become commercially viable.

It is then safe to assume that the rural market is and will continue to remain an attractive and important market both in absolute terms as also relative to urban India.

Marketing to rural India has its geographical and infrastructural challenges, which is why, despite being bigger in current market value than urban markets for many categories, it is still more expensive and less attractive to marketers.

SPENDING PATTERNS OF RURAL INDIA

The share of food versus non-food expenditure in any economy is one of the measures of the extent of consumption sophistication of the economy. On an aggregate basis, NSS data shows that in rural India the share of expenditure on food is still at a hefty 58.3 per cent of total expenditure, while non-food expenditure is at 41.7 per cent. For the top 5 per cent of the rural population by income, the share of food versus non-food expenditure is at exactly 50 per cent. For the bottom 5 per cent, the share of food expenditure is as high as 65 per cent.

The growth of food-related expenditure has been much slower than the growth of non-food expenditure—between 1993–4 and 2002–3, food expenditure has grown at 9.8 per cent as compared to non-food expenditure growth at 5.7 per cent.

The fastest growing non-food expenditure categories, however, are education, healthcare and conveyance. Education and healthcare increased their share of the rural consumer wallet from 9 per cent to 11 per cent in the ten-year period from 1993–4 to 2003–4, during which time total consumption expenditure doubled. Consumer durables are another category that is growing fast. FMCG expenditure share has, however, remained constant through 1996–2006, explaining perhaps the pain of FMCG companies.

The emerging picture of the rural consumers is that they want life-improving 'do good' products and services of real quality, or durables that enhance productivity and increase earning—like two-wheelers and cell phones. This is also a consumer base that has enough aspiration (70 per cent of R1, R2 and R3 households, which account for about half of rural India, can be reached through the mass media) and not enough amenities, thanks to government neglect. Innovations in technology and service delivery systems to deliver electricity, water, sanitation, health and other life-improving services will, therefore, be clear winners.

SEGMENTATION SCHEMES FOR RURAL INDIA: AFFLUENCE SEGMENTS, DEMAND SEGMENTS

Scattered oases of affluence: Rural India comprises 640,000 villages of varying sizes. Seventeen per cent of the villages have 50 per cent of the population and 60 per cent of the wealth. A little over one-third have hardly any developed distribution in the form of shops (Table 11.1).

Viewed through the consumer expenditure window, 20 per cent of rural India accounts for 43 per cent of expenditure, and the top 10 per cent by income are discontinuously higher spenders. However, these pockets of affluence and hence higher quality market opportunity, are scattered over a very vast geography, with no apparent logic.

Rural India has consumer deserts and oases within it that form no apparent discernible pattern. The average statistics on any count are quite dismal, but the total numbers of opportunity are very heartening. Even at the state level there is huge heterogeneity. This pattern of consumer oases and deserts is not driven by any particular development design or logic, but by

Table 11.1: Profile of Villages

Population	Distribution of Villages	
	No. of villages	Percentage of total villages
Less than 200	92,541	15.6 ⎫ Hardly any shops
200–500	127,054	21.4 ⎬ in these 220,000
501–1000	144,817	24.4 ⎭ villages
1001–2000	129,662	21.9
2001–5000	80,313	13.5 ⎫ 17% of villages
5001–10,000	18,758	3.2 ⎬ account for 50% of
		rural population and
Total no. of villages	593,154*	100.0 ⎭ 60% rural wealth

*Inhabited villages; total number of villages is 638,691
Source: Census 2001, Pradeep Kashyap, MART.

a series of localized happenings. Therefore, one model of winning in rural consumer markets is to undertake micro market planning—map each geographic sub-segment, a district or even its sub-unit, a taluka, or in some cases even villages and undertake distribution and other market development activities. LG and other Korean companies do this very well—they painstakingly isolate pockets of demand that are underserved and move in to mop it up. Hindustan Unilever looks for growth by micro market mapping media-dark and distribution-deficient areas for development, also they are in the process of developing a women's network to really penetrate such villages. There are at least 150 rural districts that have assets and amenities equivalent to urban India.

Developed and developing states: Rural India in the more progressive, higher GDP growth states is far more prosperous, well developed and close to urban India. If we were to analyse rural Consumer India's profile in the high growth, better developed states like Punjab, Haryana, Gujarat, Maharashtra, Goa, Karnataka, Kerala and Tamil Nadu, account for one-third of the population of rural India, the balance two-thirds being in the less developed states. The developed rural Consumer

India has a diamond-shaped income distribution, while the rest of rural India still has a triangle-shaped income distribution, with the maximum number of people in the lowest income group. In developed states, media reach is significantly higher, as is product penetration.

Non-Agricultural Rural Consumer India

According to NSS data, 35 per cent of households in rural India are engaged in non-agricultural activities. The data also shows that these households are far higher spenders than the 'agricultural' households. Households get classified in NSS data as agricultural or non-agricultural depending on what the major source of income is. However, an analysis of the occupation of individual household members shows that many households are engaged in both. As the sons grow up, the inability of the farm to support all of them forces them to move out of agriculture. Gradually, as the proportion of non-agricultural income increases and predominates, the character of the household changes, as does its consumption patterns. It is this change wave that contributed to the growth spurt in motorcycle sales between 1999 and 2003.

It is also this wave that changed the agricultural equipment market. As families started venturing into other businesses, they wanted more productivity even if it came at high cost as long as less time was spent at the farm. Resultantly, the demand for low cost, low productivity equipment declined.

As discussed earlier, this non-agricultural rural segment is an interesting demand segment with many sub-segments. It has not yet been specifically targeted by marketers—providing huge opportunity across sectors to create new businesses. The mindset and needs of this segment are neither entirely urban nor rural. Hence it requires custom built products and services.

AGRICULTURAL CONSUMER INDIA

The best segmenting variable for agricultural Consumer India is how the farmer thinks about his farming business.

In a study done for Mahindra & Mahindra several years ago, several segments and mindsets on agriculture emerged. There were the return on investment farmers, who thought of farming as a business and were willing to spend more to earn more. Then there was a segment that is gradually turning to non-agricultural businesses as well, who are looking at productivity maximization. Finally, there are those for whom farming is an inescapable fact—they are stuck with. They have neither the skills nor the mindset to diversify and for them the accent is on cash flow minimization.

This objective function and focus of each segment drives not just their orientation to agriculture-related products, but also to all other products and to living and spending in general. All this will again change as laws governing the agricultural sector get liberalized.

FUTURE SHIFTS: LIBERALIZING AGRICULTURE, SPECIAL ECONOMIC ZONES (SEZs)

Laws governing the sale of agricultural commodities and laws relating to corporate contract farming are in the process of being modified. As is usual of India, each of these changes seems limited and minor. However, over the last five years, we have seen significant changes, sufficient to encourage the rise of new businesses and new business models.

The new growth business that most large corporates are looking at is related to agriculture and food. ITC has demonstrated that with the use of IT they can create virtual markets for agricultural produce and farmers are ready for more sophisticated transactions, because they have more information. In some states, government acceptance of the fact that ITC can buy directly from the farmers (the law till recently said they had to sell at a government *mandis*), as long as it pays a mandi tax, has inspired more companies to test the system.

The arrival of modern retailers and the recent entry of Wal-Mart into the cash and carry segment of the market have changed the vision of agricultural supply chains altogether, incentivizing all participants to get more efficient and market driven.

All these changes will slowly transform the mindsets of farmers. This change will be different for different types of farmers in different states, eventually creating a new pattern of rural Consumer India, with yet another shake of the kaleidoscope.

And yet another shake to the kaleidoscope could come from SEZs, which are islands of world-class infrastructure, industry and residential townships in the middle of rural areas. The jury is still out on how many and what scale of SEZs we may have. But that could change agriculture, young people and rural India forever—or not, depending on how they are structured, and how much local talent they use.

12

understanding the
'bottom of the
pyramid' Consumer
India

The 'Bottom of the Pyramid' Consumer

C.K. Prahalad's book *Fortune at the Bottom of the Pyramid* created a sort of sceptical scramble within large global companies to make haste in a dispassionate manner and find the Holy Grail: A business model that can give the consumers all that they want, at the price that they want, and still be profitable. Several leading-edge global companies have started experimental projects in India to try and figure out what they should or could do for and with the Bottom of the Pyramid (BOP) consumer, a significant chunk of which lives in India.

Having been a part of many of these projects, I am not certain that there is enough conviction amongst operating managers, no matter how senior, about why such a big effort has to be made to construct such a challenging and risky business model. Serving the BOP consumer is seen to be part of corporate social responsibility and hence essential and noble, but not part of mainstream business. It is seen to be part of sustainable development and hence important, but not urgent—the planet must be saved, but not at the cost of displeasing Wall Street. The general feeling is that finding ways to serve the BOP consumer is about buying some kind of option for some not clearly recognized eventuality—a bit like prayer, essential but not mission critical to everyday living.

As a result of this level of conviction, companies have not invested a great deal of effort or energy in understanding consumers and using that as a starting point to develop appropriate business models. Most of the time, the effort is in the form of blinkered, 'inside out' approaches. At worst, it comes in the form of tinkering to strip features and create 'no frills' cheaper versions of a feature-rich expensive product, with no concern for what consumers would consider to be a frill and what an essential. At best, it has been in the form of letting R&D loose in their spare time to invent things that the poor could use—based on the stereotypical image of the poor as illiterate, uninformed and primitive. The result has been specially created new products which are low priced but which are light years behind in sophistication, In either case, they usually fail to connect with the market.

So is there really a fortune at the bottom of the Indian pyramid for anyone to seriously bother with it? If so, what are the characteristics and attitudes and value processing methods of low-income consumers in India and how can companies unlock their market potential?

Why Bother About the 'Bottom of the Pyramid' Consumer India?

- *Large value*: The size of the BOP market in India is 650 million people who individually earn less than a dollar a day, but collectively account for 30 per cent of the national income, a little over 33 per cent of consumption expenditure and a little over 20 per cent of India's savings. At current prices, in 2004–5, this amounts to a market of 650 million people, with an aggregate income of about US$165 billion (US$840 billion on a PPP basis), and consumption expenditure of about US$125 billion (US$630 billion on a PPP basis).

  The total income of BOP Consumer India is 1.4 times that of Malaysia, 1.6 times that of Singapore, equal to that of South Africa and 90 per cent that of Hong Kong. The per capita incomes are very low—and therein lies the strategic and economic challenge of BOP—an interesting-sized market on the aggregate, pathetic on per capita incomes. This is why BOP Consumer India offers a reasonable-sized fortune. However, it isn't easy to access it with current business models.

- *A dollar a day per capita is a reasonable income in India*: One US dollar a day per capita per person translates into about Rs 6750 per month for an average family of five. On a PPP basis, this would convert to a comfortable middle class living, with all the basic consumer durables and the ability to service a mortgage. Even assuming no conversion to PPP, Rs 6750, will buy only shanty dwelling in big cities, but it can buy better living conditions especially in the smaller towns. Two months of this salary can buy a good colour television set, five months of salary can buy a good second-hand motorcycle, and half a month's salary can get a cell phone connection, with the instrument and incoming calls free for life. Another Rs 200 per month can buy a pre-paid card, which is why it is not unusual to see homes with lots of consumer durables but no attached toilets.

The experience of the BOP Consumer Market in India thus far has been that of the 650 million consumers with per capita income of less than a dollar a day (in absolute terms, not PPP terms), the bottom 250 million may be very hard to integrate into the mainstream market economy, as Prahalad urges in the book.

However, the remaining 400 million are full of surprises, challenging all our mental images of what poor consumers are really like. The fact that merits repetition is that never before in the history of humanity has a consumer group having so many poor people been subjected to so much real time information, technology, and probable benefits this frequently. This creates a unique new market, which needs to be understood if it is to be addressed appropriately. It is not about transplanting best practices from the history of other markets, but about creating 'next practices' for a totally new kind of future.

- **Sensible investment for the future**: BOP markets in growing economies are very good investments to make because (a) brand emotions and aspirations that are established when consumers are poor tend to stick as they get richer, provided, of course, that relevant product offerings are available, and (b) securing the loyalty of 400 million consumers who are in an economy where real national income doubles every decade, if not earlier, makes for a very good business case for investment. This investment can be either in terms of finding the right business models that can generate a profit today and/or in terms of settling for lower profits from this target group today, to secure the future.

- **Guaranteed income growths**: Is there enough evidence that the fruits of economic growth are trickling down and will continue to do so, to lower income Consumer India? Have the incomes of the lowest income groups actually improved in this past decade and a half, and what are they likely to be in the future?

As we saw in the chapter on purchasing power (Chapter 5), when compared on a like-to-like inflation-adjusted basis, the size of the lowest income group has actually declined sharply, showing a clear upward income mobility.

In the early years of liberalization (1995–2002), the number of households in the lower income group declined at an average annual growth rate (AAGR) of 8.5 per cent in urban India, and only 2.7 per cent in rural India. This resulted from the fruits of liberalization being unevenly distributed. In the next phase (2001–06), however, both urban and rural lower income households declined at between 5 and 6 per cent each year. For the period 2005–10, the fruits of liberalization will get to rural India more concretely and rural lower income households are set to decline at 14 per cent annually. Alongside, urban India lower income households will continue to decline at 9 per cent annually. Countrywide, there will be a 10 per cent annual average decline in the number of lower income households. The bottom of the pyramid is rising quite fast in terms of absolute quantum of income earned. This data comes from NCAER, and has been discussed towards the end of Chapter 5.

- *Favourable change in social attitudes*: Post-liberalization, there has been a perceptible change in the social attitudes of the poor. An indication of this are the changing themes in the Hindi movies. The biggest attitude change has been one from demanding social justice to grabbing economic opportunity. The fear of authority (and of the rich) has now been replaced by reducing power distances and the language is one of striving, aspiration and self-esteem. The key driving force is escape velocity for their children and the entire language is about 'how to' rather than 'why not'. The hunger for information and knowledge is extreme.

All these, taken together, make for a very fertile environment to invest in this consumer group.

CHARACTERISTICS OF THE BOP CONSUMER

Poor But Not Backward Any More

BOP Consumer India has seen significant shifts in its consumption orientation in the last decade (Table 12.1). These consumers are aware of what is happening in the rest of the world—as it happens, in real time. They are aware of product options that are possible and available to others. Hence they are unwilling to settle for less and would rather like to stretch for more and better.

Table 12.1: Changing Attitudes of the BOP Consumer

From (pre-liberalization poor) ———►	To (post-liberalization poor)
• Settle for less	• Stretch for more
• Reluctance, avoidance	• Seeking experience
• Abstemiousness ('not for us')	• Affordable indulgence
• Destiny driven and resigned to fate	• Struggling and aspiring for a better life
• Simple needs	• State need of hour

Unlike the poor of the pre-liberalization socialist era, the poor today are neither resigned, unexposed nor destiny driven. Instead, they maximize benefits, like any other income group. This is where most of the 'no frills' offerings to the poor consumers go wrong. What suppliers consider to be a frill, consumers consider to be a necessity. A better wood stove is not good enough in the world of LPG, nor is a black-and-white television or even a colour one without a remote.

They live in a fast growing economy and have seen a rapid change, in terms of improved economic status in less that one generation. This makes them confident about the future and quite comfortable about aspiring for a better life, because it will, in all likelihood, happen within their lifetime. Therefore the accent is not on abstemiousness and rationalizing that 'this not for us', but, rather on affordable indulgence—of the kind that rich people have.

There is no avoidance of experiences. Instead, they are experience seeking, and struggle to have interesting consumption experiences within the economic constraints. Consumer India's cultural shifts that we discussed earlier apply to this group too— the new life-view that 'life is not a condition to be endured, but a product to be experienced'. On special occasions like weddings, low-income consumers serve the more expensive colas rather than the cheapest squashes that they normally use for everyday consumption. However, they use smaller glasses to make it more affordable.

They want illnesses diagnosed with X-rays and other tests—they will no longer be satisfied with the local doctor's intuition any more. Poor consumers would rather defer a purchase and get a better product than settle for something of a far lower standard today. Not a new moped, but a second-hand motorcycle, when they can afford it.

They Value All Kinds of Productivity Devices that Help Them Earn More

Poor consumers see access to information, knowledge, healthcare, education, transport and communication as the means to earn more. They view all these as methods by which they can widen their operations, can get more done in a day, and work smarter.

I once did a study on two-wheelers in the villages, and was puzzled to find that as the availability of public transport increased, the sales of two-wheelers also went up. On investigating, we were told by the rural consumers that when they had no public transport, they did not have anywhere to go. The arrival of public transport enabled them to start doing business or going to work outside their village; and the more they started doing that, the more they wanted to go at timings that suited them, in order to maximize their productivity—hence the need for private transport.

Most of the loans taken by poor consumers are for medical problems. Every illness, especially of the earning members, causes a drop in income and a burden of loans. Health insurance, preventive medical measures and timely control and cure of illness are services that they value greatly, because thereby the illness does not get worse, which would entail more expenses. It is this need that Philips India is trying to tap with a distance healthcare service.

ITC e-chaupal, an IT-enabled multiple services provider in the villages, decided to provide information free to rural consumers so that the desire to do business transactions would increase. And they were confident that their superior execution skills would get them the lion's share of the new market created by this information availability. Its resounding success is an indicator of the incredible ability of this segment to change given the opportunity.

It is entirely likely that the poor will be faster adopters of e-commerce and reverse auctions than the rich.

Poor Consumers Do Complicated Value Processing, Have Complicated Financial Models

Banks often assume that complex financial transactions are done by the rich and not by the poor. This is part of the 'no frills' train of thought that companies pursue when developing products for the poor. In actual fact, because of the limited resources and complicated financial balancing acts that poor people need to do, their financial transactions are a lot more complex. They borrow from several sources at several interest rates, lend when needed at different terms depending on the exigencies involved and constantly revolve sources and uses of funds. It is interesting that default rates on loan repayments are extremely low for poor consumers.

This complicated model of sources and uses of funds that poor consumers work with, with their income generation and consumption activities totally intertwined, defies many banking sector ideas of loans being for consumption or for income generation.

Poor consumers don't think that way. They calculate the value of cable television they pay for in terms of how much more the family would spend if they had to step out of the house to entertain themselves especially teenage children who are likely to spend more. They calculate the value of the interest (that appears usurious to richer customers) in terms of how the funds could help improve earnings in the longer term.

Poor Consumers Innovate Their Own Product Solutions to Make Them 'Value-right'

Necessity is the mother of innovation. The need to make a little bit of money go a long way is a powerful driver of smart solutions. Poor countries are innovative. The Hindi word for this is *jugaad*—to somehow cobble together a solution. The CEO of an Indian company that does outsourced research for a large American pharmaceutical company said that, ironically, his competitive advantage over developed countries came from the fact that most of his researchers had gone to colleges where the equipment available was far less than what was needed for the number of students enrolled. So they had learnt to do experiments in the quickest possible time, a skill that they brought to the workplace, making the Indian business faster and cheaper.

By the same logic, we find that poor consumers are far more innovative than the folks that design products and services for them. The following are examples of some such innovations by poor consumers, each one more interesting than the previous one.

- Poor consumers with cell phones do not use them to make outgoing calls as they cost money while incoming calls are free. Instead, they will give you a missed call, if they need to get in touch with you. You then need to call them back. This is all cleanly discussed. As one man turned to me and said 'Madam I will give you a "missed call" at 11 a.m. tomorrow.'
- It is not unusual in rural India to have a form of community lighting where the headlights of a jeep or a tractor are turned on, and the fuel used is a mixture of the more expensive petrol and the cheaper kerosene.

- Smaller glasses to serve cold drinks at weddings is an innovation—let us not look stingy serving a quarter of a glass of cola, let us just reduce the size of the glass itself. Poor consumers can refill, recycle and reuse almost anything. As was said once by an exasperated international durables marketer, 'It seems that the last thing that you Indians ever threw out was the British.'

- The Grass Root Innovation Network in India (GIAN) is an organization that encourages poor people who are innovators, and its work offers interesting insights about how the poor innovate solutions to their problems, since big businesses either do not feel the need or do not have the orientation to do so. I had been working for a while with a large tractor company which was engaged in developing a new small tractor that would help small farmers mechanize their farms—thus expanding the served market beyond what existing tractors could do. At the same time, I noticed that GIAN innovators had created and were locally selling a whole slew of farm mechanization equipment like post-harvest ground nut separators, areca nut cutters, cotton picking machines, paddy threshing machines, 10HP tractor, motorcycle driven plough, bicycle hoe and a tilting bullock cart. Other GIAN innovations include a washing machine operated by pedalling a stationary bicycle. The poor do not want a better stick with which to beat their clothes, but an affordable washing machine that can operate without electricity.

Poor Consumers are Technology Embracers, not Technology Rejectors

The poor may be illiterate, but they are entirely comfortable with technology and can find innovative ways to use it.

Nlogue is a Chennai based company that has a low-cost technology that enables it to put up kiosks in villages with one Internet connection and one telephone connection for around

Rs 50,000. Each kiosk is franchised to a kiosk operator: typically, not very well-educated young women from low-income families, who have to earn about Rs 4500 per month in order for the kiosk to be financially viable. Consumers found several applications of this, and soon the computer kiosk network ended up being used as a movie theatre and as a public address system for the local politician from the district headquarters. With the help of a webcam, veterinary doctors were able to provide distance treatment for cattle and a whole host of other applications were innovated. The young women were providing tech support to one another via yahoo chats in Tamil, saving the company the cost of a traditional tech support team. Now the kids are using it to practice their lessons for their exams, since content for that has been made available.

Poor consumers, like children, have no preconceived notions or inherent fear about dealing with technology. To them, technology is the great democratizer, free from human prejudices.

This is indeed good news for companies that want to mine the profit at the bottom of the pyramid, because technology-driven consumer interfaces will be an integral part of keeping costs low when servicing a network of remote locations, or when having to do a large number of transactions, each of which is a small amount of money.

A Generic Framework for Understanding Low-income Consumers Better

Linda Alwitt and Thomas Donley, in their outstanding book *The Low Income Consumer: Adjusting the Balance of Exchange,* make a compelling case for marketers to think about the low-income consumer as a distinct market, rather than as just one more consumer segment, differentiated from the rest only in terms of income.

They suggest that marketers recognize that low-income consumers are heterogeneous and need to be further segmented. They view life differently because of their circumstances and hence have different needs, and behave totally differently as consumers. Affluent consumers worry about size, style, colour and flavour. Poor consumers worry about the basic necessities—'For *which* child should I buy shoes?'

The book presents a lot of research on low-income consumers in the US. Some of the suggestions on how to better understand and market to low-income consumers are relevant to the Indian context as well.

Segmenting low-income consumers: Age, education and occupation segments are the most obvious places to start as they clearly influence consumption attitudes and values. However, these can be combined into a more interesting segmenting variable—'spell length in low-income' or how long the household or individual is likely to remain in the low-income group.

Alwitt and Donley define two low-income segments—transitory and persistent. Transitory low-income consumers are particularly valuable long-term assets for a business, where efforts to build brand equity work better. Sylvester Research, in its document *World Waves*, says, 'The consumer may be poor, but he is living in a society that is growing faster than at any time in its history. At 8 per cent growth, income will double in the next seven years. They are deciding how to spend it now. Decisions made when poor really count.'

In the Indian context, transitory low-income could be a low-income family unit with young, relatively more educated sons who have just started working (may or may not be in regular jobs, but are beginning to earn). Their disposable income may not immediately change, because of the several financial responsibilities that have to be discharged—daughters' or sisters' weddings, house acquisition, etc. Investing in such consumers makes sense since they are clearly transitory. The elderly at the stage when their children are a few years away from being settled, are another such group as they will shortly have a sudden increase in disposable income.

Understanding Spending Power and Patterns Beyond 'Annual Income'

First, since the bulk of low income Consumer India is rural and does not have a steady source of income, total annual income is not the best measure to use to understand their affluence. More variables like per capita income, number of earning members and rules of household spending, especially in joint families, etc. need to be factored in. Second, there are often swings in the income of a given family unit, which cause frequent changes in spending patterns. Agricultural income is clearly one such example.

New household unit configurations (for example the earning son who leaves to set up his own home, or an earning daughter getting married) change the spending pattern of the old unit and the new unit, neither remaining the same as it was before. The practice of borrowing also stretches income—while formal credit is often not available to this group, they are informally borrowing against future income, not in a deliberate and planned way but in a very immediate kind of way. It is either the retailer who captures that value, or the pawn shop. Further, given the interdependent nature of our society, there is a lot of borrowing from friends and relatives.

Improving buyer power. It is well known and well documented that existing retail environments extract more from the poor customers (poor neighbourhoods have less competitive retail environments pushing up prices). Low-income consumers are dependent on the retailer for credit, they end up paying more as they buy in small quantities, and getting poorer service. There is a case for opening a set of thrift stores, offering credit as well a relevant merchandise to lower income consumers, who will reward this empowerment with loyalty. Another interesting suggestion is the creation of 'buying groups', modelled after the borrowing circles set up by Mohammad Yunus of the Grameen Bank in Bangladesh.

Understanding value processing and budget balancing: Durables are obviously far more attractive items for low-income consumers than FMCG. The Indian low-income consumer is struggling to 'up-trade' on durables and is down-trading on FMCG. While they carefully look at ways to stretch budgets with 'no frills' FMCG products, there are occasional gratification purchases— for children, around festival time, or occasional treats for the family. Sylvester Research says, 'It isn't practicable [for them] to buy houses and cars [and the big stuff], so how do you flaunt new disposable income?' Their answer is "labels". Perhaps the low end branding game has latent potential—maybe store brands?'

SUICIDAL MOVES BY GLOBAL COMPANIES IN SERVING LOW-INCOME CONSUMERS

India has seen a lot of effort from global companies to quickly try and roll out products that are to be affordable for poor consumers. They reduced the price by reducing performance and assumed that this combination would work, because they thought 'doesn't everybody know that for a lower price that's all the performance that you can hope to get?' They reduced functionality, reduced styling and offered old and obsolete products with no adaptation. The consumer, as always the wiser rejected all of it. Marketers then blamed the consumer and the country for not being evolved, whereas, in reality, the consumer was way ahead in sophistication.

So what is the mantra to achieve acceptable performance at affordable prices? Does it come through product innovation or new business systems? Perhaps consumers themselves need to participate in it for best results.

13
winning in the Indian
market

The Class vs. Mass Dilemma

Most MNCs, especially those which are recent entrants into the Indian market, voice their disappointment with the total mismatch between the size of the Indian economy and the size of their own business in India. The explanation for this usually lies in the different perspectives they have when assessing market opportunity and setting financial expectations, and when developing business strategy. Their financial expectations are based on the fact that India is a nearly US$1 trillion economy, with 1 billion people, mostly young. They forget, however, that India is a large market made up of many poor consumers, and insist on deploying their tried and tested global strategy, one designed for far richer markets with different consumer psyches. This severely truncates the canvas of opportunity available to them.

Despite some concessions and adaptations in the name of localization, strategies transplanted from developed markets are relevant only to the top 10 per cent of all Indian households, or the top 30 per cent of urban Indian households, often labelled the class market. These approximately 20 million households account for less than one-third of India's consumer expenditure which is equivalent to the GDP of a small economy like Thailand, and lower in terms of per capita income. Targeting this India can typically result in a small business with revenues of US$50–100 million today, with average profitability by global standards. In order to boost these numbers, targeting the rest of the Indian consumer base, or the 'mass market', is necessary. However, this requires the development of new and innovative strategies, especially the creation of unprecedented price-performance points. Making this choice between the comfort of a familiar strategy and a modest-sized business or the discomfort of a new untested strategy and a potentially large business is what most MNCs agonize over. It can be termed the 'class versus mass dilemma', and it sits at the heart of what winning in the Indian market entails.

The argument put forward by companies reluctant to depart from their tried-and-tested business models is that there is no need to go through the considerable pain of designing new tailor-made strategies for the mass market, since the class market is one of the fastest growing consumer groups in the economy. The inevitable comparisons are made with China, where this strategy of targeting the top end of the income pyramid and growing with it results in far bigger businesses. However, in India, while a strategy designed only for the class market can deliver a business growth of a minimum of 30–35 per cent over the next five years, given the low starting point, these numbers will still be far short of the expectations triggered by the idea of a US$1 trillion economy with 1 billion consumers—and far smaller than the results in China.

The math is simple. The creamy layer of high-income consumers in China is far thicker and creamier than it is in India. Further, since India is about ten years behind China in per capita income terms, it will take far longer to achieve equivalent-sized businesses. By 2015, China will have about 110 million households with an annual household income of over $20,000 PPP, while the corresponding number for India will be only about 30 million.

Therefore, building a business that is in line with India's large GDP and population requires winning in the mass market. In order to do that, businesses must design special keys to unlock the potential of this mass market, and to accept that these keys could be quite different from those already in existence.

A final argument that is put forward by companies that do not buy the 'made for India' prescription is that they will run a small and profitable operation in the class market, and wait until the mass market gets rich enough to become a part of this. This is a deeply flawed argument because mass markets do not sit around and wait with primitive products and unfulfilled needs until they get rich enough to afford the 'real thing'. The risk of not addressing the needs of this market today is that these consumers could be lost forever as they embrace other kinds of solutions that someone else offers for them. We earlier discussed the PC business and how, instead of waiting until they got rich enough to buy big-brand PCs, consumers were buying PCs assembled in the grey market. Simultaneously, they were moving to increasingly powerful mobile phones that were still cheaper than PCs or shared grid computing services. In other markets, it could be the retailer's store brand or a smart local company with a better understanding of customers' needs that starts to develop and capture the mass market well before it becomes a class market.

There is an interesting window of opportunity that will remain open for a while longer for companies to establish dominant positions in the Indian mass market. This is because Indian businesses are, as yet, not focussed on or capable of seizing the opportunity to step in and own this market and lock out competition. For most of them this is not currently possible, because to build a large and sustainable profitable business needs global competencies and global access to raw materials, labour, markets and money. Few Indian companies have this as yet. Those who can are very focussed on establishing a global footprint for themselves in developed markets; consequently, their focus on making a big push in the domestic Indian market is low. Therefore, the party is yet to begin, and the prize is still up for grabs.

THE CHALLENGE OF GETTING IT RIGHT
FOR THE INDIAN MARKET

Winning in the Indian mass market is not about finding ways to squeeze or coax revenue and/or profitability from it, using a suboptimal strategy compensated by marketing aggression or discounted pricing. Nor is it about old-generation products or new 'no frills' products with cheaper prices but drastically reduced functionality and style.

India is a long-haul market, and what it offers is cheap entry tickets into a guaranteed long-term, slow-burn growth story. Winning in the Indian market is about being able to design the right business machine which can profitably deliver adequate quality at affordable prices to serve the mass market, which is a large base of consumers with modest incomes but sophisticated needs and demands. This machine, if correctly designed, will be robust enough to run on auto pilot and, over the next decade, capture the fruits of automatic growth of the Indian economy, locking out competition for a long while or raising their cost of entry significantly.

There are three big factors to getting it right for the Indian market:

Creating blockbuster relevance by defining business arenas in ways that make them relevant to the aspirations and problems of most Indians. For example, the heartbeat of the new India is about education, healthcare, productivity improvement, work saving, entertainment, income improvement, better management of assets, and so on. Waiting for electricity to reach villages is not the answer. Instead, the pressing need for lighting needs to be addressed by marrying LED, solar energy and nano-technology capabilities to create low-cost community lighting, before electricity gets there. Or persuade the government to use smartcards of some kind to administer a corruption-free subsidy programme, by devising robust and simple devices that will stand up to the rigours of rural India. Equally, e-governance and education and healthcare are the arenas for technology companies like Microsoft to enter in order to win in the Indian market, rather than waiting for home PC penetration to pick up, and fretting over piracy levels. And cola companies would definitely win in the Indian market if they defined their core business in India as water-and nutrition-based drinks for young children.

Creating perceived value advantage for consumers and customers who have modest incomes but are not backward in their thinking and their aspirations, especially in an environment where innovative direct competition exists and offers low costs and high benefits, and where aggressive indirect competition for the customer rupee abounds from other product categories.

Getting the business economics right in determining what business model (especially what pricing model) to go to market with, and how to produce and deliver the better-value offer at the lowest possible cost. It is necessary to keep in mind that India has (a) a fundamentally different demand structure from that of the developed markets; (b) a consumer base which expects high functionality at low cost; and (c) a patchy ecosystem where all elements of what is needed to support a business are not equally well developed. Often, there are no ready-made support systems such as appropriate retailing or specialized service providers, and creating these will require investment and partnerships.

The business economics challenge, the value challenge and the patchy-ecosystem challenge can only be resolved by designing and implementing strategies specifically made for India; strategies which represent the 'next' practice, rather than the best practice so far. This could entail new business models, new products, new pricing models, new price-performance points, new low-cost business and distribution systems, and partnerships with the existing network of small service providers in the ecosystem, or with other companies addressing the same target group or value spaces.

Are Global Companies Ready to Create 'Made for India' Businesses?

Despite the overwhelming evidence of the need to create innovative business models and new value propositions to win both the class and mass markets, MNCs, in my experience, are most reluctant to do so.

The mindset and organizational structure by which global companies are held captive makes it very hard for them to do anything differently in new markets. It requires too much dismantling of existing planning processes and governance practices.

In addition, they have a deeply ingrained belief that all emerging markets will grow up to become just like the US or Europe—that the ugly duckling will grow up to become the beautiful swan. However, there is more than enough evidence that ugly ducklings are valuable in their own right.

Until recently, I believed that with all the information available from the experiences of early MNC entrants into India, prospective new entrants would learn and accept the need to develop, from a zero base, a customized business strategy. However, each new group of MNCs exploring India seems to tread the same old path of assuming that best practices for emerging markets are the historical best practices from developed markets. In fact, one would argue that the early entrants, being the pioneers, were far more open to fresh approaches than the middle majority who are now beginning to explore emerging markets.

WHAT CAN MNCS DO DIFFERENTLY IN THEIR APPROACH TO THE INDIAN MARKET?

Ask the Right Question

Don't ask 'When will this market be ready for my "global" strategy?', but 'What is the right strategy to unlock the potential of this market, given my competencies and comparative advantages?'

Far too many companies come to India with exaggerated financial expectations based on the macro numbers of GDP and population. Equally, there are several others that come into India armed with their tried-and-tested strategies and business models and ask: 'What is the size of opportunity for this?'

Usually the answer is 'Not much'; and the company then decides that the market is underdeveloped and that they will come back later. The fact is that they have just thrown the baby out with the bathwater by asking the wrong strategic question. The question is not 'What sort of market for this [global] strategy?', but 'What sort of strategy for this [local] market?'

This is illustrated perfectly by the story of a healthcare company with impeccable global leadership credentials in the business of making glucometers to measure the blood-glucose levels of diabetics. The company explored coming into India around 1999, and decided that there wasn't enough opportunity to justify anything more than setting up a distribution outpost for global products.

Here are the facts: According to the World Health Organisation (WHO) statistics, at that time India had (and continues to have) the highest diabetic population in the world. However, it also had the world's smallest blood-glucose monitoring market, for a variety of reasons. Doctors were not asking patients to monitor their blood glucose as regularly as they do in the developed world, where the accent is on maintaining the quality of life and aggressively managing the disease. In fact, many of the general practitioners (GPs) belonged to the old school and asked patients not to get too obsessed with their blood-sugar count and to lead a normal life by not paying too much attention to the disease and letting their morale down. Patients were fatalistic and were thus casual about managing their illness. Though they knew sugar was bad for them, they felt obliged to eat the dessert served by close relatives because they did not wish to offend them.

The reasons for the small monitoring market also lay in the difficulty and expense involved in getting a two-stage glucose test. For consumers, there was more than just the cost of the test itself involved: they also had to factor in the costs of travelling to and from the pathology lab to give blood and collect results, and to the doctor to discuss the results. Existing blood-glucose meters for self-testing were too expensive for most people to buy. In other markets, the company provided the machine virtually free, and made money from recurrent use of strips; but this would not work in India. Here, people not only monitored their blood-sugar levels a lot less often, but also cut each strip into small pieces enabling multiple use.

It was not difficult to see in this case that the obvious answer was that this market was not ready. As the president of the business said, 'If the Government of India does not think this is a priority disease, if there are so few diabetes specialists, if the GPs are so old fashioned and the consumer so poor, we have no market here.'

But had the question been 'Is the market fundamentally attractive?' the obvious answer would have been 'Yes'. Not only did India have the world's highest number of diabetics, it was also poised for a large growth in its diabetic population. This is due to extensive changes in occupation and income and increased urbanization which, in turn, has led to changes for the worse in the diet and lifestyle of the average Indian. With a predicted diabetic population of 32 million by 2005 soaring to 57 million by 2025, this was the chance of a lifetime for a company that knew how to make glucometers of all shapes and sizes for all kinds of usage. However, the question that needed to be asked was: 'What kind of strategy and business model is needed to profitably serve a market with a demand structure that is different from the "usual"?' That is, rather than one comprising a few people testing a lot, a market consisting of a lot of people testing a little bit each.

One model that could have worked was to shift the business focus from serving the end-consumer to serving pathology labs—setting up these machines as 'instamatic' monitoring stations in pathology labs, which would enable the lab to charge more for instant results, and yet would save the patient the expense of marking several trips to the lab. The model could also have included establishing testing centres in the clinics of a new emerging breed of modern young GPs who were just beginning to build their practice and needed an additional source of income that would fit with their image.

However, the company would not even engage in this discussion, let alone evaluate the option seriously. It made it clear that 'the world over it had made money by targeting the pathology labs, and taking their business away.' It also made it clear that this line of the company's business was about 'stat monitoring of blood glucose at home', and not about instant monitoring in a pathology lab. It had a separate range of equipment meant for the institutional market, but that was designed for hospitals and Indian hospitals, it felt, were not sophisticated enough or rich enough to use it.

Similarly, as discussed in the introductory chapter of this book, PC and chip makers never anticipated the likelihood that the mobile revolution may overtake PCs, and the country may never be ready for their global strategy. Mass markets, like time and tide, wait for no one.

Johnson & Johnson operates in the world's most child-centric market, where the largest number of babies are produced. Yet, given the potential size of the opportunity, the length of time it has been in the Indian market and the brand respect it enjoys even with the poor, its baby-products business is minuscule. The prices it sets for its products are such that even those families that use them for the first child do not do so for the second child. The company could have created a larger, more vibrant business for India if it had asked the strategy question 'What do I need to do in order to fully exploit the potential of this market?'

On the other hand, there is Nokia which, in addition to offering a range of affordable instruments, has also focussed on promoting Hindi-language text messaging despite not being a service provider. There is also Honda that has done an aggressive 'made for India' play and built a large and profitable business, and continues to innovate, as households evolve and infrastructure contexts change. The Korean MNCs came, adapted and have, as a result, captured significant parts of the white-goods space and established a decent position in the small car market.

Eschew Value Arrogance

In the late 1990s, I worked in the Indian office of one of the 'Big Five' management consulting firms. The expatriate partner I worked with was the quintessential corporate imperialist, who firmly believed in the uniform world that MNCs would, and should, create wherever they went. He would nip in the bud every discussion about whether MNCs should review their global strategy for its applicability to the Indian market by demanding 'Why do you believe that India is different? Do Indians wear their noses on their ears? Does water flow uphill in India?'

Citing examples of the onward march of Kellogg's, Coke and United Distillers and of organized retailers all over south east Asia, he would opine that 'people don't know what they don't know' and that demand invariably followed supply in emerging markets. 'Who can resist progress?' was the subtext to his firm belief that India would soon join the ranks of 'global–standard' consumers, and we would all forget the fact that we thought we were different.

A decade later, I do see that there are a lot of consumers out there who have resisted progress. Breakfast cereals never managed to make significant consumer progress over the years, and it isn't for lack of presence or push or advertising spends from the big brands.

Kellogg's, for example, entered the Indian market with a range of breakfast cereals promoted with the proposition that they were nutritious, fat free, cereal based and a very convenient way of (not) cooking breakfast in the morning. However, the consumers' general response is typified by that of housewives in a focus group in South India who pointed out that, in their opinion, the humble *idli* was also cereal based, nutritious and fat free. What's more, it was far most cost effective in terms of 'cost per stomachful for a family of four'.

As for the convenience benefit of breakfast cereal, Indian consumers did not attach much value to the benefit of there being 'no need to cook' Kellogg's products, because the Indian kitchen is a hive of activity in the mornings, and cooking a dish or two more for breakfast was not really more work. In Indian homes a full, hot meal has to be cooked early in the morning to be packed into lunch boxes for office- and school-goers. A snacky cold meal is considered unhealthy. Any additional cooking for those who eat lunch at home, such as old people or pre-schoolers, is also done at that time. Ironic isn't it? Here is a huge consumer base all eating cereal for breakfast in some form or other but with little desire to switch to the progressive world's breakfast habit. But then cold breakfasts do not cut much ice in a holistic health-food culture that is obsessed with the heating and cooling qualities of foods, and has dos and don'ts for every kind of weather. Cold milk was not a preferred accompaniment, and with hot milk, the overall experience was, well, mushy.

The right time for cereal could well have been in the evening when kids come home from school, and when mothers are busy getting the evening organized. But then, if your business description is *breakfast* cereals, that would be a hard transition to make. The company would need to realize that its business was to leverage its core competence in cereal nutrition delivered the convenient way, whenever and however the consumer would like it. It would have to know that localizing the product but not the mindset, and offering mango-flavuored *breakfast* cereal, would not be the solution to winning in this market.

Scotch whisky, usually smuggled, abounds in the Indian market. The old joke is that there is more Scotch whisky drunk in India than is distilled in Scotland. The early MNC entrants into the Scotch market just assumed that nobody would want to drink the smuggled and cheap Scotch whisky of questionable origin, rather than the real thing. In actual fact, the Indian market is divided between the 'label pourers', and the true connoisseurs. The former are those who flaunt the brand of the whisky they serve at home in order to signal their own status and to impress visitors while the latter appreciate and savour the qualities of the whisky they drink. The former want an impressive brand at the lowest possible cost, and are not too concerned about the genuineness of the whisky they serve. The latter are usually rich enough to travel abroad frequently and buy the real thing on their trips abroad, at cheaper duty-free prices. Neither wanted genuine Scotch whisky now available in India at two and a half times the price of smuggled Scotch, or at a price higher than duty-free.

Recognize and Accept that India is a Multi-tiered and Multi-layered Market and Needs a Multi-pronged Strategy

There seems to be an implicit paradigm in the minds of MNC strategists that low-income or developing markets require less complex strategies than richer or better developed markets. India, however, does not fit into that equation because the most fundamental characteristic of the Indian market is its plurality. It is poor, and developing, but has many sub-Indias that are very different in size, in consumer sophistication and in their future evolution.

Therefore, no one segment of the market is deep enough to provide the value that makes a business financially vibrant. A one-size-fits-all unsegmented strategy will not pull in the numbers—nor will it hedge against different levels of growth that the different sub-segments will show in any given year.

Recognize and Accept that Emerging Markets are Not the Way Developed Markets Were in Their Infancy

The analogy school in which the big consulting firms love to take comfort is not valid in India. To assume that increases in per capita GDP over the period from 1995 to 2005 would produce exactly the same changes in consumption as occurred between 1975 and 1985 is not logical: available options are different, as are theories of consumption. Markets evolve in different ways—there is no set pattern of evolution, and leap-frogging happens.

Mercedes first launched in India with an old model, which was not good enough for well-heeled Indians. Liquor companies launched with faded old brands that were once famous but well past their heyday, which were also rejected. In fact, local Indian admixes were preferred as better options. An Internet-surfing fifteen-year-old in India will not play with a Rubik's Cube today just because it was a rage in the US fifteen years ago; and poor rural Indians are not queuing up to buy a black-and-white television rather a colour one, or willing to settle for old styling on motorcycles or wait for landline phones before they 'graduate' to cell phones.

Therefore, the winning game for companies is about leveraging present competencies and historical experiences in order to create for the new world.

Forget About Thresholds of Income Above Which Consumption 'Takes Off'

There is a favourite theory entrenched in the world of business and economics that there is a magic number called the 'threshold level' of income above which consumption 'takes off'. This threshold has been pegged variously at a per capita income of US$1100 or US$2 a day per person, and so on. This threshold theory, however, is based on the notion that prices of delivered goods and services will remain unchanged, and will conform to existing 'global' standards of existing companies. But consider the facts: poor people or those below the designated thresholds of income still have the same desires as those above the threshold—to eat well, educate their children, own a television, buy at a well-laid-out store, and so on. However, if someone were able to drop prices sharply *and* make products that satisfied customer expectations, then consumption could 'take off' at income levels far below the thresholds currently assumed and the market would blossom at any given income level. The threshold theory assumes that no smart new business models are possible which can achieve this. As Shakespeare would say:

'The fault, dear Brutus, is not in our stars,
But in ourselves, that we are underlings.'

The 'Global vs. Local' Power Struggle

One of the most persistent business battles being fought in India is not between competitors in the marketplace, but between MNC head offices in the US or Europe and local managers in India. Local managers (even non-Indians based in India) are keen to get access to the considerable global competencies and resources (especially in R&D) that exist in developed markets, and to develop customized products and services for the Indian market. However, those at head office are not convinced that fresh effort is needed to create for India. Their reasoning is that whatever is available on the shelves or in the archives of developed markets is good enough for an emerging market. What's more, head offices often believe that these products must be sold at international prices or thereabouts, because all markets must measure up to a global income standard.

Local managers feel that margin sacrifices or significant investments in market development must be considered because there are enormous volumes available for value-right products. They realize that it is a growth market and the payoff will be handsome, though slow. Head offices believe that if there isn't purchasing power available in this market, then it has no right to demand better benefits for its consumers at lower prices. Local managers feel that a zero-base approach could help create the right price-performance points, and the right business model. Head office feels that reinventing the wheel is quite unnecessary, and is not easily persuaded that there is lost opportunity in not doing so.

The odd thing is that this inflexible mindset exists alongside amazing pieces of thought leadership on strategy that everyone in head office celebrates. Ideas such as 'Blue Ocean Strategy', 'Competing for the Future', 'Seeing the Future First', 'Creative Destruction', and 'Creating Industry Revolution' are all examples of creative and strategy thought. The implicit assumption seems to be that the only strategic challenges caused by changes in market conditions that head office will respond to are those that happen in the developed world, not the developing world.

POSTSCRIPT

The Changing Centre of Gravity of 'Global'

A critical question that links with all of these issues is: 'What is global? What is the global standard that every new market must measure up to?'

Out of every 100 people in the world of the future, at least two-thirds will be in Asia, and most of them in India and China. One-third will be illiterate; perhaps five will have a college education, and about a quarter will be developed market consumers from Europe or America. Between now and 2025, 95 per cent of the increase in global population will be in emerging markets and their increase in consumption will be greater than that of the traditional top six developed markets.

The inescapable conclusion to be drawn from this is that the centre of gravity of what constitutes 'global' is changing, as is the picture of the typical 'global' consumer. So why should a global strategy that has worked in the past, work in the future too? Consumer India requires the creation of new solutions, rather than the transplanting of strategies from other markets. It requires companies to leverage their core competence, things that they are very good at doing, and apply it to new markets— to create winning 'made for India' solutions: new solutions for a new and different world.

afterword

N.R. Narayana Murthy

It is a pleasure for me to write the afterword for this book. For one, this is a much-needed, clear-thinking and detailed exposition of consumer India, something all of us have been missing. For the other, it comes from Rama Bijapurkar, someone I have known for several years. I have always admired Rama for her data-driven, yet simple, approach to explaining complex phenomena. My opinion has only been reinforced by reading this book!

Developing economies, with India and China at the forefront, are set to give the world economy its biggest boost in the coming years. These nations are regarded not only as the sourcing and production bases for the entire world, but also as booming marketplaces. It is estimated that, over the next decade, almost a billion new consumers from these countries will enter the global marketplace as their household incomes reach the threshold at which they would generally begin to spend on discretionary goods.

India has become an important marketplace. Economists view the Indian economic growth as a consumption-driven one. However, India, as this book insightfully points out, exists in many centuries, at multiple income levels, and with differing cultural and social patterns. It is not an easy market to fathom.

Though the average incomes of Indians are still low, the middle class is expanding very fast and creating a vast market. They would need appropriate products and services. Also, there is a marked shift in the income patterns of rural India, with people moving from agriculture based businesses to higher remunerative non-agricultural businesses. Encouraged by these trends, global firms view India as a key market. Though these firms want to expand their presence and create an impact in this market, they do not entirely comprehend the complexity and schizophrenic nature of this market. Consequently, textbook strategies or the strategies they had followed in the developed markets are often unsuccessful.

In his evergreen work, *Marketing Management*, Philip Kotler elaborates the traditional view of marketing which assumes that the company knows what to make and that the market will buy enough from the company. This may hold true in economies with homogeneous markets and non-stratified sub-markets. Kotler continues that this does not hold good in an economy with several mini markets, each with its own wants, perceptions and buying criteria. The best example of this is the Indian consumer market.

It is always possible to find facts and trends to justify a particular hypothesis on consumer profiles and behaviour, and then use it, often incorrectly, as the basis for a new argument. I find this to be particularly true in the current context of the Indian consumer markets. Global firms have steadfastly accepted the marketing and consumer behaviour axioms that had worked in the developed markets. They use data to justify these axioms and try to replicate them in India. They assume that the India of today is similar to what a developed country was in its early stages of development. To me, this is strangely naïve, because human beings and societies are strongly influenced by their social, cultural and economic histories just as much as they are influenced by real-time events. To understand consumers, you must understand their ethos. Otherwise, such strategies are unlikely to yield positive results.

Study of the Indian consumer market is extremely fascinating. However, the Indian market has always been studied and interpreted as a collection of product-markets. Marketers had assumed, quite wrongly, that different sections of the society and region are homogeneous. This is perhaps also perpetuated by the lack of high quality and well-researched literature on the subject.

This book weaves a compelling and comprehensive picture of the Indian market. It urges the development of a 'made for India' customized strategy, by making a strong case for the intrinsic diversity of the Indian market. It reminds us that never before in history has the world seen such a large and diverse consumer market. We must create new business models to win rather than merely transplanting the old tried-and-tested models that do not work. As Rama points out, the right question marketers should ask is not 'What is the size of the market that India offers for my global strategy' but rather, 'What should my local, customized strategy for the Indian market be'.

This book is a comprehensive and engaging journey through the world of consumer India, consumer perceptions, behaviour and wants. It takes examples from several regions across India giving a pan-India view which is both rare and difficult to obtain.

The author's detailed research and her expertise on the subject is validated by a text which is simple and congent, yet interesting and jargon free. For example, Rama notes that the number of middle income households in rural India is around 27 million, while the corresponding number in urban India is just a bit higher at 29 million.

Overall, this book is an engaging read that presents the socio-cultural perspective of the Indian market, how firms should understand the heterogeneity of the market and accordingly develop their winning strategies. Thought provoking and topical, this book will appeal to a variety of people, and not least to senior management in most companies. It is highly recommended for students who need credible insights and data to understand and prepare themselves for the creative market called India.

N.R. Narayana Murthy
Chairman and Chief Mentor
Infosys Technologies Ltd, Bangalore

bibliography

Appadurai, Arjun, *Modernity at Large: Cultural Dimensions of Globalization*, University of Minnesota Press, 1996.

Bery, Suman, Bosworth, Barry and Panagariya, Arvind (eds), *India Policy Forum*, Sage Publications Pvt. Ltd, 2006.

Drèze, Jean and Sen, Amartya, *India: Economic Development and Social Opportunity*, Oxford University Press, 1999.

Ghoshal, Sumantra, Piramal, Gita and Budhiraja, Sudeep, *World Class in India: A Casebook of Companies in Transformation*, Penguin Books India, 2001.

Goldman Sachs, *Dreaming with the BRICs: The Path to 2050*, Global Economics Paper No. 99, 2003.

Jhabvala, Renana, Sudarshan, Ratna M. and Unni, Jeemol, *Informal Economy Centrestage*, Sage Publications Pvt. Ltd, 288pp, 2003.

Khilnani, Sunil, *The Idea of India*, Penguin Books India, 2003.

Maira, Arun, *Remaking India: One Country, One Destiny*, Response Books, 2004.

MRUC, Hansa Research, *Guide to Indian Markets 2006*.

NCAER–*Business Standard*, *The Great Indian Middle Class*, 2005.

Pelle, Stefano, *Understanding Emerging Markets: Building Business Bric by Brick*, Sage Publications Pvt. Ltd, 2007.

Prahalad, C.K., *The Fortune at the Bottom of the Pyramid: Eradicating Poverty Through Profits*, Wharton School Publishing, 2004.

Silverstein, Michael J. and Stalk, George (eds), *Breaking Compromises: Opportunities for Action in Consumer Markets from The Boston Consulting Group*, John Wiley & Sons, 2000.

Tharoor, Shashi, *India: From Midnight to the Millennium*, Penguin Books India, 1998.

Varma, Pavan K., *Being Indian: The Truth About Why the 21st Century Will Be India's*, Penguin Books India, 2006.

Varma, Pavan K., *The Great Indian Middle Class*, Penguin Books India, 1999.

Velayudhan, Sanal Kumar, *Rural Marketing: Targeting the Non-Urban Consumer*, Sage Publications Pvt. Ltd, 2002.

index